Monstrous Things

Monstrous Things

*Essays on Ghosts,
Vampires, and Things That
Go Bump in the Night*

JEFFREY ANDREW WEINSTOCK

McFarland & Company, Inc., Publishers
Jefferson, North Carolina

ISBN (print) 978-1-4766-8829-9
ISBN (ebook) 978-1-4766-4784-5

LIBRARY OF CONGRESS AND BRITISH LIBRARY
CATALOGUING DATA ARE AVAILABLE

Library of Congress Control Number 2022049998

© 2023 Jeffrey Andrew Weinstock. All rights reserved

No part of this book may be reproduced or transmitted in any form or by any means, electronic or mechanical, including photocopying or recording, or by any information storage and retrieval system, without permission in writing from the publisher.

Cover image © Shutterstock/Raggedstone

Printed in the United States of America

*McFarland & Company, Inc., Publishers
Box 611, Jefferson, North Carolina 28640
www.mcfarlandpub.com*

Table of Contents

Introduction: Monstrous Musings 1

Act I: Ghosts 7
    The American Ghost Story 9
    Introduction: The Spectral Turn 23
    Doing Justice to Bartleby 30
    Ten Minutes for Seven Letters: Reading Beloved's Epitaph 50

Act II: Vampires 71
    American Vampires 73
    The Vampire Cinema 91
    Circumcising Dracula 107
    Vampire Suicide 120

Act III: Monsters 139
    American Monsters 141
    Introduction: A Genealogy of Monster Theory 157
    Invisible Monsters: Vision, Horror, and Contemporary Culture 189
    What Is IT? Ambient Dread and Modern Paranoia in *It* (2017), *It Follows* (2014), and *It Comes at Night* (2017) 206

Index 225

Introduction: Monstrous Musings

I have a soft spot for anthology horror movies—movies comprising several different stories such as *Dead of Night* (1945) with its multiple directors, Mario Bava's *Black Sabbath* (1963), Freddie Francis's *Torture Garden* (1967), George A. Romero's *Creepshow* (1982), and, more recently, Ryan Spindell's *The Mortuary Collection* (2019). Often loosely held together by the connective tissue of some thin framing device, such as characters thrown together at a carnival attraction hearing their fates predicted by showman Dr. Diabolo (Burgess Meredith) in *Torture Garden* (reprising a similar device from Francis's *Dr. Terror's House of Horrors* two years earlier), a mortician spinning tales of gruesome supernatural deaths in both *Tales from the Hood* (Rusty Cundieff, 1995) and *The Mortuary Collection*, or even disturbing events witnessed by a cat in *Cat's Eye* (Lewis Teague, 1985), such films tend to feel less like feature-length motion pictures and more like scary stories told around the campfire. Indeed, what I enjoy most about such films—in keeping with anthology television programs such as *The Twilight Zone*, *Tales from the Crypt*, and even *The Simpsons* Halloween "Treehouse of Horror" episodes—is that the short form of the individual tales licenses experimentation, creativity, and often campiness that would conceivably be harder to sustain for a complete film. Thus, Nathan Grantham (Jon Lormer) can have his cake and eat it too in *Creepshow*, we can get the zombie point of view in *V/H/S/2* (Gregg Hale's segment, 2013), and the dangers of unprotected sex are made abundantly clear in *The Mortuary Collection*!

I have conceived of this collection as a kind of anthology horror film—not as campy as one might wish for perhaps, but nevertheless telling tales of ghosts, vampires, and monsters in three segments linked by some thin connective tissue. These essays hail from disparate places, some of which are now hard to access, including scholarly journals (one of which has been defunct for some time) and expensive anthologies, and the goal

1

is to make them available in one place at a price that doesn't require a trust fund or winning lottery ticket to afford.

Assembling this volume has also been a chance for me to take stock of an academic career thus far cobbled together around what some might consider "questionable" topics: Gothic horror, cult films, and monsters mostly (with things like *South Park*, *Welcome to Night Vale*, and Monty Python somehow tossed into the mix). I've grouped the essays into three clusters—ghosts, vampires, and monsters—with each cluster introduced by an essay on the topic in relation to American texts (reflecting the fact that my background is as an Americanist). Included are a few of my earliest published pieces: "Circumcising Dracula," for example, began (un)life as a conference paper at the International Conference for the Fantastic in the Arts in 1997 before eventually being published in *The Journal of the Fantastic in the Arts* in 2001, while both "Doing Justice to Bartleby" and "Ten Minutes for Seven Letters: Reading *Beloved*'s Epitaph" developed out of my PhD dissertation. Also included are some very recent essays (at least at the time of this writing). "What Is IT? Ambient Dread and Modern Paranoia in *It* (2017), *It Follows* (2014), and *It Comes at Night* (2017)" and "Introduction: A Genealogy of Monster Theory" from *The Monster Theory Reader* are both from 2020.

In broad strokes, the clusters mark a trajectory of developing foci. My earliest interest—and continuing passion—has been with ghost stories. I'm sometimes asked if I believe in them, a question that always reminds me of the reply Edith Wharton references to the question in the introduction to her collected ghost stories: "No, I don't believe in ghosts, but I'm afraid of them" (7). This succinctly encapsulates my own relationship with ghosts growing up. As a kid, I had no real interest in zombies or serial killers, but ardently sought out ghost stories and attractions. The Haunted Mansion ride at Walt Disney World made a deep impression on me, as did a collection of ghost stories titled *Alfred Hitchcock's Haunted Houseful* that I found in my primary school library and the Disney made-for-television film *Child of Glass* (John Erman, 1978). I didn't believe in ghosts, but nevertheless found it prudent to secure my closet doors firmly just in case (because non-existent ghosts, if they decided to materialize, would naturally emerge from the closet). I later dragged my indulgent grandfather with me to see *Poltergeist* (Tobe Hooper, 1982) and made my younger brother go with me to see *Ghostbusters* (Ivan Reitman, 1984), which may have scarred him for life because he was quite young and found it quite scary. To this day, there is still nothing I enjoy more than a well-done ghost movie or film. It was, therefore, a natural development for me to make ghost stories a focus of academic investigation.

I had already started to develop this interest in ghostly narratives in graduate school when I crossed paths with scholar Jeffrey Jerome Cohen at a conference in Cincinnati in the spring 1994. His keynote address at the event,

"In a Time of Monsters," was to become his foundational "monster theory" chapter, "Monster Culture (Seven Theses)," in his edited collection *Monster Theory: Reading Culture*. What I also discovered at the conference was that Jeffrey would be joining the faculty that fall at the George Washington University where I was doing my graduate work. Our shared interest in monsters led to my working closely with him toward my eventual dissertation on spectrality and language, with a focus on "dead letters": letters from the living that go astray and letters from the dead that arrive. I ended up mining the dissertation for articles, which yielded the essays on Herman Melville's "Bartleby" and Toni Morrison's *Beloved* included in this volume; my edited collection of scholarly essays, *Spectral America: Phantoms and the National Imagination*, and my first monograph, *Scare Tactics: Supernatural Fiction by American Women*, also developed out of the dissertation. Reprinted here from *Spectral America* is the introduction, "The Spectral Turn," which summarizes *fin-de-siècle* ghostly goings-on in literary theory and American culture. *Scare Tactics* makes the case for what was at that point an unacknowledged tradition of feminist-themed supernatural fiction by American women in the second half of the nineteenth and first part of the twentieth centuries.

While ghost stories remain my first love, the spectral turn took a vampiric twist for me around 2009 when I was invited by Wallflower Press (now an imprint of Columbia University Press) to contribute a volume on vampire films to their "Short Cuts" book series covering different genres and aspects of filmmaking. I had previously published a book on *The Rocky Horror Picture Show* for Wallflower as part of their "Cultographies" series, which, I assume, is why I got the nod for the vampire book, given that my vampire street cred was flimsy, resting primarily on the "Circumcising Dracula" essay. In those pre-on-demand days of yore, I put a lot of energy (and cash!) into tracking down used copies of more obscure vampire film titles—many on VHS. (If you are interested in a well-loved "preowned" VHS copy of *Dead Men Walk* [Sam Newfield, 1943] or *Dance of the Damned* [Katt Shea, 1989], drop me a line.) An intensive period of vampire research and film watching ensued (a tough job, but someone's got to do it, right?!) culminating in the publication of *The Vampire Film: Undead Cinema* in 2012, a book that considers the ways cinematic vampires reflect human anxieties and desires related to sex, technology, race, and class. Subsequent to the publication of *The Vampire Film*, I've had several more opportunities to write on vampires, including the chapters on American vampires, cinematic vampires, and suicidal vampires represented here in the vampires cluster.

By virtue of dealing with ghosts and vampires (and having flirted here and there with zombies, witches, and, of course, Lovecraftian cosmic dread), I had by default been working with monsters for a good while, which led to an invitation in 2010 to edit the *Ashgate Encyclopedia of Literary and Cinematic*

Monsters. This I blame on scholar of fantasy and speculative literature Brian Attebery, who was then general editor of *The Journal of the Fantastic in the Arts* for which I had been serving as book reviews editor. Brian apparently recommended me for the gig, which turned out to be quite the undertaking. Compiling the encyclopedia began with finding "subject area experts" to help advise me concerning inclusions, then generating a list of entries, and then finding authors to write them. The volume ended up a couple-three years later with around 200 entries starting with "Angel" and ending with "Zombie" involving about half as many authors and twenty-some illustrators. Due to its heft, it's a very good book indeed if one actually needs to fend off a monster (or prop open a door) and, as a bonus, I got to talk about Bugs Bunny in the introduction (because, as Bugs explains in the classic "Water, Water Every Hare" episode, monsters are the most interesting people!)

The monsters encyclopedia is probably what marked me most as a "monster guy" and that's the phase that has more or less persisted up to the present day as a number of my more recent publications have dealt in broad strokes with monsters and the idea of monstrosity. This includes the four essays presented here as part of the monsters cluster: "American Monsters," "Introduction: A Genealogy of Monster Theory," "Invisible Monsters: Vision, Horror, and Contemporary Culture," and "What Is IT? Ambient Dread and Modern Paranoia in *It* (2017), *It Follows* (2014), and *It Comes at Night* (2017)." "American Monsters" and "Invisible Monsters" were published as chapters in edited collections of scholarly essays, "What Is IT?" came out in the academic journal *Horror Studies*, and "A Genealogy of Monster Theory" is the lengthy introduction to *The Monster Theory Reader* collection that I edited for the University of Minnesota Press.

I'm happy to say that the future looks full of monsters. On the one hand, I will be serving as the general editor for the six-volume Bloomsbury Academic "Cultural History of Monsters" series. On the other hand, I'm working together with scholar Scott Brewster on the *Routledge Handbook to the American Ghost Story*. And, on the other other hand (when you deal with monsters, you can have three hands), there are some pieces on vampires in the works. Since this introduction is a letter to ghostly future readers, maybe these works have already appeared or perhaps never materialized for one reason or another. Ghosts may gesture toward a future yet-to-come as Derrida proposes in *Specters of Marx*, but generally remain tight-lipped about it!

The one thing we can all be sure of, however, is that we will continue to be plagued by devilishly delightful monsters because, as Cohen makes clear, monsters are expressions of the anxieties and desires of particular moments and locations—they give shape to the fears and longings of a particular time, feeling, and place (Cohen 4). Some familiar monsters will continue to do the same cultural work they have done for centuries or

Introduction: Monstrous Musings

longer: ghosts, for example, will no doubt continue to reflect fears of death and the hope that something will come after. Changing circumstances, however, will result in the repurposing of familiar monsters and the birth of new ones as future monsters develop to reflect emerging fears and shifting desires. Monsters inevitably limn the human, and as we change, so do they. May your monsters be mild!

As this introduction has suggested, I have been greatly assisted over the past … years by many wonderful people who deserve thanks. Foremost among them is Jeffrey Jerome Cohen whose work has been a source of inspiration and whose support has been unwavering. Brian Attebery as well is among the most gracious people in the world, as is Lenny Cassuto, without whose help I don't think my first monograph, *Scare Tactics*, would have been published. I have had the great good fortune to collaborate with excellent people in various monstrous capacities including Sarah Higley on *Nothing That Is: Millennial Cinema and the* Blair Witch *Controversies*, Isabella van Elferen on *Goth Music: From Sound to Subculture*, Carl Sederholm on *The Age of Lovecraft* and our special edition of *The Journal of the Fantastic in the Arts* on Lovecraft, Catherine Spooner on *Return to Twin Peaks: New Approaches to Materiality, Theory & Genre on Television*, Kate Egan on *And Now for Something Completely Different: Critical Approaches to Monty Python*, and, more recently, Regina Hansen on the *Giving the Devil His Due: Satan and Cinema* collection and Lorna Piatti-Farnell on a current project on the Gothic and Disney. Richard Morrison at Fordham University Press, Douglas Armato at Minnesota, Marjorie Mather at Broadview, and now Gary Mitchem at McFarland have all been supportive and great to work with, and Simon Bacon has frequently given me the opportunity to develop essays for his many collections. Then there are all those who have contributed to the collections I have edited, the students and colleagues who have helped me develop and refine my thinking, and, of course, my family. Thanks to you all!

Specific acknowledgment for permission to reprint the essays included here also must be extended as follows. My thanks to all these presses and journals for permitting inclusion of material this context. Special thanks as well to Sabrina Cunningham for assisting with conversion of the PDF documents.

- "The American Ghost Story" originally appeared in *The Routledge Handbook to the Ghost Story*, edited by Scott Brewster and Luke Thurston and published by Routledge in 2018. It is reproduced with permission of Taylor and Francis Group LLC (Books) U.S. through PLSclear.
- "Introduction: The Spectral Turn" is originally from *Spectral America: Phantoms and the National Imagination*, edited by

Jeffrey Andrew Weinstock. It is reprinted by permission of the University of Wisconsin Press. © 2004 by the Board of Regents of the University of Wisconsin System. All rights reserved.
- "Ten Minutes for Seven Letters: Reading *Beloved*'s Epitaph" originally appeared in *The Arizona Quarterly* vol. 61, no. 5, 2005, and is reproduced here with permission of *The Arizona Quarterly*.
- "American Vampires" was originally published in the *Edinburgh Companion to the American Gothic*, edited by Jason Haslam and Joel Faflak and published in 2015. It is reproduced here by permission of Edinburgh University Press.
- "The Cinematic Vampire" is allegedly forthcoming from Edinburgh University Press and is included here with the press's knowledge and permission.
- "Circumcising Dracula" was originally published in *The Journal of the Fantastic in the Arts* vol. 12, no. 1, 2001, is reproduced with permission of *The Journal of the Fantastic in the Arts*.
- "Vampire Suicide" originally appeared in *Suicide and the Gothic*, edited by Andrew Smith and Bill Hughes, and published by Manchester University Press in 2019. It is reproduced with permission of Manchester University Press.
- "American Monsters" originally appeared in *A Companion to the American Gothic*, edited by Charles L. Crow and published by Wiley-Blackwell in 2014. It is used by permission.
- "Introduction: A Genealogy of Monster Theory" originally appeared in *The Monster Theory Reader*, edited by Jeffrey Andrew Weinstock and copyrighted by the Regents of the University of Minnesota Press, 2020. It is used by permission.
- "Invisible Monsters: Vision, Horror, and Contemporary Culture" originally appeared in *The Ashgate Research Companion to Monsters and the Monstrous*, edited by Asa Mittman and Peter Dendle and published in 2011. It is reproduced with permission of Informa UK Limited through PLSclear.
- "What Is IT? Ambient Dread and Modern Paranoia in *It* (2017), *It Follows* (2014), and *It Comes at Night* (2017)" was originally published by *Horror Studies* vol. 11, no. 2, 2020, and is reproduced with permission of *Horror Studies* through PLSclear.

Works Cited

Cohen, Jeffrey Jerome. "Monster Culture (Seven Theses)" in *Monster Theory: Reading Culture*, edited by Jeffrey Jerome Cohen, University of Minnesota Press, 1996, pp. 3–25.

Wharton, Edith. *The Ghost Stories of Edith Wharton*. Scribner's, 1973.

Act I

Ghosts

Welcome to Act I of this horror anthology! As the introduction explains, ghost stories are where my interest in monsters started and they remain my favorite category in fiction, film, and other media. (If you like to listen to ghost stories, I recommend the podcast *Palimpsest* and the "How to Summon the Butter Street Hitchhiker" episode of the *NoSleep Podcast*; the most beautifully haunting game I have ever played is *What Remains of Edith Finch*.) Ghosts are also extremely helpful when it comes to illustrating the premise that our monsters reflect human anxieties and desires because their objectives are often obvious. The immediate encounter with the ghost is frightening because ghosts violate rationalist understandings of the world and, neither fully alive nor dead, are exemplary of what Cohen calls "category crisis" (see Cohen, 6–7). Ghosts, however, also are very much figures of desire, reflecting deep-seated longings to believe that consciousness doesn't wink out of existence at the moment of death, that justice will not be thwarted, that lost things can be recovered, and so on.

The four essays included in this cluster address the many manifestations and functions of ghosts in contemporary literature, film, and popular culture. The first two pieces, "The American Ghost Story" from *A Companion to the Ghost Story* and "Introduction: The Spectral Turn" from *Spectral America: Phantoms and the National Imagination*, offer broader overviews. The latter two pieces, "Doing Justice to Bartleby" and "Ten Minutes for Seven Letters: Reading *Beloved*'s Epitaph," address the ideas of ghosts and hauntings in Herman Melville's "Bartleby the Scrivener" and Toni Morrison's *Beloved* respectively. The pieces, both of which are older essays that developed out of my doctoral dissertation, are somewhat unusual in the context of this collection both in limiting their attention to a single primary text (for maximum utility, most of the essays included here are broader surveys) and in the theoretical framing used to address the idea of haunting. Both pieces, however, are ones that I think do useful work in elaborating the relationship of the ghost to questions of ethics—of our relationships to the past and to other people. Failures of language in both give rise to ghosts and they ask us how we can act when confronted by the specters of loss and incompleteness.

Work Cited

Cohen, Jeffrey Jerome. "Monster Culture (Seven Theses)" in *Monster Theory: Reading Culture*, edited by Jeffrey Jerome Cohen, University of Minnesota Press, 1996, pp. 3–25.

The American Ghost Story

There is a tongue-in-cheek meme that circulates on social media stating, "The USA is having so many disasters and tragedies you'd almost think it was built on thousands of ancient Indian burial grounds" (@shutupmikeginn). To get the joke requires conversance both with American history and with American popular culture. One first has to be aware of the long, tragic American history of mistreatment of and discrimination toward indigenous populations. Colonization of North America by European nations went hand-in-hand with displacement of and war against Native American tribes who were deprived of their lands, consigned to reservations, and, at times, slaughtered. From a certain perspective, the USA *is* an extensive Indian burial ground. One then has to be aware of the recurring motif in American horror novels and films of the dangerous consequences of violating the sacred space of Indian burial grounds. In an article titled "Why Every Horror Film of the 1980s Was Built on 'Indian Burial Grounds,'" Dan Nosowitz notes the ubiquity of the theme in twentieth-century works including Jay Anson's *The Amityville Horror* (1977) and Stephen King's novels *The Shining* (1977) and *Pet Sematary* (1983). Nosowitz goes on to assert that, by the end of the 1980s, the connection in American literature and media between paranormal experiences and violation of sacred indigenous spaces was so firmly established that pop culture fans assumed (and continue to assume) it to be present in narratives even where it is not, such as Tobe Hooper's film *Poltergeist* (1982) in which homes are built over a cemetery, but not a Native American one. "The concept of the Indian Burial Ground is so strong," he writes, "that it finds its way into places it doesn't even belong" (Nosowitz). In fact, the trope has become such a cliché that it now functions primarily in a comic register—*The Simpsons*, *South Park*, *Buffy the Vampire Slayer*, and *Parks and Recreation* have all used it in this way, and the tweet with which this chapter starts is a case in point.

Precisely because it has become such a cliché, this connection in the imagining of America between Native American burial sites and ghosts and hauntings is a particularly useful one to frame this chapter, because it highlights the ways in which a population's ghosts reflect a specific set of historically conditioned anxieties and desires. Terror inevitably reflects *terroir*. In Mary Lambert's 1989 adaptation of King's *Pet Sematary* (1983), this is almost literally the case as benevolent ghost Victor Pascow (Brad Greenquist) warns protagonist Louis Creed (Dale Midkiff) away from the cursed Micmac Indian burial ground by telling him, "the ground is sour." The character of a place is formed by its history and is reflected by its ghosts. To develop this idea in the American context, this chapter will focus on three broad and interconnected roles that ghosts and ghost stories play in American culture: the creation of national myths, the highlighting of patterns of exclusion that critique those national myths, and the offering of consolation, particularly in light of historical ruptures and trauma. Ghosts of course perform these general functions in other regional, national, and cultural traditions; what therefore differs are the particular ways in which American authors and, later, filmmakers put ghosts to work, and the ways in which those ghosts reflect the specific *terroir* of their historical contexts.

Gray Champions and Watchful Eyes

Because ghosts are inextricably interconnected with ideas of violence and death, their presence usually signals a problem that needs to be addressed. The return of the dead may have to do with travesties of justice—murder, usurpation, neglect leading to death, and so on—or it may have to do with neglected or improper burial rituals and observances. Ghosts and ghost stories, however, can also participate in the project of nation building through the establishment of a kind of a national mythology. This is arguably the role that ghosts play in several early American ghost stories, including two of the most famous: Washington Irving's "The Legend of Sleepy Hollow" (1820) and "Rip Van Winkle" (1819). Published together in Irving's *The Sketch Book of Geoffrey Crayon, Gent.* (published serially throughout 1819 and 1820), the two stories use ghosts in the same way: to invent a national mythology giving shape to a new nation. In "Legend," the "dominant spirit" said to haunt the "enchanted region" of Sleepy Hollow, New York, is "the apparition of a figure on horseback without a head" (273). According to local myth, he is "said by some to be the ghost of a Hessian trooper, whose head had been carried away by a cannon ball, in some nameless battle during the revolutionary war" (273). Hessians were German mercenaries hired by the British to fight against the colonists during the American Revolutionary War. This ghost haunting the

American landscape thus originates together with the birth of the country. He is in this sense the first U.S. ghost—and the country is already haunted at the moment of its birth!

Similarly, in "Rip," the languid protagonist escapes from his shrewish wife with his dog and his gun into the Catskill Mountains, where he may have downed a pint with the spirits of explorer Henry Hudson and his crew. Upon his return twenty years later, most dismiss Rip's tale of having been asleep as nonsense. Old Peter Vanderdonk, however, corroborates Rip's story: "He assured the company that it was a fact handed down from his ancestor the historian, that the Kaatskill mountains had always been haunted by strange beings. That it was affirmed that the great Hendrick Hudson, the first discoverer of the river and country, kept a kind of vigil there every twenty years, with his crew of the Half Moon—being permitted in this way to revisit the scenes of his enterprize and keep a guardian eye upon the river and the great city called by his name" (40). Whether it is in the guise of a galloping Hessian who lost his head during the formation of the country or the watchful, paternalistic spirit of one of the first explorers who charted the North American contours, Irving, aware of himself as writing in a newly formed nation lacking its own national literature, populates the American landscape in "The Legend of Sleepy Hollow" and "Rip Van Winkle" with specifically American ghosts of European origin.

Nathaniel Hawthorne does something similar in his lesser-known tale, "The Gray Champion" (1837). Within the story, a ghostly Pilgrim-esque "gray patriarch" (240) manifests in eighteenth-century New England to protest British abuses of power and then vanishes. His denunciations inspire similar indignation among the colonists and look toward the American Revolution. Hawthorne ends the story by suggesting that this spirit of defiance, "the type of New-England's hereditary spirit," may appear again "should domestic tyranny oppress us, or the invader's step pollute our soil" (243). As with Irving, Hawthorne invents a kind of ghostly mythology that participates in the project of nation building. The Gray Champion, a sort of spectral superhero who appears in times of need, embodies the bold character of the new nation.

Sour Ground

It is important to note, however, that Irving and Hawthorne develop their ghostly nationalistic mythologies by overwriting or effacing competing histories—most notably, those of indigenous people who are consistently dematerialized in such narratives and either folded into national myth as supernatural creatures or displaced altogether. Indeed, as early as

1787, the colonial poet Philip Freneau in his "The Indian Burying Ground" had imagined America exactly as an ancient Indian burial ground populated by restless Native spirits. Although the Native presence in 1787 was still significant and considered a pressing colonial concern, Freneau's poem proleptically speaks of Indians in the past tense and, looking ahead to the cursed ancient Indian burial ground conceit so common in contemporary American culture, Freneau warns the reader to tread softly: "Thou, stranger, that shalt come this way, / No fraud upon the dead commit—/ Observe the swelling turf, and say / They do not lie, but here they sit" (17–20). One must be respectful of the indigenous people and their traditions—now that they are gone.

In Irving's fiction, Native Americans are similarly transformed into supernatural creatures associated with legend and the past. One less prominent explanation for the bewitched character of the Sleepy Hollow area in "Legend" is that "an old Indian chief, the prophet or wizard of his tribe, held his powwows there before the country was discovered by Master Hendrick Hudson" (273). Similarly, in "Rip," Rip himself delights in telling children "long stories of ghosts, witches, and Indians" (30). No reference is made to Indians at all in Hawthorne's "The Gray Champion," a tale of eighteenth-century New England and Colonial resistance to the British, but his "Young Goodman Brown" (1835) has Brown nervously speculating that "there may be a devilish Indian behind every tree" (277).

Early American literature thus "ghosts" American Indians, transforming them either literally or figuratively into spirits that haunt the landscape and absorbing them into part of American mythology as supernatural creatures of a bygone era that still haunt the forests as shades—a dematerialization of indigenous populations that arguably facilitated policy decisions resulting in the disenfranchisement of Native tribes. Ghosts, however, seldom rest easy and this same spectralization of indigenous peoples—either lumped in with ghosts, witches, and the devil or haunting the margins as an absent presence haunting the tale—as part of the establishment of a national mythology gets turned on its head by American authors and filmmakers, and deployed in the twentieth century as a form of cultural critique that contests those same founding myths, highlighting the contradictions inherent in a *Constitution* asserting the equality of all men while in practice privileging white male landholders over everyone else. The twentieth-century "ancient Indian burial site" literalizes the Freudian convention of the return of the repressed and, in keeping with the irony often associated with the ghost, affords agency in death where it was denied in life.

In most cases, it should be pointed out, this modern haunting is indirect; rather than actual Indian ghosts appearing in the Lutzes' basement in

The Amityville Horror (1977), or stalking through the halls of King's Overlook Hotel in *The Shining* (1977) or the Micmac burial site in *Pet Sematary* (1983), the sour ground of these places fosters bad dreams, worse luck, and a range of supernatural phenomena and encounters. This is the return of the repressed in the form of a ghostly curse visited upon those who violate sacred spaces of indigenous interment, but its rise to prominence reflects a significant postmodern American cultural shift in the wake of the various civil rights and pride movements of the 1960s and 1970s toward acknowledging past social injustices and valuing diversity. While the cursed Indian burial ground trope remains in many ways problematic—Native Americans remain stereotyped as mystical creatures of the past connected with satanic forces—the motif nevertheless demonstrates a shift toward acknowledging past injustices.

Terrors of the Known

A key role played by ghosts in many cultural traditions is precisely to bring to light travesties of justice that dispute the official record. The story the ghost bears is often one of violence and exclusion, and the narrative associated with it therefore often functions as a form of cultural critique calling into question the completeness or truthfulness of the "official record." American ghost stories function in this capacity not only in relation to indigenous people, but other historically disenfranchised groups as well, including women and persons of color.

As I address in *Scare Tactics: Supernatural Fiction by American Women* and elsewhere, in the hands of American women, the ghost story form has presented an effective means to convey allegories of gender oppression testifying to the "terrors of the known" (Weinstock, "American Ghost Story" 408)—that is, the forms of violence and exclusion women were subject to within patriarchal culture that limited their autonomy. In such works, terror is invested more in husbands and fathers than in the spectral presences that haunt their pages. These works thus participate in the larger project of what has come to be called the Female Gothic—texts that, as outlined by Andrew Smith and Diana Wallace, articulate "women's dissatisfactions with patriarchal society" (1). Within the American tradition, the use of the ghost story form to contest women's oppression proved particular fertile during the second half of the nineteenth century and the first quarter of the twentieth. This was a period during which the professionalization of women's writing gained increasing acceptance and the rapidly expanding American literary marketplace provided venues in which women could publish. In addition, beginning with the Seneca Falls women's rights convention in 1848 in New York State and culminating in the achievement of national suffrage for women in 1920, this was a period of increasing feminist consciousness and agitation—which found expression, sometimes directly and sometimes obliquely, in the supernatural fiction of many American women writers, including Harriet Beecher Stowe, Harriet Prescott Spofford, Sarah Orne Jewett, Mary E. Wilkins Freeman, Charlotte Perkins Gilman, Ellen Glasgow, Kate Chopin, and Edith Wharton. I will address Gilman and Wharton briefly here, whose works represent clearly the ways in which American women put ghosts to work contesting female oppression.

While American sociologist, social reformer, and author Charlotte Perkins Gilman is best known today for her often-anthologized short story, "The Yellow Wall-paper" (1892), her lesser-known and more straight-forwardly ghostly story "The Giant Wistaria" (1891) uses ghosts to offer a counter-narrative to the historical record by emphasizing the lost stories of oppressed women. "The Giant Wistaria" opens with a scene of domestic distress as a young unwed mother wearing a small carnelian cross and fingering the leaves of a young wisteria plant is deprived of her child and scolded by her Puritan father. To hide the shame the bastard child has brought upon the family, the girl will be married off to a "coarse" cousin she has "ever shunned" and they will all return to England where her disgrace can be concealed (125). "She weddeth him ere we sail to-morrow, or she stayeth ever in that chamber" degrees the stern Puritan patriarch (125).

The story then jumps ahead to Gilman's present of 1891 and introduces three young married couples who are renting a New England home for the summer—one notable in particular for the giant wisteria vine that covers the front of the house, the trunk of which strikes one of the women as looking "for all the world like a writhing body—cringing—beseeching!" (126). Following their first night in the house, the couples meet in the morning and compare notes about nocturnal disturbances including a female figure wearing a little red cross holding a bundle in her arms and the sound of the old chain to the well in the cellar. Drawing up the well's bucket reveals the corpse of an infant, while workmen pulling up the wisteria plant discover entwined with its roots "the bones of a woman, from whose neck still hung a tiny scarlet cross on a thin chain of gold" (130).

"The Giant Wistaria" is a ghost story that literally shows the roots of American women's oppression in the sour ground of patriarchal Puritanism. In *Scare Tactics*, I approach "The Giant Wistaria" as a rewriting of Hawthorne's *The Scarlet Letter* (1850) in which the girl's carnelian cross substitutes for Hester Prynne's scarlet letter and the outcome is not redemption but infanticide and either suicide or murder. The critique offered by the story, however, can be extended easily to encompass nationalistic works such as "The Gray Champion" in which the heroic spectral Puritan protesting infringements upon the liberty of the brave colonists is shown himself to be a hypocrite who claims freedom on the one hand while oppressing women on the other. Like an Indian burial ground, the New England home rented by the three couples in "The Giant Wistaria" is shown to be a kind of sacred space bearing the traces of historical injustice. To dig into the stony soil is to recover the story of violence toward which the ghost bears evidence.

Although not nearly as strident in her critique of patriarchal culture as Gilman, Edith Wharton nevertheless used the ghost story format as a means to foreground the kinds of abuses to which women were subjected—most notably in marriage, which is the focus of several of her ghostly tales, including "Afterward" (1910), "Kerfol" (1916), and "Pomegranate Seed" (1931). The conceit of "Afterward" is that the Tudor estate named Lyng purchased by Americans Edward and Mary Boyne comes with a ghost, but one that is only recognized as such after the fact. Following Edward's disappearance, Mary not only discovers evidence of her husband's shady dealings as concerns a Midwestern U.S. mine but that she herself naively directed the shade of a suicide victim—a man apparently cheated by Ned out of his share in the mine—toward her husband. The ghost at Lyng apparently mirrors the *lying* of its inhabitants, as Mary discovers the dubious basis of their material success and the truth of the mine's sour ground comes to light. "Pomegranate Seed" is related to "Afterward" in emphasizing the husband's concealment of information important to marital contentment. Within the story, Charlotte Ashby is a second wife who becomes convinced her husband Kenneth is receiving occasional letters from his deceased first wife. Kenneth refuses to confide in her and in the end, as with Edward in "Afterward," he disappears.

"Kerfol" is a much more direct tale of ghostly revenge that lays bare the oppressive nature of patriarchy. Within the story, a recovered manuscript details the tragic story of Anne de Cornault, wife of Yves de Cornault, lord of Kerfol in Brittany. Suspecting his wife of infidelity, Cornault methodically strangles her beloved dogs before he himself is killed, apparently by the ghosts of the dogs he has strangled—dogs that then appear once a year. "Kerfol"—which means "crazy house" in Breton but also suggests the need for women to be "careful"—thus serves as a commentary on the forms of victimization to which women are subject in patriarchal culture. Barring supernatural intervention, Cornault is free to terrorize his wife with impunity—to keep her confined and to murder that which she loves the most. As in Gilman's "The Giant Wistaria," present-day forms of oppression can be excavated from the rocky soil of the past.

In the same way that American women writers used ghosts to materialize forms of gender oppression, in the hands of American ethnic writers, ghost stories have served as a powerful means through which to challenge the accuracy and completeness of the historical record and to highlight the forms of violence and discrimination to which minorities have been subject in American culture. Among the many ethnic American authors who have developed narratives of what Kathleen Brogan calls "cultural haunting" (4)—works in which ghosts act as agents both of "cultural memory *and* cultural renewal" (Brogan 12)—are Louise Erdrich, Sandra Cisneros, Leslie Marmon Silko, August Wilson, Nora Okja Keller, Christina García, Maxine Hong Kingston, Amy Tan, Gloria Naylor, and Paule Marshall. In contrast to ghost stories such as those making use of the Indian burial ground plot that adopt the white, middle-class perspective and emphasize the exoticness otherness of different traditions, these are works written from the perspective of members of ethnic American communities attempting to grapple with their history and negotiate their place within the larger culture. Toward this end, spectral presences within such works participate in the "process of ethnic invention and revision" (Brogan 29).

Among the most celebrated ghost stories to fall into this category is Toni Morrison's 1987 Pulitzer Prize-winning novel, *Beloved*, which takes as its central focus American slavery and its aftermath and makes clear the connection between terror and *terroir*. Based on the historical account of a woman named Margaret Garner, the novel's protagonist is Sethe, a slave who escaped from a Kentucky plantation with her children to her mother-in-law's home in Ohio (a free state) prior to the Civil War. When a posse of white men arrived to retrieve her and her children, she attempted to kill them rather than allow them to be remanded back into slavery; she was successful in killing one, a two-year-old girl whose gravestone memorializes her simply as "Beloved." When many years later a strange woman appears at Sethe's home calling herself Beloved, Sethe and the reader come to believe that she is Sethe's murdered daughter returned to her, and her arrival precipitates a battle for Sethe over preserving not only her identity, but the possibility for a future.

The complexity of Morrison's novel is that the character Beloved is simultaneously Sethe's daughter returned and an embodiment of the "Sixty Million and more" Africans and their descendants referenced by the novel's epigraph who died as a consequence of the Atlantic slave trade. The immense question Beloved as ghost of slavery poses is how to grapple with profound historical trauma—trauma that continues to be felt but that can never be known fully—while retaining hope for a future. The vexing nature of this task presented by the ghost is made clear through the narration's thrice-repeated characterization of the story as "not a story to pass on" (260)—a statement that can be read either as suggesting that the story cannot be passed on to another or cannot be passed up or by. Morrison's ghost story, finding its basis in the bloody earth of American slavery, thus confronts us with the paradox of needing to tell the impossible story, and asks how a person, group, or culture can move through trauma toward a future when still haunted by ghosts of the past that can—and should—never be fully exorcised. American slavery may have ended in 1865 and anyone alive then has since passed away, but—like a ghost—its effects still linger, shaping the nation's understanding of itself and directing, in ways both shadowy and explicit, its prospects for a future.

Terrors of the Unknown

Beloved is also, at least initially, a story of a haunted house—when the story opens, prior to the arrival of Beloved in physical form, Sethe's house is haunted by the ghost of the baby she killed. As a haunted house story, it therefore participates in another well-established American subcategory of the ghost story—one that ranges at least from Edgar Allan Poe's "The Fall of the House of Usher" (1839) to Mark Z. Danielewski's *The House of Leaves* (2000) and beyond. And, in keeping with the haunted house motif in general, the ghost in Sethe's house foregrounds the historical ripples created by acts of horrific violence that spread outward in time. The ghost marks the site of violence—of injustice done—and the haunted house, "latent with memory and pregnant with malice," as Rebecca Janicker puts it in her study of the haunted house, typically emphasizes suspect inheritance, usurpation, and "the dark side of domesticity" (Janicker 3). To the extent that one wishes to read Hawthorne's *The House of the Seven Gables* (1851) as a ghost story, for example, the narrative finds its grounding—literally—in the unjust seizure of land by Judge Pyncheon from the accused "wizard" Matthew Maule and the latter's curse upon the Pyncheon family. Foregrounding domestic violence, Ambrose Bierce's "The Middle Toe of the Right Foot" (1890), akin to Wharton's "Kerfol," is a ghoulish tale of supernatural revenge in which a man who has murdered his wife and two children is subject to justice from beyond the grave.

Here I will focus briefly on two famous American haunted house tales that foreground not the terrors of the known—of husbands, fathers, and the forms of violence inherent in patriarchal culture—but rather of uncertainty: Henry James's *The Turn of the Screw* (1898) and Shirley Jackson's *The Haunting of Hill House* (1959). Another powerful function performed by the ghost is to call into question one's ability to distinguish between fact and fancy and to raise questions about the nature of reality itself.

Such stories are of particular interest—and particularly unsettling to—an American political system founded on the principles of Enlightenment rationalism that presumes individuals to be able to draw logical conclusions based on empirical data. *The Turn of the Screw* and *The Haunting of Hill House* each confront their protagonists and readers with unanswerable questions that call into question the extent to which human beings can know their own motivations and trust their senses.

In Tzetvan Todorov's famous study of the fantastic, he proposes that, when faced with what seems supernatural, the fantastic occupies the duration of hesitation while protagonist and reader try to determine whether there has in fact been some violation of the laws of reality as we know them (the fantastic marvelous) or whether there is some real-world explanation (the *Scooby-Doo* ending) to make sense of what has occurred (the fantastic uncanny). Only rarely do works sustain that fantastic tension all the way through—and James's *The Turn of the Screw* is one of those works (see Todorov 43). Within the work, a newly installed unnamed governess takes over the care of two young children—Miles and Flora—on the isolated estate of Bly. Left to her own devices—the children's parents are dead and their Uncle neither present nor interested—the governess reaches the conclusion that she must protect the two children from the menacing ghosts of the previous governess, Miss Jessel, and a manservant, Peter Quint, who abused the children in unspecified ways and remain hungry for them. The story ends with the death of Miles—the exact cause is left uncertain.

As legions of readers and literary critics have appreciated, *The Turn of the Screw*, told from the perspective of the governess, leaves the reality of the apparitions unconfirmed as no irrefutable evidence for their existence is ever supplied. It may very well be that, as the governess steadfastly asserts, Quint and Jessel have returned from the grave "For the love of all the evil that, in those dreadful days, the pair put into them. And to ply them with that evil still, to keep up the work of demons, is what brings the others back" (47). It equally may be the case that, as Edmund Wilson asserted in his 1934 essay, "The Ambiguity of Henry James," "the young governess who tells the story is a neurotic case of sex repression, and the ghosts are not real ghosts at all but merely the governess's hallucinations" (385). Or, in yet another turn of the screw, the story may be simultaneously one of neurotic sex repression *and* of ghosts. This uncertainty is exactly the point—what is most unsettling about *The Turn of the Screw* is that the prospect of ghosts and the governess's response to them raise questions about our abilities as human beings to trust sensory data, to know what motivates us to do the things we do, and to understand our universe. There may be ghosts or there may not—how can we be sure and, in the absence of certainty, how should we act?

These questions about the nature of reality are similarly raised by Shirley Jackson's *The Haunting of Hill House*, which, in many respects, is clearly indebted to James's tale. In Jackson's story, a repressed spinster named Eleanor is invited to the purportedly haunted Hill House to participate in an investigation into the paranormal. There, Eleanor experiences a variety of strange compulsions and experiences, some of which are witnessed or shared by other participants, such as a message to "help Eleanor come home" (146) painted on the walls and thunderous pounding on the door to the room she shares with another character. None of the events, however, is beyond rational explanation and, at the end of the story when Eleanor crashes her car into a tree, questions remain as to whether she does so in the grip of some kind of supernatural force or whether she is compelled by her own unconscious forces.

Jackson indeed foregrounds the lack of certainty that is the nature of human existence from the novel's famous first lines: "No live organism can continue for long to exist sanely under conditions of absolute reality; even larks and katydids are supposed, by some, to dream. Hill House, not sane, stood by itself against its hills, holding darkness within; it had stood for eighty years and might stand for eighty more. Within, walls continued upright, bricks met neatly, floors were firm, and doors were sensibly shut; silence lay steadily against the wood and stone of Hill House, and whatever walked there, walked alone" (3). From the very start, Jackson's *Hill House* highlights the intermeshing of truth and dream in human experience and the limitations of human knowledge and then, reprising these lines as the conclusion to the narrative, she makes clear that, while we can summarize the story, we can't say for certain what happened. James's *Turn of the Screw* and Jackson's *The Haunting of Hill House* both in this way use haunted houses to unsettle rationalist paradigms asserting the knowability of the universe and the reliability of our senses. The specific ghostly presences in each stand in for the more general hauntingness of uncertainty.

Consolation

However, if ghosts can raise vexing questions about the past, about the accuracy of the historical record, and about the human ability to be certain about anything, they can also serve the exact opposite function: to answer questions about death and the future, and in this way to offer consolation to the anxious and to the bereaved. In the American context, "friendly ghosts" did this for the American Puritans, as "elegies made the onslaughts of Satan seem more bearable by assuring mourners that the invisible world remained well stocked with friendly ghosts who longed for the redemption of the living" (Hammond 40). Nineteenth-century Spiritualism on both sides of the Atlantic was premised on the possibility of establishing communication with the dead that would usher in a new age of progress. In the American context, a resurgence of Spiritualism following the conclusion of the American Civil War in 1865 helped reassure the families and friends of the some 750,000 soldiers killed in combat that their loved ones had passed on to a higher plane (see Braud), and a rosy view of Heaven as a perfect version of earthly life and a place to redress squandered opportunities made Elizabeth Stuart Phelps' trilogy of "Gates" books—*The Gates Ajar* (1868), *Beyond the Gates* (1883), and *The Gates Between* (1887)—best sellers. Ghosts in contemporary American literature and media, as evidenced by films such as *Ghost* (Jerry Zucker, 1990) and *1408* (Mikael Håfström, 2007), continue to console the living through the premise that death is not the end and that there is more to the universe than what we can see and touch.

Indeed, *1408* is a useful text to round out this condensed consideration of the American ghost story for the ways it not only brings together much of the preceding discussion but foregrounds the appeal of the ghostly tale more generally. Stephen King's short story, "1408" (1999), is a relatively uncomplicated ghostly tale that takes as its focus author Mike Enslin, a writer of guidebooks to haunted places who finally encounters the real thing when he attempts to stay the night in the Hotel Dolphin's room 1408. In the hands of director Mikael Håfström, however, King's take on the "Ghostly Room at the Inn" story (King 457) expands into a moving meditation on the nature of haunting. As in the short story, the film's Mike Enslin (John Cusack) is an author of guidebooks to ghostly places; we discover, however, that, as a consequence of the death of his daughter some years before, he is a cynical doubter in God and the supernatural. He has never encountered an actual ghost and the experiences he details in his guidebooks are complete fabrications for gullible readers. What becomes apparent is that Enslin's visits to haunted places are in fact the desperate acts of a man confronting an existential crisis. Beneath Enslin's cynicism is a profound need to believe in the persistence of spirit beyond death and in something beyond the material world—to believe that his daughter's death was meaningful and that she did not simply cease to exist at the moment her heart stopped beating. Enslin's search to be proven wrong—to be shown something that will undermine his atheistic materialism—demonstrates part of the powerful appeal of the ghost story: the desire to find evidence of life after death.

Ghosts in American literature and media thus perform roles similar to those they play in other regional and cultural traditions: they participate in the creation of national myths, they point to gaps in and revisions to the historical record, and they console the living with the prospect of persistence after death. They perform these roles, however, in narratives shaped by and reflecting specific historical contexts and concerns: the American frontier, the abuse of indigenous populations, American slavery, the American Civil War, and gender discrimination, and so forth. Terror shaped by *terroir*—the ghost, while often giving shape to widely shared anxieties about mortality and meaning, nevertheless is always an expression of the anxieties and desires of its place and time.

Works Cited

@shutupmikeginn. FunnyTweeter.com. http://funnytweeter.com/the-usa-is-having-so-many-disasters-and-tragedies-youd-almost-think-it-was-built-on-thousands-of-ancient-indian-burial-grounds/.

Braud, Ann. *Radical Spirits: Spiritualism and Women's Rights in Nineteenth-Century America*. Beacon Press, 1989.

Brogan, Kathleen. *Cultural Haunting: Ghosts and Ethnicity in Recent American Literature*. University Press of Virginia, 1998.

Freneau, Philip. "The Indian Burying Ground." *Poetry Foundation*, https://www.poetryfoundation.org/poems/46094/the-indian-burying-ground.

Gilman, Charlotte Perkins. "The Giant Wistaria" in *Restless Spirits: Ghost Stories by American Women, 1872–1926*, edited by Catherine A. Lundie. University of Massachusetts Press, 1996, pp. 123–30.

Hammond, Jeffrey. "Friendly Ghosts: Celebrations of the Living Dead in Early New England" in *Spectral America: Phantoms and the National Imagination*, edited by Jeffrey Andrew Weinstock. University of Wisconsin Press, 2004, pp. 40–56.

Hawthorne, Nathaniel. "The Gray Champion" in *Hawthorne: Tales and Sketches*, edited by Roy Harvey Pearce. Library of America, 1982, pp. 236–43.

———. "Young Goodman Brown" in *Hawthorne: Tales and Sketches*, edited by Roy Harvey. Pearce. Library of America, 1982, pp. 276–89.

Irving, Washington. "The Legend of Sleepy Hollow" in *The Sketch Book of Geoffrey Crayon, Gent*. Penguin, 1978, pp. 272–97.

———. "Rip Van Winkle" in *The Sketch Book of Geoffrey Crayon, Gent*. Penguin, 1978, pp. 28–42.

Jackson, Shirley. *The Haunting of Hill House*. Penguin, 2006.

James, Henry. *The Turn of the Screw*, edited by Deborah Esch and Jonathan Warren. Norton, 1999.

Janicker, Rebecca. *The Literary Haunted House: Lovecraft, Matheson, King and the Horror in Between*. McFarland, 2015.

King, Stephen. "1408" in *Everything's Eventual*. Pocket Books, 2002, pp. 457–510.

Morrison, Toni. *Beloved*. Plum, 1987.

Nosowitz, Dan. "Why Every Horror Film of the 1980s Was Built on 'Indian Burial Grounds.'" *Atlas Obscura*, 22 Oct. 2015, https://www.atlasobscura.com/articles/why-every-horror-film-of-1980s-was-built-on-indian-burial-grounds.

Smith, Andrew, and Diana Wallace. "The Female Gothic: Then and Now." *Gothic Studies*, vol. 6, no. 1, 2004, pp. 1–7.

Todorov, Tzetvan. *The Fantastic: A Structural Approach to a Literary Genre*, translated by Richard Howard. Cornell University Press, 1975.

Weinstock, Jeffrey Andrew. "The American Ghost Story" in *A Companion to the American Short Story*, edited by Alfred Bendixen and James Nagel. Blackwell, 2010, pp. 408–24.

———. *Scare Tactics: Supernatural Fiction by American Women*. Fordham University Press, 2008.

Wharton, Edith. "Afterward" in *The Ghost Stories of Edith Wharton*. Simon & Schuster, 1973, pp. 58–91.
———. "Kerfol" in *The Ghost Stories of Edith Wharton*. Simon & Schuster, 1973, pp. 92–117.
———. "Pomegranate Seed" in *The Ghost Stories of Edith Wharton*. Simon & Schuster, 1973, pp. 219–53.
Wilson, Edmund. "The Ambiguity of Henry James." *Hound & Horn*, vol. 7, 1934, pp. 385–406.

Introduction: The Spectral Turn

Spectral America

Our contemporary moment is a haunted one. Having now slipped over the edge of the millennium into the twenty-first century, it seems that ghosts are everywhere in American popular and academic culture. Beginning in the 1980s with *Poltergeist* (1982)—directed by Tobe Hooper and produced by Steven Spielberg—and Bill Murray and Dan Aykroyd in *Ghostbusters* (1984), American cinema has witnessed a spate of big-budget ghostly features including *Ghost* (1990) starring Patrick Swayze and Demi Moore, *The Sixth Sense* (2000) starring Bruce Willis, *What Lies Beneath* (2000) starring Harrison Ford and Michelle Pfeiffer, and *The Others* (2001) starring Nicole Kidman.[1]

On television, late-twentieth- and early-twenty-first-century programs such as *The X-Files*, *Buffy the Vampire Slayer*, *Ally McBeal*, and, more recently *Tru Calling*, *Dead Like Me*, *The West Wing*, and *NYPD Blue*, more or less regularly featured and continue to include ghosts and supernatural intervention. On cable, *Crossing Over with John Edwards*, a program that features a psychic who communes with the dead, has become one of the Sci Fi channel's most popular programs. In contemporary literature, Stephen King, an author of supernatural tales, remains one of America's—and the world's—most popular authors, while even such "highbrow" authors as Toni Morrison, Louise Erdrich, Maxine Hong Kingston, and Gloria Naylor routinely imbricate the spectral realm with the world of profane reality (Morrison's ghost story *Beloved* won the Pulitzer prize for literature in 1988). On the American stage, two 1990s productions featuring ghosts won Pulitzer prizes for drama: August Wilson's *The Piano Lesson* in 1990 and Tony Kushner's *Angels in America, Part One: Millennium Approaches* in 1993.

Contemporary academia has followed suit in this preoccupation with ghosts; while studies of the supernatural in literature and culture are not new to academia, the late 1980s also marked the beginning of heightened interest in ghosts and hauntings in cultural and literary criticism.[2] Concerned specifically with accounts of "real" ghosts, F.C. Finucane's *Ghosts: Appearances of the Dead and Cultural Transformation* was published in 1996; Jean-Claude Schmitt's *Ghosts in the Middle Ages: The Living and the Dead in Medieval Society*, originally published in French in 1994, was introduced in English in 1998; and Gillian Bennett's *Alas Poor Ghost! Traditions of Belief in Story and Discourse* followed in 1999. As concerns ghosts in American literature and film, one can look to the following monographs issued with increasing velocity over the last twenty years: Howard Kerr, John W. Crowley, and Charles L. Crow's edited collection *The Haunted Dusk: American Supernatural Fiction, 1820–1920* (1983); Lynette Carpenter and Wendy K. Kolmar's edited collection *Haunting the House of Fiction: Feminist Perspectives on Ghost Stories by American Women* (1991); Katherine A. Fowkes' *Giving Up the Ghost: Spirits, Ghosts, and Angels in Mainstream American Comedy Films* (1998); Kathleen Brogan's *Cultural Haunting: Ghosts and Ethnicity in Recent American Literature* (1998); Lee Kovacs's *The Haunted Screen: Ghosts in Literature and Film* (1999); Dale Bailey's *American Nightmares: The Haunted House Formula in American Popular Fiction* (1999); and Renée Bergland's *The National Uncanny: Indian Ghosts and American Subjects* (2000).

Perhaps even more intriguing is the "spectral turn" of contemporary literary theory. Because ghosts are unstable interstitial figures that problematize dichotomous thinking, it perhaps should come as no surprise that phantoms have become a privileged poststructuralist academic trope. Neither living nor dead, present nor absent, the ghost functions as the paradigmatic deconstructive gesture, the "shadowy third" or trace of an absence that undermines the fixedness of such binary oppositions. As an entity out of place in time, as something from the past that emerges into the present, the phantom calls into question the linearity of history. And as, in philosopher Jacques Derrida's words in his *Specters of Marx*, the "*plus d'un*," simultaneously the "no more one" and the "more than one," the ghost suggests the complex relationship between the constitution of individual subjectivity and the larger social collective.

Indeed, the figure of the specter in literary and cultural criticism has become so common that one may refer to contemporary academic discourse as, in some respects, "haunted." The end of the millennium witnessed a proliferation of publications focused specifically on specters and haunting, including Jacques Derrida's *Specters of Marx* (1994), Jean-Michel Rabaté's *The Ghosts of Modernity* (1996), Avery Gordon's *Ghostly Matters: Haunting and the Sociological Imagination* (1997), Peter Buse and Andrew Stotts's *Ghosts: Deconstruction, Psychoanalysis, History* (1999), and Peter

Schwenger's *Fantasm and Fiction* (1999). And, if one begins to consider contemporary poststructuralist theory more generally—for instance, the recent preoccupation with "trauma" in which the presence of a symptom demonstrates the subject's failure to internalize a past event, in which something from the past emerges to disrupt the present—the ubiquity of "spectral discourse" becomes readily apparent.

The question of why American popular culture and academia finds itself in the midst of this spectral turn is complex and, in various ways, the essays included in this volume will each address different aspects of the needs and desires that ghosts fulfill. However, I will briefly suggest here that the current fascination with ghosts arises out of a general postmodern suspicion of meta-narratives accentuated by millennial anxiety.

As I have indicated above, the idea of the ghost, of that which disrupts both oppositional thinking and the linearity of historical chronology, has substantial affinities with post-structural thought in general. The ghost is that which interrupts the presentness of the present, and its haunting indicates that, beneath the surface of received history, there lurks another narrative, an untold story that calls into question the veracity of the authorized version of events. As such, the contemporary fascination with ghosts is reflective of an awareness of the narrativity of history. Hortense Spillers observes that "[events] do occur, to be sure, but in part according to the conventions dictating how we receive, imagine, and pass them on" (176). This is to say that there are multiple perspectives on any given event and one perspective assumes prominence only at the expense of other, competing interpretations. To write from a perspective other than the authorized one and "to write stories concerning exclusions and invisibilities" is, to quote Avery Gordon, "to write ghost stories" (17). The usefulness of the ghost in the revisioning of history from alternate, competing perspectives is one reason why tales of the spectral have assumed such prominence in contemporary ethnic American literature.[3] The ubiquity of ghost stories in our particular cultural moment is connected to the recognition that history is always fragmented and perspectival and to contestations for control of the meaning of history as minority voices foreground the "exclusions and invisibilities" of American history.

It is also no coincidence that the contemporary American fascination with ghosts seems to have reached a high-water mark at the turn of the millennium and has yet to abate. Ghosts, as all the essays in this volume argue, reflect the ethos and anxieties of the eras of their production. In this respect, the spectral turn of American culture should be read as a mark of millennial anxiety. As a symptom of repressed knowledge, the ghost calls into question the possibilities of a future based on avoidance of the past. Millennial specters ask us to what extent we can move forward into a new millennium when we are still shackled to a past that haunts us and that we have yet to face and mourn fully. The millennial explosion of supernatural cultural production thus seems to suggest that what is as frightening as the unknown field of the future is the tenacious tendrils of a past we cannot shake.

And yet it needs to be acknowledged that our ghosts are also comforting to us. They represent our desires for truth and justice (not to mention the American way), and validate religious faith and the ideas of heaven and hell. They speak to our desire to be remembered and to our longing for a coherent and "correct" narrative of history. We value our ghosts, particularly during periods of cultural transition, because the alternative to their presence is even more frightening: If ghosts do not return to correct history, then privileged narratives of history are not open to contestation. If ghosts do not return to reveal crimes that have gone unpunished, then evil acts may in fact go unredressed. If ghosts do not appear to validate faith, then faith remains just that—faith rather than fact; and without ghosts to point to things that have been lost and overlooked, things may disappear forever. How can we get it right if we do not know that we have gotten it wrong? That ghosts are particularly prominent in our cultural moment indicates that we are particularly vexed by these questions. The ghosts that we conjure speak to these timely, context-bound fears and desires—they can do nothing else.

America's Spectral Turn

To be spectral is to be ghostlike, which, in turn, is to be out of place and time. Ghosts, as noted above, violate conceptual thinking based on dichotomous oppositions. They are neither fully present nor absent, neither living nor dead. The ghost is the mark or trace of an absence. As Avery Gordon puts it, ghosts are "one form by which something lost, or barely visible, or seemingly not there to our supposedly well-trained eyes, makes itself known or apparent to us" (8). Phantoms haunt; their appearances signal epistemological uncertainty and the potential emergence of a different story and a competing history.

This volume foregrounds the growing interest in the importance of ghosts and hauntings—of spectrality—to American cultural configurations, and it aims to address a salient gap: the absence of any sustained diachronic attention to the role of the spectral in American culture. In the general body of criticism on American literature, attention has historically been paid to the supernatural writings of individual authors, such as Edgar Allan Poe and Henry James, and individual articles have appeared here and there noting spectral motifs in virtually every time, region, and ethnic group in the United States. Studies have also focused on American ghost stories during discrete blocks of time (Kerr), ghost stories written by specific populations (Brogan; Carpenter and Kolmar; Lundie; Neary; Patrick), ghost stories with particular thematic foci or political orientations (Bergland), and cinematic ghost stories (Fowkes, Kovacs).

However, despite the development of what I am tempted to term "spectrality studies" in the 1990s, and the pronounced contemporary interest in ghosts and hauntings, what is lacking in American studies, literary studies, and cultural studies is any sustained approach to the importance of phantoms to the general constitution of North American national identity and consciousness.[4] That is, while there are specific studies of particular authors and bodies of literature, what all these isolated studies point to the need for, and what precisely is missing, is an analysis of the general importance of phantoms and haunting to the constitution of the "American imagination." *Spectral America: Phantoms and the National Imagination* speaks to this gap by assembling scholars who focus on how phantoms and hauntings have exerted their influences in literary and popular discourses across the span of American history and have shaped the terrain of American consciousness. This is an immense topic, of course, and it is not one that any single volume can hope to exhaust. However, it is my hope that the essays contained within this volume will begin to outline broad parameters for future investigation.

Taken together, the essays included in Spectral America demonstrate the ways in which phantoms have been a part of American culture since its inception, and the manner in which the preoccupation with the supernatural has been a defining American obsession—but one that has persistently been appropriated and redeployed to accommodate changing American sociohistorical anxieties and emphases. *Spectral America* thus reveals the idea of the ghost as one that has remained consistently vital to American culture, but demonstrates the ways in which particular ghostly manifestations are always constructions embedded within specific historical contexts and invoked for more or less explicit political purposes. What the contributions to this volume confirm is that America has always been a land of ghosts, a nation obsessed with the spectral. Part of the American national heritage is a supernatural inheritance—but each generation puts this inheritance to use in different ways and with differing objectives. This is to say that ghosts do "cultural work," but that the work they perform changes according to the developing needs of the living. Phantoms participate in, reinforce, and exemplify various belief structures. To investigate the role of the spectral in American life, therefore, is to engage with changing parameters of religion and science and to explore the ongoing importance of the liminal in the constitution of American subjectivity. Examining our ghosts tells us quite a bit about America's hopes and desires, fears and regrets—and the extent to which the past governs our present and opens or forecloses possibilities for the future.

NOTES

1. One could supplement this list with Michael Keaton in *Beetlejuice* (1984), Spielberg's *Always* (1989), Kevin Costner in *Field of Dreams* (1989), Brandon Lee in the cult hit *The Crow* (1994), Kevin Bacon in *Stir of Echoes* (1999), big-budget 1999 remakes of both *The Haunting* and *House on Haunted Hill*, the re-release of *The Exorcist*, Tim Burton's version of *Sleepy Hollow* (2000) and *The Ring* (2002), and, depending upon one's interpretation of the ghostly elements, one could include *The Blair Witch Project* (2000).
2. Older studies of the supernatural in literature include Dorothy Scarborough's seminal survey, *The Supernatural in Modern English Fiction* (1917); H.P. Lovecraft's increasingly cited *Supernatural Horror in Literature* (1945), and Julia Briggs's *Night Visitors: The Rise and Fall of the English Ghost Story* (1977). There are also, of course, studies of the use of supernatural conventions in individual authors such as Poe and Irving and a large body of information on the Gothic novel.
3. See Hayes in this volume, as well as Brogan and Gordon, for studies of contemporary ethnic American ghost stories as forms of political critique. For discussions of feminist ghost stories, see Carpenter and Kolmer, Lundie, Neary, Patrick and Salmonson.
4. Bergland comes closest to this objective in her study of the importance of Native Americans as spectral to the constitution of American cultural identity.

WORKS CITED

Bailey, Dale. *American Nightmares: The Haunted House Formula in American Popular Fiction.* Bowling Green State University Press, 1999.
Bennett, Gillian. *Alas, Poor Ghost! Traditions of Belief in Story and Discourse.* Utah State University Press, 1999.
Berland, Renée L. *The National Uncanny: Indian Ghosts and American Subjects.* University Press of New England, 2000.
Briggs, Julia. *Night Visitors: The Rise and Fall of the English Ghost Story.* Faber, 1977.
Brogan, Kathleen. *Cultural Hauntings: Ghosts and Ethnicity in Recent American Literature.* University Press of Virginia, 1998.
Buse, Peter, and Andrew Scott, eds. *Ghosts: Deconstruction, Psychoanalysis, History.* St. Martin's, 1999.
Carpenter, Lynette, and Wendy K. Kolmar, eds. *Haunting the House of Fiction: Ghost Stories by American Women.* University of Tennessee Press, 1991.
Crow, Charles L., ed. *American Gothic: An Anthology 1787–1916.* Blackwell, 1999.
Derrida, Jacques. *Specters of Marx: The State of Debt, the Work of Mourning, and the New International,* translated by Peggy Kamuf. Routledge, 1994.
Finucane, R.C. *Ghosts: Appearances of the Dead & Cultural Transformation.* Prometheus, 1996.
Fowkes, Katherine A. *Giving Up the Ghost: Spirits, Ghosts, and Angels in Mainstream Comedy Films.* Wayne State University Press, 1998.
Gorden, Avery. *Ghost Matters: Haunting and the Sociological Imagination.* University of Minnesota Press, 1997.
Higley, Sarah, and Jeffrey Andrew Weinstock, eds. *The Nothing That Is: Millennial Cinema and the Blair Witch Controversies.* Wayne State University Press, 2004.

Kerr, Howard, John W. Crowley, and Charles L. Crow, eds. *The Haunted Dusk: American Supernatural Fiction, 1820–1920*. University of Georgia Press, 1982.

Kovacs, Lee. *The Haunted Screen: Ghosts in Literature and Film*. McFarland, 1999.

Kushner, Tony. *Angels in America: A Gay Fantasia on National Themes. Part I: Millennium Approaches*. Theatre Communications Group, 1992.

Lovecraft, Howard Phillips. *Supernatural Horror in Literature*. 1945, Reprint by Dover, 1973.

Lundie, Catherine A. "Introduction" to *Restless Spirits: Ghost Stories by American Women 1872–1926*, edited by Catherine A. Lundie. University of Massachusetts Press, 1996, pp. 1–24.

Morrison, Toni. *Beloved*. Plume, 1988.

Neary, Gwen Margaret. *Disorderly Ghosts: Literary Spirits and the Social Agenda of American Women, 1870–1930*, PhD diss. University of California, Berkeley, 1994.

Patrick, Barbara Constance. *The Invisible Tradition: Freeman, Gilman, Spofford, Wharton, and American Women's Ghost Stories as Social Criticism, 1863–1937*, PhD diss. University of North Carolina, Chapel Hill, 1991.

Rabaté, Jean-Michel. *The Ghosts of Modernity*. University Press of Florida, 1996.

Salmonson, Jessica Amanda. "Preface" to *What Did Mrs. Darrington See? An Anthology of Feminist Supernatural Fiction*, edited by Jessica Amanda Salmonson. The Feminist Press, 1989, pp. xv–xxxvi.

Scarborough, Dorothy. *The Supernatural in Modern English Fiction*. 1917, reprint by Octagon, 1978.

Schmitt, Jean-Claude. *Ghosts in the Middle Ages: The Living and the Dead in Medieval Society*, translated by Teresa Lavender Fagan. University of Chicago Press, 1998.

Schwenger, Peter. *Fantasm and Fiction: On Textual Envisioning*. Stanford University Press, 1999.

Spillers, Hortense J. "Notes on an Alternative Model: Neither/Nor" in *The Year Left 2: An American Socialist Yearbook*, edited by Mike Davis. Verso, 1987, pp. 176–94.

Wilson, August. *The Piano Lesson*. Plume, 1990.

Doing Justice to Bartleby

Herman Melville's 1853 short story "Bartleby" is a text about haunting and a text that haunts. It is a tale that intimates that there are some secrets that never can be revealed and therefore raises the important question of how one can act and react in the face of incomplete knowledge and the possibility of total loss. It structures a desire for meaning that never can be fulfilled—as such, it foregrounds lack, which is the nature of haunting and, in haunting, intimates that to be human is precisely to be haunted.

"Bartleby" is a short story that explicitly traffics in ghostly dead letters. Within the tale, the only piece of background information uncovered about the narrator's uncanny scrivener is the posthumously reported "rumor" that he served for a time as a subordinate clerk in the Dead Letter Office in Washington. The lawyer appends this "vague report" as an epilogue that he cannot substantiate. However, the supplemental status of the epilogue and its equation of dead letters with dead men compels a reevaluation of the narrative as a whole and encourages the reader to consider Bartleby himself as a type of "dead letter," and his story as itself a rumor, an unsubstantiated report. The question that the ghostly scrivener raises for the narrator whom he haunts is how can one act in the absence of understanding? The more general question that the narrator's dilemma raises is the question of how one is to "do justice" to another when the other will always escape reduction to a singular narrative, will always escape knowing in full. What finally does it mean to do justice to Bartleby, to this uncanny dead letter that resists all attempts at understanding?

"Bartleby" ultimately raises the possibilities that some things may not be knowable or may be lost forever—that history may not be recoverable, that secrets may remain unrevealed. Beyond this, the tale intimates that the possibilities of misinterpretation, of "dissemination," are intrinsic to language in general. The conclusion (or lack thereof) of "Bartleby" points to the unsettling realization that every letter is potentially a "dead letter"—that, as famously proposed by Jacques Derrida, a letter can always not arrive at its destination. Meaning can always go astray. If this is an inherent possibility of language, then "Bartleby" finally raises the question of what it means for meaning to arrive—of what it in fact means for something to mean at all.

Correspondences

The dead letter office account at the end of the narrative refers the reader back to the narrative's beginning, in which the lawyer introduces his subject as one that he precisely cannot narrate. The first paragraph of "Bartleby" opens,

> I am a rather elderly man. The nature of my avocations, for the last thirty years, has brought me into more than ordinary contact with what would seem an interesting and somewhat singular set of men, of whom, as yet, nothing, that I know of, has ever been written—I mean, the law-copyists, or scriveners. I have known very many of them, professionally and privately, and, if I pleased, could relate divers histories, at which good-natured souls might smile, and sentimental souls might weep. But I waive the biographies of all other scriveners, for a few passages in the life of Bartleby, who was a scrivener, the strangest I ever saw, or heard of [13].

Here, the narrator, the unnamed lawyer, begins his first-person narration by positioning himself—an elderly man having encountered many scriveners—and then telling the reader what he will not recount: what he will not provide is a romantic or sentimental account of any of a "singular set" of men about whom nothing has been written but who could serve as the subjects of satisfying biographical narratives. Rather, from this singular set of men, the narrator will single out one singular being for discussion.

The narrator continues:

> While, of other law-copyists, I might write the complete life, of Bartleby nothing of that sort can be done. I believe that no materials exist, for a full and satisfactory biography of this man. It is an irreparable loss to literature. Bartleby was one of those beings of whom nothing is ascertainable, except from the original sources, and, in his case, those are very small. What my own astonished eyes saw of Bartleby, *that* is all I know of him, except, indeed, one vague report, which will appear in the sequel [13].

The narrator reveals that he will not provide what he potentially could narrate—the satisfactory biography of any representative member of the singular set of scriveners. And since nothing yet has been written (as far as the narrator knows) of this group, the law-copyists, the narrator thus forfeits his opportunity to produce a "full and satisfactory" biographical account. Instead, the lawyer will attempt to tell what he knows cannot be told—the biography of someone for whom the necessary materials for the telling of that biography do not exist. Or rather, he will not in fact provide a biography, but report in a "few passages" what is rumored about and what he observed of his subject.

In this first paragraph of the text, the important themes of loss of origin and confusion of original and copy that organize the text as a whole are already apparent. What cannot be done is to tell the story of Bartleby. The lawyer, the originator of legal documents that he employs scriveners to copy, indicates that he here will recount the story of just such a copyist by writing what he saw and heard. In this retrospective reporting of events witnessed, the narrator will not originate but reproduce what has already transpired. He will copy what he has seen and heard of his copyist—his copyist who does not copy and who is an original among the singular set of copyists. This confusion of original and copy, that persists throughout the narrative, ultimately calls into question the sanctity of all originals.

Even before Bartleby is hired to serve as a law-copyist, confusion of original and copy and the power of law to sanction or authorize particular narratives are already concerns of the text. The reader is informed prior to Bartleby's arrival that Nippers, another one of the narrator's scriveners, evidences ambition in excess of his current post that takes the form of "an unwarrantable usurpation of strictly professional affairs, such as the original drawing up of legal documents" (16). Nippers, who is not a lawyer, is therefore not empowered by the law to produce original legal documents. Both he and his documents in this respect are "false copies." They aspire to a level of authenticity that they cannot attain. The lawyer, however, does not seem particularly concerned with his scrivener's actions (perhaps because they do not directly impact upon him) and appears to accept them as he does the idiosyncrasies of his other employees, Turkey and Ginger Nut. It is Bartleby who manages to provoke a response from the narrator—not through the production of unauthorized original documents, but rather through his refusal to verify his copies as exact copies of an authorized original. Whereas Nippers tries to pass off fake documents as real—or rather unauthorized as authorized—Bartleby's refusal to verify leaves the documents he produces (like a rumor) in a spectral limbo-space between real and fake, authorized and unauthorized. This prospect of unverified copy raises the unsettling question of how in fact one distinguishes between original and copy in the first place.

As Maurice Blanchot proposes, the theory of mimesis rests on a fundamental paradox—the only perfect imitation of an object would in fact be that object itself. Leslie Hill summarizes, "Before any object may be perceived as an exact, mimetic copy of another, a margin of alterity must first have differentiated object from copy in order that the relation of resemblance between the two may be instituted at all" (64). It may be said that it is this "ineliminable residue" that remains, that exceeds the mimetic process, that accounts for the uncanniness of the double, of two things that are the same, yet are not the same (65). In the space of the law office, this uncanniness of the double, the threat of confusion between original and copy is contained by a strict process of accounting. The lawyer produces the original document and signs it. The copies can be distinguished by the handwriting of the scrivener and by the fact that they remain unsigned until verified. Once the copy is signed, however, it will act as an original. The authorizing signature enacts a metamorphosis—it "activates" the scrivener's inactive copy and transforms it into an original. The copy as copy therefore only exists as an interstitial stage in the creation of duplicate originals.

Bartleby's refusal to verify his copy raises the possibility that an "inaccurate" copy might be activated as an original—that the original might then differ from itself. According to J. Hillis Miller, Bartleby's refusal to verify his copy "makes what he has copied into something more ominous and uncanny. He makes them into words that have meaning but have been drained of their efficacy and made into ghosts of themselves. They have been etiolated, whitened, neutralized-neither words nor nonwords" (159). Miller characterizes unverified copy as a type of dead letter, "of no more use than a blank sheet of paper" (157). However, Bartleby's unauthorized words are anything but null and void. On the contrary, they are remarkably potent and present a marked threat to the sanctity of the original. They possess the power to act as unauthorized forces, outside of the system of law. It is precisely the process of verification that neutralizes the disruptive possibilities of the copy by authorizing it to act as a "lawful" original. Until this process of verification takes place, it is not in fact clear that Bartleby has not produced another original, a different original, a document that differs in content from the model it is supposed to duplicate. It is in fact the process of verification that makes of Bartleby a copyist. Until that point, Bartleby's documents are not "dead letters," but rather the more uncanny and threatening "living dead letters," letters that raise concerns about the ability of law to delimit alternative interpretations. What the system of law must repress is the possibility that the "original original" may already differ from itself—that in spite of the legal system's hyperawareness of the possibility of misinterpretation, this possibility can never be foreclosed entirely.[1]

Machine in the Ghost

"Bartleby," as I have already begun to detail above, is insistently about the tenuous distinctions between original and copy, real and fake, and authentic and forgery. Bartleby after all is a copyist who first refuses to verify his copy so that it can be approved as an "authentic copy" and then refuses to copy at all. In the process, according to John Carlos Rowe, Bartleby both "raises the possibility that the 'original' text may be led astray, [and] that the 'copy' may take the place of its model" (126); that is, Bartleby calls into question the very mechanisms that distinguish between original and copy. In addition, "Bartleby" also confounds the opposition between life and death. Bartleby himself is an uncanny spectral presence, is in fact a "forgery," a simulacrum of the human. It is Bartleby's "betweenness," his liminality that provides the narrative with its heightened charge or aura of the uncanny. Bartleby's "textualization," that is, the identification of him with an unreadable letter, points to the ways in which all human subjects are "texts," are socially constructed and endowed with meaning by virtue of their places within language and culture. His ghostliness indicates the ways in which this imposition of symbolic meaning from without results in the "fading" of the subject beneath the weight of the signifying chain of language. The narrator's final expostulation generalizing Bartleby's condition as the inevitable fate of all humanity suggests that all subjects of language are, in a sense, dead letters, texts that never can be completely read, texts that always resist and exceed the imposition of determinate meaning.

That there is something strange about Bartleby is evident from his first appearance in the narrative. The lawyer observes, "In answer to my advertisement, a motionless young man one morning stood upon my office threshold.... I can see that figure now-pallidly neat, pitiably respectable, incurably forlorn! It was Bartleby" (19). That Bartleby should first appear as an "it" on the threshold is appropriate for Bartleby is himself a "threshold figure," a liminal entity somehow other than human. That Bartleby should just appear one morning, as if conjured magically out of thin air, coincides with Bartleby's lack of history, the fact that nothing (with the notable exception of the dead letter office rumor) is recoverable about Bartleby's past.

Bartleby does not in fact arrive at the lawyer's office; he is not coming from anywhere. Rather, he is first not there and then suddenly there. The description of him as standing "motionless" adds to the impression that he has simply materialized out of nowhere, while simultaneously suggesting the opposite—that he has instead always been standing there, overlooked—an impression reinforced by the lawyer's later emphatic observation that one "prime thing" about Bartleby was that "he was always there" (26), always present in the office, at least after his initial discovery. That Bartleby should be "motionless" further indicates Bartleby's remove from the sphere of common humanity—in contrast to the activity and emotions of the lawyer and his employees, Bartleby is still, lacking in vitality and emotion, thing-like. He is not a "who," but rather a "what" left like a basket on the lawyer's doorstep. His motionlessness and thing-like nature is reinforced by the passivity of the construction "it was Bartleby."

Robert E. Abrams, in his article "'Bartleby' and the Fragile Pageantry of the Ego," characterizes Bartleby's unworldliness by describing him as a "close cousin of the silent movie automaton" (494). Bartleby indeed initially is depicted as a sort of automaton, working ceaselessly and without emotion. The lawyer observes that

> [a]t first, Bartleby did an extraordinary quantity of writing. As if long famishing for something to copy, he seemed to gorge himself on my documents. There was no pause for digestion. He ran a day and night line, copying by sunlight and by candle-light. I should have been quite delighted with his application, had he been cheerfully industrious. But he wrote on silently, palely, mechanically [19–20].

As in the lawyer's prior description, Bartleby here remains otherwise than human—a thing, a machine, now in motion, but mechanical and repetitive.[2] It is as if Bartleby has all at once been activated, "switched on." The lawyer's use of the adverbs "silently" and "palely" resonates with his earlier description of the "pallidly neat" Bartleby's silent, motionless appearance upon the threshold of the office. Bartleby will be figured repeatedly throughout the narrative as "pale," "pallid," "cadaverous," and, as he is increasingly distanced from the living, as an "apparition" and as a "ghost."

In *Through the Custom-House: Nineteenth-Century American Fiction and Modern Theory*, Rowe notes that Bartleby figures what Freud describes as the "uncanny" in psychic experience (129), "that class of the terrifying which leads back to something long known to us, once very familiar" (Freud, "Uncanny" 20). Indeed, one of the remarkable things about "Bartleby" is the extent to which the tale condenses multiple manifestations of the uncanny as detailed by Freud including confusion between man and machine, the presence of spirits and ghosts, and manifestations of involuntary repetition. What "Bartleby" in fact makes apparent is the uncanny automatonism of ghosts.

Freud observes in "The Uncanny" that the sensation of the uncanny is excited in the highest degree "in relation to death and dead bodies, to the return of the dead, and to spirits and ghosts" (47). He conjectures that this is so because the mind retains the primitive belief that "the deceased becomes the enemy of his survivor and wants to carry him off to share his new life with him" (48). In *Totem and Taboo*, Freud expands upon this point, speculating that the hostility the dead are presumed to bear toward the living is actually the result of a psychic displacement of the guilt borne by the living for the repressed wish for the death and unconscious satisfaction at the death of the now-deceased.

However, beyond displaced guilt, the fear of the dead is also related to fear of death more generally. In her close reading of Freud's essay on the uncanny, Hélène Cixous proposes that "the direct figure of the uncanny is the Ghost. The Ghost is the fiction of our relationship with death, concretized by the specter in literature. The relationship to death reveals *the highest degree* of the *Unheimliche*. There is nothing more notorious and uncanny to our thought than mortality" (542). The ghost is the uncanniest of figures because it makes death present and death, according to Cixous, is something that cannot be known, the ultimate secret. Death is "that which signifies without that which is signified. What is an absolute secret, absolutely new and which should remain hidden, because it has shown itself to me, is the fact that I am dead; only the dead know the secret of death" (543). The ghost, as a "memento mori," as a reminder of death as both the most proper of human possibilities and simultaneously an impossibility, an experience never accessible as such for any human subject who is effaced in dying, haunts the living as a prophecy of the inevitable rendezvous with the unknown. The ghost thus reminds one of what one knows intimately but constantly tries to forget—the inevitability of death.

Yet the ghost, in its return from death, from the beyond, transgresses the limit of death. According to Cixous, it is in fact this "betweenness" that is most tainted with strangeness. "What is intolerable is that the Ghost erases the limit which exists between two states, neither alive nor dead; passing through, the dead man returns in the manner of the Repressed" (543). As such an interstitial "threshold" entity, the ghost is "impure" in the sense of impurity developed by Mary Douglas in *Purity and Danger*—it is an uncanny figure that violates classificatory boundaries and disrupts orderly categorization of forms. The ghost is the confusion of life and death—a marginal figure, invested with the taboo of the in-between. The taboo nature of the interstitial leads one back to Bartleby, the ghostly "threshold" figure poised between life and death and man and machine.

As numerous critics have observed, Bartleby is precisely such a ghostly entity—in Abrams's words, "in the world, but not of the world" (490).[3] As noted, Bartleby is persistently figured by the text as spectral—as an "apparition," as "cadaverous," and as a "ghost." His extreme uncanniness derives from this ghostly betweenness, the fact that he occupies an impossible position between life and death. In a sense, his dying at the end of the text is only the "official" recognition of what has been the case throughout the whole of the text itself—that Bartleby is already dead. Miller, in an important chapter on Bartleby in *Versions of Pygmalion*, writes:

> What Bartleby brings ... is the otherness that all along haunts or inhabits life from the inside. This otherness can by no method, such as the long series of techniques the narrator tries, be accounted for, narrated, rationalized, or in any other way reassimilated into ordinary life, though it is a permanent part of that ordinary life. Bartleby is the alien that may neither be thrust out the door nor domesticated, brought into the family, given citizenship papers. Bartleby is the invasion of death into life, but not death as something from outside life. He is death as the other side of life or the cohabitant with life [172].

What "Bartleby" dramatizes, in Miller's opinion, as well as that of Rowe, is "the way man keeps secret what is most familiar to him" (Rowe 132), that is, death at the heart of life.

Bartleby's "otherness" is the strangeness of loss. His spectral presence dramatizes the unknowability of death. Bartleby and his story are intimately connected: Bartleby will not recover and there can be no recovery of his story. Both are lost—and dramatize the loss at the heart of language and life. What the narrator of Bartleby's story, the lawyer, is attempting to do is to account for him, to make sense of him. But, as Poe's epigraph to "The Man of the Crowd" points out, "there are certain books which will not permit themselves to be read," certain stories which can never be told. Bartleby's history is just such an unreadable text and, as Miller observes, "The narrator's writing is also an attempt at a reading, a failed attempt to read Bartleby" (173). What Bartleby as unrecoverable text makes apparent is the way in which death operates in language itself, language that is defined by absence.

Indeed, the character of Bartleby in a certain sense is doubly uncanny, condensing as he does confusion both of living and dead and man and machine. Or rather what is most uncanny about Bartleby is that, in contrast to the long-standing distinction between the body as a machine and the spirit as the divine element in man, Bartleby is not a spiritual machine, but a *machine-like* spirit. Bartleby as uncanny automaton reverses the familiar notion of the "ghost in the machine" to reveal the machinic in the ghost—the ghost not as a figure for independent autonomy, but of programmed repetition. "Bartleby" reveals ghosts to be repeating machines that persist in their impossible demands.

Hauntings in literature generally persist until a certain end is realized—revenge, redress of a crime, recovery of some lost story or object, etc. Slavoj Žižek considers this aspect of the return of the dead in *Looking Awry* when he writes, "Why do the dead return? The answer offered by Lacan is the same as that found in popular culture: *because they were not properly buried*, i.e., because something went wrong with their obsequies. The return of the dead is a sign of a disturbance in the symbolic rite, in the process of symbolization; the dead return as collectors of some unpaid symbolic debt" (23). The dead return, according to Žižek, as traces or reminders of a violation of symbolic codes. The ghost of Hamlet's father returns, for example, to "settle symbolic accounts" (23). In the case of Hamlet's father, there has been a violation of law—a crime has been committed, and the danger exists that this crime will go unknown and unredressed. Hamlet's father returns from the dead to demand revenge. The ghost of Hamlet's father is a repeating machine functioning as an agent of symbolic law. The uncanniness of the ghost is thus related not only to its interstitially—the way in which it disturbs categorical classification, the way in which it makes the unknowability of death present, but also to its mechanical nature, the way in which it repeats.

Bartleby is, of course, defined by repetition (his persistent reiteration of the phrase "I prefer not to"), and Bartleby precisely has the effect of making others feel as if they are dreaming, as if they are caught up in a dream from which they cannot escape. Indeed, the narrator, approximating Freud's description of the fatefulness or inescapability of uncanny repetition experienced as if in a dream, begins to feel that his troubles with the scrivener "had been all predestinated from eternity and Bartleby was billeted upon me for some mysterious purpose of an all-wise Providence" (37). Ann Smock captures this dream-like or mesmerizing aspect of Bartleby when she writes of the narrator, "It would seem that, as sometimes happens in dreams, he is running as hard as he can and remaining in place, unable to move either forward or back" (85). Milton R. Stern observes that, like a character in a dream—and in contrast to the narrator—there is something "unreal" about Bartleby. Stern writes that

> the lawyer and Bartleby are characters from two distinctly different modes of fiction. The narrator comes from a recognizable world and can be measured in terms of that world: he is the kind of character who inhabits the province of realist fiction. Bartleby, however, in every way inhabits a world other than the narrator's. He comes from the province of allegorical fiction, or romantic fiction, or both. The narrator is a human character; Bartleby is a metaphor [29].

Stern concludes that "the science-fiction and gothic impingement of alien worlds gives 'Bartleby' its weirdness. One does not expect the preternatural or the preternaturalistic to be accommodated into simultaneous existence with the realistic or the naturalistic" (29).

There is no denying that Bartleby is alien (alien is also Miller's word for him), that he does not belong to the world of the lawyer. However, I would suggest one significant emendation to Stern's assessment here: the problem with Bartleby is not that he is a metaphor, but that he refuses to be a metaphor. Stern concludes that Bartleby is a "metaphor" based on his sense that Bartleby is "fixed." He writes, "[t]he vehicle for the allegorical character is typalism. Bartleby is given metaphoric weightings by which he is recognized, mysterious qualities independent of verisimilitude or realistic statistication.... [T]he inhabitant of the typal world is fixed. In speech, action, and possibility Bartleby *as character* is as rigidly fixed as a corpse" (29). Yet a metaphor is that which carries or transports. The difficulty with Bartleby is that he *fails* to be a metaphor; despite the ghostly rhetoric the narrator employs to describe him, Bartleby is rather too solid, too concrete.

The whole problem with Bartleby is that he is *too there*, he will not move, he will not budge. There is an opacity to Bartleby, a persistent materiality—neither the narrator nor the reader can "see through" him, understand his motivations. Indeed, in a certain sense, "Bartleby" is all about the faculty of vision—and seeing beyond or beneath the surface of things. When questioned as to his intractability, Bartleby's response is simply "do you not see the reason for yourself?" But the narrator and the reader cannot—or will not—see the reason. Nothing about Bartleby is transparent. The question that Bartleby puts to the narrator and that the text puts to the reader is how does one grapple with the opaque, inscrutable thing? Rather than a metaphor, conveying or communicating meaning, Bartleby, in this story of "Wall Street," is himself a type of wall blocking the conveyance of meaning. There is a certain paradox here—to say that Bartleby is a "wall" blocking meaning is still to characterize him metaphorically—but it is not to say what he *means* but what he *does*, how he functions. Bartleby acts as an "anamorphic blot" in the narrator's frame of reference. He is an inscrutable and disturbing object that should not be there and that cannot be viewed aright by the narrator except by looking awry—which would involve the distortion of the rest of the narrator's world. He is simultaneously spectral, diffuse, haunting, and somehow also ultra-dense—a "black hole" of meaning. This is his ghostliness, his uncanniness—he is both a fragile physical thing, potentially knowable, and the terror of the unknown, of death made manifest. Why are ghosts so scary? Because to see a ghost is not just to see a translucent material entity, barely there, always on the verge of going out of existence, but to confront the positive consistency of lack and the terror of the real, of death, absence, the unknowable made manifest. Bartleby in this sense is all too evident.

Bartleby's opacity, his resistance to serving as a metaphor, however, generates fear and prompts attempts to contain him, to fix him—to impose meaning upon him, which is to avoid reading him as the blockage of meaning. Bartleby as "stain" or "blot" *produces* meaning. Gordon E. Bigelow characterizes him—and the story more generally—as a "generator" of meaning (350). Donald H. Craver and Patricia R. Plante concur when they characterize "Bartleby" as suggesting a whole group of meanings with no single meaning exhausting the text's "connotativeness" (129). One might in fact wish to consider "Bartleby" as a "technology" of interpretation, as a text that produces continuous interpretations. However, this "compulsion to find meaning" (Bigelow 348) in "Bartleby" derives precisely from the fact that the meaning is not obvious, that a residue of ambiguity resists all reading, all interpretation. Bartleby fails to communicate determinate meaning—he resists being turned into a metaphor.

In a similar manner, Bartleby's repeated responses "I prefer not to" and "I am not particular" disrupt the rules of language that attempt to fix meaning, to pin signifier to signified, to differentiate clearly between sign and referent, original and copy. The problem with Bartleby's responses is that he does not seem to say what he means. When he says that he "prefers not to," what he really *seems* to mean is that he *will* not. And when he says that he is not particular, it is clear that he is very particular indeed. The reader and the lawyer are in the same untenable position when it comes to interpreting Bartleby's statements: what should one make of this discrepancy between statement and action? How can one "read" Bartleby, interpret his statements, when he does not seem to mean what he says? For the lawyer, this discrepancy is especially problematic because he makes his living by seeking to limit the disseminative power of language—the realm of law is one in which language is very carefully controlled to limit interpretive possibilities. Bartleby introduces an intolerable ambiguity into the realm of the law—he raises the disturbing possibility that a gap can always exist between what one says and what one means.

Law is also a realm in which words *act*, cause things to happen. In contrast, Bartleby's "I prefer not to"

> cannot be assimilated to any dialectical or oppositional way of thinking. You can neither deny it nor accept it. It is neither constative nor performative, or perhaps it might be better to say that it is an exceedingly disquieting form of performative. It is a use of words to make something happen, but what it makes happen is to bring about the impossibility of making anything happen with words. It performs the blockage of performative language by which the narrator lives and makes his living [Miller 156].

As a result of this blockage, the narrator is left *stunned* each time, "thunderstruck," unable to connect what Bartleby says with what he seems to mean. Language and meaning seem to have been disconnected. At one point, the narrator attempts to force the issue, to force Bartleby to say exactly what he means:

> "Bartleby," said I, "Ginger Nut is away; just step around to the Post Office, won't you?" (it was but a three minutes' walk) "and see if there is anything for me."
> "I would prefer not to."
> "You *will* not?"
> "I *prefer* not" [25].

Here, the lawyer's attempt to elicit a firm yes or no response from Bartleby is thwarted by the scrivener's perverse refusal to accede to ready intelligibility. However, far from doing nothing with words, or making words do nothing, as Miller suggests, Bartleby's frustrating responses are, as Marvin Hunt points out, remarkably *potent* (280). In place of communicating meaning, they communicate a shock. And in place of conscious knowing, Bartleby's responses somehow find their way into the unconscious of others. Bartleby's responses act to render the narrator like Bartleby and to infect the speech of others.

That the narrator and the other workers unconsciously begin to copy Bartleby becomes evident in the way in which his language "infects" their own. Ironically, although Bartleby's responses demonstrate breakdowns of communication, his language itself is *communicable*, and although he refuses to copy, others copy him. The narrator observes that, "somehow, of late, I had got into the way of involuntarily using this word 'prefer' upon all sorts of not exactly suitable occasions" (31), and it becomes evident that Bartleby has also "turned the tongues" of Nippers and Turkey as well (31). Here again, Bartleby is correlated with dreams, mesmerism, and the realm of the unconscious. He manages to "get under the skin" of those around him in such a way that they begin to copy him without being aware of it.[4]

Beyond adopting Bartleby's language, the lawyer's response to Bartleby is to approximate the latter's own ghostliness and silence. He is "turned in to a pillar of salt" (21) by Bartleby's refusal to examine his copy and considers himself rendered "impotent" and "unmanned" (27) by Bartleby's upending of the traditional office hierarchy.[5] However, it is the narrator's encounter with Bartleby on the Sunday morning when the narrator has expected Bartleby to have departed the premises that makes the transformation most apparent. The narrator writes, "I was thunderstruck. For an instant I stood like the man who, pipe in mouth, was killed one cloud less afternoon long ago in Virginia, by summer lightening; at his own warm open window he was killed, and remained leaning out there upon the dreamy afternoon, till someone touched him, when he fell" (34–35). This image of the thunderstruck man presents another example of confusion between life and death and original and copy. In the same way that Bartleby manipulates language, both by refusing to verify his copy and by refusing to say what he means such that the utterances inhabit a liminal space between active and passive, authorized and unauthorized, life and death, and in the same way that Bartleby himself is figured as an uncanny spectral presence inhabiting the space between life and death, the effect that he has upon others is to infect them with a similar confusion between life and death. *The effect that he has is to turn others into copies of himself.* The reversal here is complete—the lawyer, the boss, bows to the "wondrous ascendancy" which the "inscrutable scrivener" has over him and momentarily becomes a copy of his copyist (35).

The narrator's parable of the thunderstruck man parallels the action of "Bartleby" in even more significant ways: the account foregrounds both uncanny resemblance and the power of touch. The thunderstruck man literally is hit by something "out of the blue," a shock that kills him while he stands at the window of his own home. Then, he continues to masquerade as the living, to appear alive, until he is touched and he falls. That the narrator should figure himself as just such a thunderstruck man foreshadows his ultimate conclusion—his resignation to the fact that Bartleby's hopelessness is the general condition of humanity, that all of us are in a sense thunderstruck, awaiting the touch that will awaken us to our true status as beings-toward-death. And what prompts this realization—the narrator's "fall"—is precisely that, in the absence of comprehension, he is "touched" by Bartleby, moved by another "child of Adam."

Love Letters

The paradox of Bartleby, which is also the paradox of language, is that he both kills and enlivens. His active passivity both disarms others and goads them into action. His "cadaverous" language leaves the narrator both "thunderstruck" and "burning." For Rowe, Bartleby is in fact the essence of the uncanny; he is "a dramatization of the way man keeps secret what is most familiar to him" (132). This secret that the spectral Bartleby dramatizes is "the repression of death that operates in language as both its desire and its dread, its resource and its fear" (132).

This is a good description for it gets at both poles—the desire and the dread—of the narrator's relation to Bartleby. As is evident throughout the text, while the narrator is persistently frustrated and irritated by Bartleby's intractability, the scrivener exercises some attraction, some hold over the narrator. Patricia Barber makes the assertion in her article "What if Bartleby Were a Woman?" that "Bartleby" is a story of "failed love" (214), that it is "essentially a love story, a story about a man who is confined in an office setting that forbids intimacy and who comes to love a person he cannot save" (223). But what is this "love" that the narrator feels for Bartleby? Is it merely the anxious fascination that the uncanny exerts by reminding us of something long forgotten? Is the narrator's simultaneous attraction to and repulsion by Bartleby simply the narcissistic tug of a part of himself that he has repressed? If he "loves" this person whom he cannot save, does he love him precisely because he cannot save him? What would it mean finally to "save" Bartleby? Can one love someone whom one is called upon to save? And is Bartleby the (only) one who needs saving?

The rhetoric of "saving" operates here in two registers: the spiritual or religious and the economic. Barber proposes that "the story evokes our sense of pity and helplessness in the confrontation with this isolato [Bartleby]" (219). For the narrator to "save" Bartleby in Barber's sense would presumably mean for him to penetrate Bartleby's impassive façade, to elicit some emotion from him, and, on a basic level, to learn Bartleby's story. After all, the narrator virtually pleads with Bartleby for the latter to impart even the smallest detail of his background or history. The sense that one receives is that if Bartleby would volunteer even the tiniest bit of information, if he would, in the narrator's words, be even "a little reasonable" (30), the course of his destiny would be diverted—he would be "saved" from dying forlorn and alone.

However, saving Bartleby in this spiritual sense for the narrator means saving him in an economic sense as well. To prevent Bartleby from being the "wasted" man the narrator sees lying dead on the grass at the end of the story, to prevent his story from being an "irreparable *loss* to literature," the narrator requires that Bartleby be used, put to use, useful. To save Bartleby would be to *account* for Bartleby, to call him to account, to hold him accountable—and, as such, re-countable. But Bartleby will not account for himself, he will not be held accountable for his copying, he will not recount his history, and he will not settle accounts with the narrator (the money the narrator tries to give him remains untouched).

The tenderness that the narrator bears toward Bartleby is related precisely to Bartleby's unaccountability. If Bartleby would only be a "little rational," if he would engage in a relationship of exchange with the narrator, the narrator could replace tenderness with legal tender. He repeatedly reports that if only Bartleby would demonstrate some engagement with him and the world, then ironically, the narrator could end his engagement with Bartleby. After Bartleby's first refusal to verify his copy, the lawyer notes that "had there been the least uneasiness, anger, impatience or impertinence in his manner; in other words, had there been anything ordinarily human about him, doubtless I should have violently dismissed him from the premises" (21). Because Bartleby is unresponsive, the narrator cannot respond. Or rather, the narrator's non-response is a result of his emotional response to Bartleby and his non-responsive ness.

Ironically, Bartleby's "non-response," his refusal to respond is a powerful response indeed—one that both "touches" and "disconcerts" the lawyer. Following Bartleby's "I would prefer not to," the narrator explains, "With any other man I should have flown outright into a dreadful passion, scorned all further words, and thrust him ignominiously from my presence. But there was something about Bartleby that not only strangely disarmed me, but, in a wonderful manner, touched and disconcerted me. I began to reason with him" (21). Here it is evident, as in the last quotation, that if Bartleby would be reasonable, if he would accede to "common usage and common sense" (22), then the narrator could in fact relinquish reason himself, "scorn words" and give in to his "dreadful passion" to "violently dismiss" Bartleby. But because Bartleby is unaccountable, he cannot be summarily dismissed. The narrator cannot settle accounts with Bartleby—Bartleby will not allow the narrator to acquit himself of the debt to or responsibility he feels for Bartleby. Because Bartleby is unreasonable, the narrator struggles to retain his own reason—he is particularly reminded of this when he considers the "tragedy of the unfortunate Adams and the still more unfortunate Colt" (36), that is, when thoughts of violence momentarily enter his head. In fact, throughout the tale the narrator attempts to reason with himself, to rationalize his inability to confront and dismiss Bartleby. But he cannot rationalize his response to Bartleby because Bartleby's irrationality has "touched" him—he has been "moved" by the scrivener's stillness. If Bartleby is "a little *luny*" (22), a bit "touched," his lunacy (like his language), is communicable; he touches others, and renders them unreasonable. The narrator, "an eminently *safe* man" (13) who considers his primary virtues "prudence" and "method" (14), and who prior to his encounter with Bartleby has never experienced "aught but a not unpleasing sadness," now finds himself seized by an "overpowering stinging melancholy" (28). The narrator's safe—or rather in this story of "Wall Street," his wall—has been cracked. Instead of a sadness he can enjoy, instead of doing charity for the sake of his own soul, he now finds himself no longer in control of his reason. Instead of communicating meaning, Bartleby has evoked pathos. Indeed, Bartleby has forced the narrator out of his comfortable retreat, his safe circuit of conveyance. The narrator, a bachelor, a man seemingly without close friends or family, attempts to run from Bartleby, but he cannot quit himself of Bartleby, he cannot leave Bartleby behind. He seems to carry Bartleby wherever he goes.

According to Dan McCall, the "deepest" question surrounding the story is "what you do with Bartleby" (113). Miller arrives at a similar conclusion when he observes that the story of "Bartleby" is the story of the narrator's "responsibility," which is also the story of his "ethical relation, or failure of ethical relation, to Bartleby" (142). Miller's gloss on "Bartleby" is that the process of taking responsibility for another, of fulfilling one's obligation to the other, is dependent upon knowing the story of the other. He writes,

> "Bartleby the Scrivener" is the story of the failure of the narrator to tell the complete story of Bartleby. It is also the story of the corollary of this failure: the narrator therefore cannot determine his ethical responsibility toward

Bartleby and act on it. The moral or message of "Bartleby," if there is one, seems to be the following: I cannot determine what my ethical obligation to my neighbor is, and then act on that obligation, unless I can identify him by telling his story [142].

While I agree with Miller's characterization of "Bartleby" as the "story of the failure of the narrator to tell the complete story of Bartleby," I must take issue with his conclusions. First of all, in the same way that Bartleby's silence is *telling*, that his *impassivity* moves, one can say that the story of "Bartleby" succeeds in failing to tell the story of Bartleby. After all, one does receive Bartleby's story—the narrator does succeed in telling a story about the failure to tell Bartleby's story. But beyond this, Miller's reading of the story leaves an ethical void—if Bartleby as dead letter demonstrates that every letter can go astray, that stories can be lost, that misinterpretation is always possible, and that dissemination is intrinsic to writing, then on what basis can an ethics based on an historical narrative of identity be founded? The narrator's final expostulation at the end of the text is so powerful in this respect because it equates all humanity with Bartleby and indicates that all subjects of language are, in a sense, "ghostly" like Bartleby. If all stories are as potentially lost as Bartleby's, if no stories are transcendentally grounded in truth, on what basis is an ethics of responsibility possible?

To a certain extent, Miller does recognize this dilemma. Toward the end of the chapter, he recapitulates, this time as his own assertion rather than a gloss on Melville, "We cannot identify our ethical responsibility to a person we cannot identify, whose story we cannot tell. None of this is possible with Bartleby" (174–75). He then continues:

On the other hand, in his ghostly way, Bartleby demands with calm authority that the narrator take responsibility for him.... The narrator's inability to fulfill his responsibility to Bartleby is analogous to our inability to read this text in the sense of providing a satisfactory interpretation based on what the text says. On the one hand the story demands to be read, with an authority like that of Bartleby himself over the narrator. On the other hand it cannot be read. It demands an impossible task, and the reader remains paralyzed by the text, called upon to act but unable to act [175].

And yet Miller has acted, just as I and literally hundreds of others have acted, on a certain level, to "take responsibility" for the text in attempting to "work" with "Bartleby." Miller equates the "taking of responsibility" with the attempt to "do justice" to the other. He writes:

If the narrator can encompass Bartleby with words, if he can do justice to him, he may simultaneously have accounted for him, naturalized him after all, and freed himself from his unfulfilled obligation. He will have made an adequate response to the demand Bartleby has made on him. The narrator, that is, may have justified himself while doing justice to Bartleby.

> This is impossible because Bartleby cannot be identified. His story cannot be told [173].

This impasse, the imperative yet impossible task of telling the untellable, the "aporia" of justice, is precisely the ethical moment. What it suggests is that justice itself is not reasonable—that it demands the impossible. Doing justice to Bartleby—to the other, to any ghostly figure that haunts—entails recognizing the impossibility of doing justice to the other and then assuming the burden of the responsibility anyway, knowing that there will always be a remainder, an undomesticatable strangeness. Ultimately, the terrible and terrifying responsibility lies in the *attempt* at the telling of the impossible story and justice is approached through the recognition of this impossibility. Indeed, a certain *injustice* lies in believing that one has told the story of the other, captured the essence of the other in a singular narrative.

At base, "Bartleby" asks how one can respond in the face of incomplete knowledge. How can one act ethically toward others—and how can one deal with ghosts—if their stories are not ultimately knowable and if history is not always recoverable? In Miller's terms, "Bartleby" asks how justice can be served if the other cannot be "identified" and narrativized. "Telling" someone's story, "summarizing" an identity through narrative, is not to "do justice" to that individual. As "Bartleby" in fact makes clear, the "original" is never self-identical and the copy never exact. The story is not the individual nor can one presume "truly" to "know" an individual by "reading" his or her story.

According to Miller, "Bartleby" demands the impossible from the reader. "Imperiously, imperatively, it says, 'Read me!' On the other hand, it cannot be read. It demands an impossible task, and the reader remains paralyzed by the text, called upon to act but unable to act" (175). However, to accept "paralysis" in the face of an inescapable hermeneutic circle is to accept injustice and to abandon oneself to nihilism. As Derrida indicates in "Force of Law," the "impossibility of justice in the present" needs to be taken as an imperative toward action rather than an impediment. The narrator attempts to do justice to Bartleby precisely by recounting the story of why his story cannot be told. Rather than attempting to neutralize Bartleby's strangeness, to contain his otherness within a narrative that presumes to know Bartleby, to explain his actions, the narrator ultimately leaves Bartleby to himself, recognizes Bartleby's strangeness, his lostness—and therefore attempts to mourn him *as lost*. What Bartleby compels the narrator to do is to tell the story of why he cannot tell the story of Bartleby. In a sense, this is all that the narrator can do with the "crumbs," the *mors*, the bits that Bartleby leaves behind. To recognize this is to recognize justice beyond the economy of law, a different model of justice in which there is always something left over, always a remainder, something that escapes accounting—something left out. The narrator attempts to do justice to Bartleby, to remember him, to acquit some debt that he feels toward him, yet words fail to account for Bartleby—they fail to encompass either his fullness or his lack—and the absence he leaves behind.

This is why I think one must consider the story of Bartleby as a type of love letter from the narrator to Bartleby. The absent Bartleby stands behind the narrator, close upon him, pointing over his shoulder as he composes the story of Bartleby. He floats there in memory as the now elderly lawyer recounts the story of the unaccountable person who touched him, who penetrated his walls. If every letter can be a dead letter, perhaps every letter can also be a love letter, a desirous reaching out to someone not present, across space and time. Ultimately, the narrator has been *moved to write* by Bartleby. His story of Bartleby is a letter to Bartleby, an attempt to fill in a void with words, in spite of the fact that words themselves are governed by a lack all their own. The narrator's narrative ultimately is an inscription of loss and the title of the narrative, "Bartleby," is also an epitaph as the narrator is moved to mourn the lost Bartleby.

Notes

1. The inherent possibility of misinterpretation leads to an even more unsettling conclusion: that there is no single self-present original, but always multiple differing originals. Barbara Johnson describes this in *A World of Difference* as the way "A is always already different from A." In the realm of law, this means that there is no ultimate authority, no system transcendentally grounded in truth. Rather, as Derrida describes in "Force of Law," what law must rigorously strive to repress (or "mystify") is its own lack of foundation, the way in which any system of law is always dependent upon the violent performative imposition of the system. For a deconstructive approach to legal studies, see Drucilla Cornell and Tom Keenan.

2. Louise K. Barnett in "Bartleby as Alienated Worker" also observes the mechanical nature of Bartleby's production, but she takes Bartleby to be representative of the plight of the proletariat. The question of Bartleby's "representativeness" in fact has dichotomized the bulk of the scholarship on the text into two categories: Marxist readings that take Bartleby to be representative of the alienation of the worker from the means of production and existentialist readings that take Bartleby to be representative of the alienating effects of modernity. In the first case, Bartleby's behavior is considered to be a response to the conditions under which he labors; in the second, to his empathic understanding of the meaninglessness of existence.

3. Bruce R. Bickley, for instance, links "Bartleby" to Poe's "The Man of the Crowd," as part of the tradition of the " mysterious stranger" (30); Stanley Brodwin characterizes Bartleby as "living death itself" (177); Maurice Friedman observes that Bartleby is a man who has "placed himself outside the realm of the human" (68); Ronald Wesley Hoag characterizes Bartleby as a memento mori, an "abiding icon of death" (119), and refers to him (with unexamined Coleridgean overtones) as "dead-in-life" (127); J. Hillis Miller describes Bartleby in *Versions of Pygmalion* as a ghost (163–65).

4. However, in contrast to Bartleby, it should be pointed out that the lawyer and his other employees use the verb "prefer" to express specific, positive preferences. Unlike

Bartleby's negative "prefer not," the lawyer, for example, tells Nippers that "I'd prefer that you would withdraw for the present" (31). Although Bartleby touches those around him, "unmans" them, infects them, he does not drain them entirely of their beliefs in personal autonomy and the efficacy of human action. In expressing positive preferences, those around Bartleby refuse his nihilism.

    5. That the lawyer is "turned into a pillar of salt," as is Lot's wife, as well as rendered "impotent" and "unmanned" by Bartleby's refusal, here raises the issue of gender. The narrator is of course correlating authority with masculinity—one is "unmanned" when one allows one's subordinates to dictate a course of action. However, what is intriguing about the narrator's choices of adjectives is that, in a sexual sense, the narrator as impotent and unmanned is rendered *unable to reproduce*. As I will develop below, Bartleby's potency ironically lies in his refusal to reproduce copy, that has the effect of turning others into copies of himself.

WORKS CITED

Abrams, Robert E. "'Bartleby' and the Fragile Pageantry of the Ego." *ELH*, vol. 45, no. 3, 1978, pp. 488–500.
Barber, Patricia. "What if Bartleby Were a Woman?" in *The Authority of Experience: Essays in Feminist Criticism*, edited by Arlyn Diamond and Lee R. Edwards. University of Massachusetts Press, 1977, pp. 212–223.
Barnett, Louise K. "Bartleby as Alienated Worker." *Studies in Short Fiction*, vol. 11, no. 4, 1974, pp. 379–386.
Bickley, Bruce R., Jr. *The Method of Melville's Short Fiction*. Duke University Press, 1975.
Bigelow, Gordon E. "The Problem of Symbolist Form in Melville's 'Bartleby the Scrivener.'" *Modern Language Quarterly*, vol. 31, no. 3, 1970, pp. 345–358.
Blanchot, Maurice. *The Writing of the Disaster*, translated by Ann Smock. University of Nebraska Press, 1986.
Brodwin, Stanley. "To the Frontiers of Eternity: Melville's Crossing in 'Bartleby the Scrivener'" in *Bartleby the Inscrutable: A Collection of Commentary on Herman Melville's Tale "Bartleby the Scrivener,"* edited by Thomas M. Inge. Archon, 1979, pp. 174–196.
Cixous, Hélène. "Fiction and Its Phantoms: A Reading of Freud's *Das Unheimliche* (The 'uncanny')," translated by Robert Dennomé. *New Literary History: A Journal of Theory and Interpretation*, vol. 7, no. 2, 1976, pp. 525–548.
Cornell, Drucilla. *The Philosophy of the Limit*. Routledge, 1992.
Craver, Donald H., and Patricia R. Plante. "Bartleby, or The Ambiguities." *Studies in Short Fiction*, vol. 20, no. 2-3, 1983, pp. 129–131.
Derrida, Jacques. "Force of Law: the 'Mystical Foundations of Authority'" in *Deconstruction and the Possibility of Justice*, edited by Drucilla Cornell, Michel Rosenfeld, and David Gray Carlson. Routledge, 1992, pp. 3–67.
Douglas, Mary. *Purity and Danger: An Analysis of the Concepts of Pollution and Taboo*. Routledge, 1966.
Freud, Sigmund. *Totem and Taboo: Resemblances Between the Psychic Life of Savages and Neurotics*, translated by A.A. Brill. Random House, 1918.
_____. "The Uncanny." *Studies in Parapsychology*, translated by Alix Strachey, edited by Philip Rieff. Collier, 1963. pp. 19–62.
Friedman, Maurice. "Bartleby and the Modem Exile" in *Melville Annual 1965, A Symposium: Bartleby the Scrivener*, edited by Howard P. Vincent. Kent State University Press, 1966, pp. 64–81.
Hill, Leslie. *Blanchot: Extreme Contemporary*. Routledge, 1997.
Hoag, Ronald Wesley. "The Corpse in the Office: Mortality, Mutability and Salvation in 'Bartleby, the Scrivener.'" *ESQ: A Journal of the American Renaissance*, vol. 38, no. 2, 1992, pp. 119–142.
Hunt, Marvin. "*That's* the Word: Turning Tongues and Heads in 'Bartleby, the Scrivener.'" *ESQ: A Journal of the American Renaissance*, vol. 40, no. 4, 1994, pp. 275–292.

Johnson, Barbara. *A World of Difference*. Johns Hopkins University Press, 1987.
Keenan, Thomas. "Deconstruction and the Impossibility of Justice" in *Critical Encounters: Reference and Responsibility in Deconstructive Writing*, edited by Cathy Caruth and Deborah Esch. Rutgers University Press, 1995, pp. 262–274.
McCall, Dan. *The Silence of Bartleby*. Cornell University Press, 1989.
Melville, Herman. "Bartleby, the Scrivener" in *The Piazza Tales and Other Prose Pieces, 1839–1860*. Northwestern University Press, 1987, pp. 13–46.
Miller, J. Hillis. *Versions of Pygmalion*. Harvard University Press, 1990.
Poe, Edgar Allan. "The Man of the Crowd" in *The Unabridged Edgar Allan Poe*, edited by Tam Mossman. Running Press, 1983, pp. 799–803.
Rowe, John Carlos. *Through the Custom-House: Nineteenth-Century American Fiction and Modern Theory*. Johns Hopkins University Press, 1982.
Smock, Ann. "Quiet." *Qui Parle*, vol. 2, no. 2, 1988, pp. 68–100.
Stern, Milton R. "Towards 'Bartleby the Scrivener,'" in *The Stoic Strain in American Literature: Essays in Honor of Marston LaFrance*, edited by Duane J. MacMillan. University of Toronto Press, 1979, pp. 19–41.
Žižek, Slavoj. *Looking Awry: An Introduction to Jacques Lacan Through Popular Culture*. MIT Press, 1991.

Ten Minutes for Seven Letters: Reading Beloved's Epitaph

> You haven't really read something until you've read
> it as an epitaph, said a friend of a friend of mine
> to whom I told this title. Tell them that.
> —Cynthia Chase, "Reading Epitaphs" (52)

"Tell them that," the last reported words from an anonymous "friend of a friend." Taken by itself, the command raises ambiguity to its highest level—the imperative for someone to tell something to others. Read contextually, the implied "you" of the imperative "Tell" is Cynthia Chase. The "them" is the audience at the 1993 New York University conference "Deconstruction is/in America" listening to Chase's "Reading Epitaphs" presentation. The "that" is "You haven't really read something until you've read it as an epitaph." Yet the "that" of Chase's related comment raises even more questions: what is an epitaph? How does one read it? How and why does this reading differ from normal reading—or rather, how does reading something as an epitaph constitute reading in its essence such that texts read otherwise aren't "really read"? And how can something that is not an epitaph be read as an epitaph?

One can begin to approach the dilemmas posed by the idea of reading epitaphs by observing that to read something as an epitaph, as written on a gravestone, is, first of all, to make the relationship between language and death explicit—epitaphs are always curious types of dead letters that mediate the relationship between the living and the dead. Reading something as an epitaph forces one to consider the strange materiality of language, the way in which the sign can persist in the absence of both its producer and addressee. The epitaph marks a site of memory, a powerful zone of contact between the living and the dead. It performs the complicated function of calling to mind the departed as departed, that is, of foregrounding the present absence of the beloved. To read the epitaph is to remember its referent, to conjure the dead, while at the same time to be struck by the ephemerality of living. The materiality, the weightiness, the persistence of words literally etched in stone contrast with the fleetingness and fragility of life.

However, can one ever really "read" an epitaph? If the epitaph functions to refer beyond itself, to call to mind the departed, then to read the text of the epitaph as *text*, divorced from its referential function, is not to read it as epitaph. To read an epitaph as a poem, for instance, to celebrate the beauty of its composition rather than to reflect on the absence of the deceased, is not to read it as an epitaph. Contrarily, to read the epitaph as epitaph, as that which commemorates the deceased and insistently gestures towards the present absence of its referent, is not to read the epitaph as text. The question of reading the epitaph therefore introduces an ethical dimension to reading. Is it ethical to consider an epitaph as "literature" and to perform the same critical analyses and manipulations one might apply to, say, a "normal" poem? Can an epitaph be aestheticized and still be an epitaph? The reverse of this question also applies, especially in light of my *epigraph*: can one consider the "normal" poem as *epitaph*? At bottom here is the vexed question of the relationship of language to that which exists outside language. If, as Hegel suggests, the word is the death of the thing, then is not every word, in some sense, an epitaph? The imperative to read as epitaph suggests that somehow reading is connected to absence, that to read is always to recognize or undergo an experience of loss.

In order to approach the subject of spectrality in Toni Morrison's *Beloved* and its relation to language and to the possibility of justice for the living and the dead, one must start with the complex mediation performed by the epitaph, because, from start to finish, *Beloved* is a story about an epitaph, the name "Beloved," "the one word that mattered" etched into "dawn-colored stone" (5). Everything in *Beloved*, from title to last word, circles around the name, the ways in which the word "beloved" connotes both the most intense intimacy and communal gatherings, the celebration of new life together and the sundering of bonds by death. To read *Beloved*'s epitaph, to read *Beloved*, as epitaph, is to confront the haunting limitations of language and to engage in a process of mourning that inevitably will fail to capture or reconstitute the other. However, the frightening recognition of loss that the epitaph compels serves as the precondition for learning to live and for the opening of the future as something other than a repetition of the present.

Ten Minutes for Seven Letters

What Derrida says in *Given Time* of Baudelaire's short story "Counterfeit Money," that "it is as if the text did nothing but play with its title"

(97), can also be said of Morrison's *Beloved*. From start to finish, as Deborah Horvitz has observed, Morrison's text is "enveloped" by the presence of a problematic *name*—the epitaph "Beloved" carved onto the gravestone of Sethe's "crawling already?" baby, named only in death (157). Prostituting her body to the engraver, "her knees wide open as any grave," Sethe exchanges "ten minutes for seven letters" (5), ten minutes of sex for the inscription of the word "Beloved" on the tombstone of her murdered child. This complicated transaction functions as a nexus of sex, time, and writing, love, lust, hatred, and death. It thus figures in microcosm many of the key terms of the text as a whole.[1] Sethe, in this relationship of exchange, is the lover, her dead child, the beloved, and the engraver the third party who will mediate this relationship between living and dead through language. The relationship between Sethe and her departed child is contrasted with the relationship between Sethe and the engraver, which is not one of tenderness but of tender, of capital. What this contrast foregrounds is the insistent theme of Morrison's text that there is no beloved of a transaction. One of the most dramatic movements of Morrison's text is its insistence that love relationships must exist outside of the economy of exchange and possession.

The irony of the phrase "ten minutes for seven letters" lies in the disparate valuations of the epitaph to the engraver, to Sethe, and to the reader. The seven letters that she chooses mean nothing more to the engraver than the opportunity to vent his lust, while they, as epitaph, as "the one word that mattered" from the preacher's eulogy, as an expression of love, mean significantly more to Sethe—a value not reducible to a cost per letter. And, beyond Sethe's desire to remember her daughter, these same seven letters govern the entire momentum of the text for the reader, serving as its title, the text's last word, and designating one of its central characters. The overwhelming irony of the reduction of "Beloved" to ten minutes is most evident when one observes that Beloved herself is symbolic of the "sixty million and more" Africans who died during the Middle Passage of slavery. The whole structure of Morrison's text works to counter this tragic reduction that seeks to measure lives in terms of minutes (in this respect, it is significant that Beloved's tombstone bears no dates), or to calculate the value of lives in terms of units of material exchange.

The overdetermination of the epitaph "beloved" functions on several levels to foreground the mediation of language between self and other and living and dead. As Caroline Rody observes, the term "expresses at once the greatest anonymity and the dearest specificity" (104). It is the private name each person gives to his or her most intimate relations and personal treasures. However, in addition to serving as "an address conferred by the lover on the object of affection," the term "beloved" also names everyone in the impersonal rhetoric of the Church and, as noted by May G. Henderson, is "used in matrimonial and eulogistic discourse, both commemorative, linguistic events: the former prefiguring the future, the latter refiguring the past" (67). In the "Dearly Beloved" of the marriage ceremony and the funeral eulogy, the term "beloved" unites the celebrants or mourners in a present moment of anticipation or commemoration. In its public contexts, it functions simultaneously in two capacities, marking both the specific relationship of the affianced to each other or the bereaved to the deceased, and the general relation of the Church to all. In its various uses, the term thus connects public with private, the intimacy of the individual love relationship with communal gatherings of both celebration and grief. The term also structures a tension between the timeless present of one's most intimate encounters and the communal marking of time through the rememoration of significant events in the lives of individuals—particularly the joining of marriage and the passing of death. The use of the term, at least in its public contexts, thereby marks a vacillation, a wavering in time, the fullness of a present marked by a past-and an openness to a future beyond the event.

The name "Beloved" thus acts on several levels, as Valerie Smith remarks, as "a site where a number of oppositions are interrogated" (350). As an epitaph on a tombstone, the "public inscription of a private memorial" (Henderson 67), as well as an element of Church rhetoric and a term that everyone deploys to identify her or his own most intimate relations, it serves to link public to private. In its use in public contexts, it serves to foreground the presentness of both the past and the future. However, as Smith observes, the word "beloved" itself is a site of opposition and ambiguity. "Simultaneously adjective and noun, the world [sic] problematizes the distinction between the characteristics of a thing and the thing itself" (350).

This instability of the word, a word that deprived of context can be either noun or adjective, that vacillates in time, that figures both intimate moments and public gathering, arises from the fact that, as Morrison's text is well aware, "beloved," by itself, is nothing. For there to be a beloved, or for someone to be beloved, there must be a lover. Conversely, if there is a lover, there must be a beloved. Herein lies the ambiguity and imperative of Morrison's title: the starkness of this overdetermined epitaph demands some sort of context. Beloved of whom? Morrison's text does a neat spin on this question by making both it and its inverse, "who is Beloved?" two of the most important questions of the text. The answers to both these questions replicate the tendency of the term "beloved" itself to vacillate between private and public, to slip beyond the borders of any singular context.

The term "beloved" thereby functions metonymically, always gesturing beyond itself toward some other term. Separated from the rest of the preacher's funeral eulogy, "Beloved" points backward to "Dearly" and forward to the rest of the oration. Sethe wonders, "With another ten could she have gotten 'Dearly' too?" (5). What Sethe is able to purchase with her body is a link from a longer chain of language addressed to the community in general. Her extraction of the term "beloved" from the rest of the funeral eulogy, her mistaking the "Dearly Beloved" as an address to her dead child rather than to the assembled crowd (Rody 104), and, finally, the decontextualized "Beloved" of the epitaph, function as failures of language—failures that figure the complex relationship of public to private in the novel and implicate the community in the circumstances of her daughter's demise and subsequent return—that complicate but do not efface Sethe's own accountability for her actions.

The text of *Beloved* enacts a movement from public to private as Sethe withdraws from the world following Beloved's return, and then shifts from private back to public as Denver steps out into the yard to seek assistance from the community—the same community initially connected to the events leading up to primal scene of Beloved's murder. What is important about this is that Beloved is thus both Sethe's personal ghost and a communal problem. Indeed, Beloved's return and expulsion ultimately result in the reintegration of Denver, and, to a certain extent, Sethe, into the community. The return of the dead thus acts on a personal level for Sethe as the disruption of social bonds and simultaneously acts on a communal level as an imperative toward cooperation and healing.

Beloved, as a ghost story, turns on the various significations and resonances of its title. To read *Beloved*, one therefore must engage in the vexing task of reading epitaphs—which is to allow oneself to be haunted by the absence toward which the epitaph gestures. This situation is made even more complicated by Morrison's use of the term "beloved" to designate both one and many. Caroline Rody observes that, although the name "Beloved" refers to everyone in the rhetoric of the Church and names everyone who is intimately loved, it "does not name the forgotten" (104). She continues, "Morrison has the name perform precisely this last function; the novel's defining conceit is to call the unnamed 'beloved.' Part of Beloved's strangeness derives, then, from the emotional burden she carries as a symbolic compression of innumerable forgotten people in one miraculously resurrected personality, the remembering of the 'sixty million' in one youthful body" (104).

What Rody refers to as Beloved's "strangeness," the fact that she simultaneously incarnates the return of Sethe's murdered child and symbolizes the African holocaust of the Middle Passage, the "Sixty Million and more" of Morrison's dedication, one might also consider as the complexity of the novel itself its allegorical overlay. Beloved, inseparable from her name, is both one and many, and Beloved the ghost, like "beloved" the epitaph, mediates between private and public, self and other, and living and dead. The haunting she performs pushes Sethe, her community, and the reader toward the momentous recognition of the possibility of loss and, as a result, introduces the necessity of mourning-mourning that fails to domesticate the strangeness of absence and thereby introduces a "chance for the future."

The Social Structuration of Haunting

Avery Gordon, in her *Ghostly Matters: Haunting and the Sociological Imagination*, insists that "haunting is a constitutive feature of social life" (23). A haunting describes "how that which appears to be not there is often a seething presence" (8). Gordon explains, "A disappearance is real only when it is apparitional because the ghost or the apparition is the principal form by which something lost or invisible or seemingly not there makes itself known or apparent to us" (63). The ghost, in other words, functions as the trace of an absent presence, the "evidence of things not seen" (195). And, as Gordon points out, only that which has not been completely forgotten can return as a ghost. Ghosts are products of uneasy minds—of problematic knowing—not complete ignorance.

In the case of the specific story of Sethe's murder of her daughter, Beloved can be read as the return of Sethe's murdered "crawling already?" baby. However, to read Beloved's return as solely the "return of the repressed" of Sethe is mistaken. As Sally Keenan observes, "Sethe has not forgotten either her daughter or the fact that she killed her ... suggesting that remembering or acknowledgment is not the problem, but, rather, how to forget, how to lay the past to rest, is" (71).[2] Importantly, this past is not purely Sethe's past, nor can she "lay it to rest" on her own. Indeed, the moral dilemma intrinsic in the attempt to judge Sethe's actions—a difficulty evident in the ways in which the huge mass of critical literature carefully evades even the question of Sethe's accountability for her crime—lies in the complex web of social forces that result in the act.[3] Sethe's "tough response to the Fugitive Slave Bill" (171), her decision to kill her children rather than allow them to be remanded back into slavery, is the culmination of her personal experience as a black woman living in the social context of the existence of black slavery. She is placed in an impossible situation—the only way to keep her children is to lose them, the only place where they will be safe is in death (164). Additionally, her actions also result from the failure of the black community to warn the residents of 124 of the approaching horsemen. Jan Furman observes that the black community in *Beloved* "fails its obligation" to Sethe when it "betrays Baby Suggs and her family by failing to warn of what they instinctively know is trouble" (72). This failure of communication is then continued when Sethe extracts the one word "beloved" from the funeral eulogy and uses it, at least in part, as a *weapon* against the community, as an answer to "one more preacher, one more abolitionist, and a town full of disgust" (5).

Sethe's actions, therefore, cannot be extricated from the social context in which they occur, and the return of Beloved, the presence of the ghost, the "fearful claim of the past on the present" (Rody 104), is not an isolated event affecting Sethe, but a social phenomenon implicating the community and the culture at large that facilitated Sethe's action. Beloved's return affects the community since it, through "spite, jealousy, and meanness" (Furman 72), allowed the conditions for Sethe's act to develop. Ultimately, it is the community that must come together at the end of the novel to expel Beloved, which points to the social constitution of haunting and the collective nature of memory itself.

That haunting is a social phenomenon is most readily apparent in *Beloved* when one considers Beloved as the symbol for the millions who died during the Middle Passage. As Gordon observes, *Beloved* "is about the lingering inheritance of racial slavery, the unfinished project of Reconstruction, and the compulsions and forces that all of us inevitably experience in the face of slavery's having even once existed in our nation. Slavery has ended, but something of it continues to live on.... Such endings that are not over is what haunting is about" (139). Beyond the particular story of the return of Sethe's murdered child, beyond even the implication of Sethe's community in her crime and its results, *Beloved*, as a contemporary ghost story, as an effort at "reclamation" (Morrison, "A Conversation" 199), is the attempt to address a contemporary haunting, the social trauma of slavery that lives on in American culture. Implicit in Morrison's project of reclamation of black history is the objective of healing. Keenan remarks that "if Beloved's spectral return into the slave family represents within the narrative the eruption of that which has lived on as memory but has remained unspoken, the text, *Beloved*, signals a current discursive renegotiation with their history by African Americans which amounts to a contestation of the ways that past has been erased or subsumed within the historical discourse of hegemonic culture" (48). Reclaiming or revisioning this history in the present is thus proposed as part of a healing process directed at the wounds of a traumatic past. However, as I will argue below, the most dramatic recognition prompted by Beloved's uncanny irruption is that the forgotten, and, by extension, the past itself, cannot he recovered or recover. The opening of a future-yet-to-come, a future different from that which can be envisioned today, is contingent upon learning to read epitaphs, on learning to preserve the alterity of the other by mourning the lostness of the lost.

The Oppressed Past

Caroline Rody writes that "*Beloved* is manifestly about the filling of historical gaps" (93) and suggests that one consider fiction such as *Beloved* as "structures of historiographic desire," that is, as "attempts to span a vast gap of time, loss, and ignorance to achieve an intimate bond, a bridge of restitution or healing, between the authorial present and the ancestral past" (97). Morrison herself speaks of this process as one of "assuming responsibility" ("In the Realm" 247) for the forgotten and the dispossessed. This responsibility is one of "artistically burying" the unburied ("A Conversation" 209), that, Morrison acknowledges as "just one step" in the process of the reclamation of black history ("Interview with Toni Morrison" 413). However, the pressing questions here are how does one remember the forgotten? How can one bear witness to what one has not experienced? And to what extent can a work of fiction, a ghost story, participate in these endeavors?

In an interview with Christina Davis, Morrison explains that:

> The reclamation of the history of black people in this country is paramount in its importance because while you can't really blame the conqueror for writing history his own way, you can certainly debate it. There's a great deal of obfuscation and distortion and erasure, so that the presence and the heartbeat of black people has been systematically annihilated in many, many ways and the job of recovery is ours. It's a serious responsibility and one single human being can only do a very very tiny part of that, but it seems to me to be both secular and non-secular work for a writer ["Interview with Toni Morrison" 413].

Morrison is thus participating in, to quote Walter Benjamin, the "fight for the oppressed past" ("Theses" 263). She recognizes, with Hortense Spillers, that "[events] *do* occur, to be sure, but in part according to the conventions dictating how we receive, imagine, and pass them on" (176). This is to say that there are multiple perspectives on any given event and one perspective assumes prominence only at the expense of other, competing interpretations. In the rewriting of the event, the revisioning of history that the ghost prompts, Gordon observes that "a different story or history is made possible" (163). For Gordon, the encounter with the ghost is the moment at which one no longer can stand divorced from history and objectively survey its field. Rather, in experiencing a haunting, the wheels of history stop and one is faced with uncertainty, with the disturbing realization that something is missing, that the story is incomplete.

The ghost, as the trace of an absent presence, thus has ethical ramifications for Gordon; it is both "the symptom of something missing" and a "loss," but also "a future possibility, a hope" (64). It can "lead you toward what has been missing" (58) and "mak[e] you see things you did not see before" (98). Ultimately, it "forces a reckoning" (130). The ghost as such is a "living force" (179) that pushes those who encounter it toward a "something to be done" (203). Yet how can a work of fiction, a ghost story, participate in the task of historical reclamation and prompt this something to be done? How can *Beloved* fight for the oppressed past?

In her essay, "The Site of Memory," Morrison comments explicitly on the line between history and fiction in her writing, a negotiation that she describes as "literary archeology." She writes, "on the basis of some information and a little bit of guesswork you journey to a site to see what remains were left behind and to reconstruct the world that these remains imply. What makes it fiction is the nature of the imaginative act: my reliance on the image—on the remains—in addition to recollection, to yield up a kind of truth" (112). Morrison thus attempts to reconstitute a life from an epitaph—in a sense, to summon spirits—to imagine what is missing based on the remains.

Intriguingly, in this process of imaginative reconstruction, Morrison does not oppose truth and fiction. Rather, she writes, "the crucial distinction for me is not the difference between fact and fiction, but the distinction between fact and truth. Because facts can exist without human intelligence, but truth cannot" (113). To gain access to the interior life of historical subjects, to "rip the veil drawn over 'proceedings too terrible to relate'" (110), to get at the truth of historical silences and forgettings, "Only the act of the imagination can help" (111). Attempting to get at the truth, to do justice to the dispossessed, and, in the process, to live more justly oneself, therefore depends precisely upon the act of imagining. What Morrison indicates is that sometimes fiction paradoxically can be more "truthful" than facts. Or rather, the imagination "animates the remains," brings "dead" facts to life in such a way so as to turn "inhuman" facts into a living narrative. The imagination thereby provides a framework for learning, for comprehending indigestible facts. And yet to read a story as epitaph is to remember not only that any story is never the whole story, that the real, the other, always exceeds, escapes language, but also that the imaginative animation of the remains cannot help but to foreground what is missing. The task of recovery, of reclamation, therefore also entails a letting go, a recognition of loss, and healing, learning to live for the future, requires a mourning of and for the past. Reading epitaphs is both about remembering the dead and remembering to live before one joins them. Reading epitaphs is about summoning spirits and coming to terms with ghosts, not about exorcising them.

Learning to Live

In this respect, philosopher Jacques Derrida's comments in the "Exordium" to his *Specters of Marx* are particularly striking. Derrida begins by writing, "someone, you or me, comes forward and says: *I would like to learn to live finally*" (xvii)—a remarkably strange turn of phrase, as Derrida himself notes. Why does anyone need to learn this? And how? And from whom? And why "finally"? The phrase implies that one can be alive without living, that, paradoxically, living needs to be learned, and that this learning is a task. The weight that Derrida places on this task is suggested by the finality of the "finally": at the end of it all, after having lived without living—or having forgotten how to live—to be left with living. The finality of "finally" implies that one can only learn to live by encountering the end, the limit of life, by and through death, through "com[ing] to terms with death" (xviii). Derrida writes, "If it—learning to live—remains to be done, it can happen only between life and death. Neither in life nor death *alone*" (xviii). Life, by itself, is meaningless. Without the fact of mortality, learning to live is impossible, for life would not be a gift, and living would lack all urgency. For Derrida, this task of learning to live is "ethics itself" (xviii) and "has no sense and cannot be *just* unless it comes to terms with death" (xviii).

Learning to live and coming to terms with death can only happen in the between, in an uncanny space between life and death—which is the space and time of the ghost. Derrida continues, "What happens between two, and between all the 'two's' one likes, such as between life and death, can only *maintain itself* with some ghost, can only *talk with or about* some ghost [*s'entretenir de quelque fantôme*]. So it would be necessary to learn spirits" (xviii). Learning to live thus means to "learn spirits," to learn to live *with* spirits, which is to learn to live with a restless past and one's own being-towards-death. And this "being-with specters," this acceptance of spirits, which also amounts to a "*politics* of memory, of inheritance, and of generations" (xix), allows one to live "otherwise" and "more justly" (xviii)—because justice entails a *responsibility* both to the dead and the still to be born: "No justice ... seems possible or thinkable without some responsibility, beyond all living present ... before the ghosts of those who are not yet born or who are already dead" (xix).

Derrida goes on to identify the classes of these already dead to which one owes some debt, toward which one bears some responsibility: "victims of wars, political or other kinds of violence, nationalist, racist, colonialist, sexist, or other kinds of exterminations, victims of the oppressions of capitalist imperialism or any of the forms of totalitarianism"(xix). The ghosts that come back to haunt, "these unburied, or at least unceremoniously buried" dead (Morrison, "A Conversation" 209), victims of the most extreme acts of violence, raise the question of the possibility of justice in its starkest form—how can justice be served? How can one discharge a debt to the dead? How can hurt be undone? These are not happy spirits or friendly ghosts that return. The question that Derrida raises here—and that *Beloved* forcefully engages—is the question of how to live with these spirits, victims of brutal violence, victims of the Middle Passage. How does one live with a history or an inheritance that is too painful or shameful to be remembered—one that an individual or a community or an entire culture desperately wishes to forget—and yet which is too important to be forgotten? How can one do justice to the dead and, if this is the task that is required to live justly, or to learn to live at all, is learning to live even possible?

For Derrida, the opening of the future as something other than a repetition of the present is dependent precisely upon the work of mourning, and, importantly, on mourning that never succeeds fully in working through or domesticating the trauma of loss, mourning that fails in "introjecting" the absent loved one. The absence of the other remains and this absence, this loss, can never be filled with words, can never itself be articulated completely. The epitaph gestures toward the absence that remains.[4] Against this absence of the other, narcissism reaches a limit as "we realize that, will what we might,' we cannot rewrite the other back into life, remaking history so that she is still with us. She is gone. In her very absence we feel the pull of otherness" (Cornell 73). One can remember, but not recall to life. For Derrida, one cannot eliminate the absence of the other that propels one to mourn.

However, as Drucilla Cornell notes, "Ironically, it is only through this failure to fully recollect the Other that we 'succeed' in mourning the Other as Other" (73). To mourn the "Other as Other" is to recognize the otherness of the other, to understand, in a sense, the fullness of the other that exceeds all knowing, overflows all attempts at circumscription and containment. Derrida writes, "we learn that the other resists the closure of our interiorizing memory. With the nothing of this irrevocable absence, the other appears as other" (*Memoires* 34). The absence of the other that cannot be overcome points to a fullness of the other that cannot be recreated by memory or language. The recognition of this loss, this absence that remains is, according to Derrida, a strange type of success, a gesture of respect toward the otherness of the other: "the *failure succeeds*: an aborted interiorization is at the same time a respect for the other as other, a sort of tender rejection, a movement of renunciation that leaves the other alone, outside, over there, in his death, outside us" (*Memoires* 35).

In mourning, one confronts the "remains," the "beyond," that which exists outside of systems of representation that which resists conscious knowing, resists articulation-that which can only be experienced as loss. But, as Cornell writes, "it is the very failure of mourning as mimetic interiorization that allows us to attempt fidelity to the remains. The inevitable failure of memory to enclose the Other, opens us to the 'beyond'" (73). Mourning thus becomes both crucial and, in a sense, impossible. One must grapple with absence, with the past, knowing that loss can never be eliminated or overcome fully. This painful experience of loss and the resistant residue of otherness opens one to the "beyond," to the recognition of incompleteness, to the recognition of the limitations of signifying systems, and to the frightening yet potentially liberating prospect of other ways of thinking. An openness to or opening of the beyond is the openness to difference, to a different future, a future yet to come.[5] Only where the possibility of loss exists can things be found. Cornell concludes that "the chance for the future ... is preserved in the work of mourning which ironically remembers the remains through the experience of the limit of interiorization, through the very finitude of memory that makes 'true' mourning impossible, and yet so necessary" (75).

Justice, in Cornell's reading of Derrida, is "our singular responsibility to the Other" (143), and "doing justice" to the *memory* of the other takes place through incomplete mourning, through the absence of the other that remains, through the otherness of the other that resists assimilation to the same. *Beloved*, I suggest, in its attempt to do justice to the memory of the lost and dispossessed, is not about the process of filling in historical gaps, as Caroline Rody contends (93). Nor is it a project of "historical recovery" (Krumholz 395). Both these descriptions imply that a coherent, singular, "truthful" narrative of history could be established if only certain missing pieces could be unearthed. A project of "historical recovery" suggests that history is in some sense an organic body, sick or lost, but potentially sound, whole, and present.[6]

On the contrary, Morrison's narrative suggests that history will not recover, that, as Morgenstern asserts, there is "no easy cure" (117), and I do not believe that *Beloved* is about the "filling in" of anything. I suggest that it is instead about loss, about emptiness, about emptying. To the extent that it is about recovery, it is precisely about first recovering or experiencing the "beyond" as *loss*: the loss of history and history as loss. This process of recovering lostness, as opposed to the filling in of gaps, means to recognize and appreciate gaps as gaps, to recognize the terrifying fact that some things can be lost forever. It necessitates a coming to grips with the fact that certainty is never possible, and that action must take place precisely in the absence of cognitive mastery. Finally, the idea of filling in gaps which I would describe as the denial of the possibility of loss—is also the attempt to side-step the painful process of mourning—indeed, to avoid the frightening prospect of an interminable mourning that will never succeed fully in "closing the circle" around lost experience. But it is this encounter with lostness and the necessity of mourning that are crucial if the opening of a different future is to be envisioned. Morrison's text, I suggest, in juxtaposing Sethe's "recovery" of narrative with Beloved's breakdown of narrative, proposes that it is only by *having* loss, owning lostness, that one can avoid *being lost* altogether. Ghosts in this sense are symptomatic of failures of mourning, the failure to recognize loss. The ghost points to a gap, a loss, an absence. *Beloved* demands that one mourn the lost as lost, to preserve their lostness, their disappearance, even as one seeks to "resurrect" their stories—to remember the lost in their lostness so as to open the possibility of a different future—a just future, a future of justice yet-to-come.

Necessary Impossible Telling

Alongside of the specific story of Sethe's murder of Beloved, there is another story, a twofold tragedy of disappearance and forgetting—the deaths of the "sixty million and more" Africans during the Middle Passage. Baby Suggs points out to Sethe, "There's more of us they drowned than there is all of them ever lived from the start of time" (244). Of these millions, Morrison writes, "No one praised them, nobody knows their names, nobody can remember them, not in the United States or Africa. Millions of people disappeared without a trace, and there is not one monument anywhere to pay homage to them, because they never arrived safely on shore. So it's like a whole nation that is under the sea" (qtd. in Furman 80). It is from this place of forgetting that Beloved emerges and, as Karla Holloway observes, she is "not only Sethe's dead daughter returned, but the return[ed] of all the faces, all the drowned, but remembered, faces of mothers and their children who have lost their being because of the force of that EuroAmerican slave-history" (qtd. in Furman, 73).[7] Or, as Susan Bowers concisely puts it, "Beloved is the embodiment or the collective pain and rage of the millions of slaves who died on the Middle Passage" (66). But Morrison's attempt at reclamation, at remembering the disremembered, at telling the story of the forgotten again raises the issue of her distinction between truth and fact and the issue of the ethics of memory.

How can Morrison use fiction in the "fight for the oppressed past"? How can Morrison do justice to the departed? And, in reference to historical catastrophes such as slavery, is it in fact ethical to attempt to reintegrate the events into narrative memory, to force them into stable, communicable, comprehensible configurations? Cathy Caruth raises these same questions in her discussion of *Hiroshima, Mon Amour* when she poses the questions of the ethics of narration and of how not to "betray" the past (*Unclaimed* 27). What Caruth proposes, following Shoshana Felman and Claude Lanzmann, is that the possibility of a "faithful" history arises out of an "indirectness of telling" (27) and a "creative act of listening" ("Introduction" 154). As numerous critics have noted, Beloved provides the former and demands the latter.

Beloved is not a text that progresses from start to finish in a linear fashion. Neither does it have a singular, stable narrator. Rather, like Sethe in her kitchen, attempting to tell Paul D something for which she has no words, for which words fail—why she killed her daughter—the text "circles" around its subjects. Philip Page remarks that "[Sethe] cannot say directly what she did or why, so the narration does tell the story directly.... The novel is like the circle Sethe spins, collecting, omitting, repeating fragments.... It tends to drop an unexplained fact on the reader, veer away into other matters, then circle back with more information about the initial fact, then veer away again, circle back again, and so on" (140–141). And part of the novel's "obliqueness" (141) is its multiple and overlapping points of view. This "deviousness" (141) of the text, the resistance of the narrative, is most evident during the middle section of the text in which identity dissolves as the voices of Sethe, Denver, and Beloved intertwine, and especially during Beloved's monologue, in which the text itself threatens to unwind altogether.[8]

What Beloved's disarticulated monologue reveals is the impossibility of telling, the impossibility of recovering the stories of the dispossessed, of explaining the horror of the Middle Passage, of articulating death. Morgenstern observes that "what most needs to be said in the novel defies narrative form" (118), and Beloved's monologue is the moment in the story when the text literally falls apart through the introduction of spatial gaps and the absence of punctuation. Here, where logic fails, the historical power of trauma is experienced in and through the experience of a gap, of a not knowing. Valerie Smith writes that "this section of the novel resists explication. It prompts, rather, the recognition that what is essentially and effectively unspoken can never be conveyed and comprehended linguistically" (352). Mobley proposes that the literal gaps left in the text during this section "signal the timelessness of [Beloved's] presence as well as the unlived spaces of her life" (362), but they also figure the resistance of trauma to telling, of the secrets of the unknown to being solved.[9] One might wish to consider Beloved's monologue figuring both her individual death and the Middle Passage of slavery as the horrific Middle Passage of both the text and of language itself. Her monologue actualizes on the levels of text and language fears of fragmentation, of exploding and being swallowed up (133). On this leaky ship of language, meaning slips away through the cracks.

However, one may ask, as Derrida does of translation, what if this "disadjustment," this disarticulation of the text, is in fact the very condition of attempting to do justice to the victims—or the memory of the victims—of the Middle Passage? (*Specters* 19–20). What Morrison avoids doing in Beloved's monologue is making any attempt at rendering either Beloved's experience of death or the deaths of millions readily intelligible. Rather than to try to represent coherently horror that exceeds intelligible frameworks, Morrison attempts to convey or transmit horror, to allow the reader to experience horror, through the performative "breakdown" or "breakage of words."

In *Testimony*, Shoshana Felman discusses the resistance of the Holocaust to intelligibility. Any attempt to explain it can only result in reduction. For Felman, it is the "breakage of words" that *acts* (39). When language breaks down, when gaps are introduced, when comprehension is problematized, language begins to act, to enact, to perform, rather than report. Following Felman, one may propose that the "breakage of words" of Beloved's monologue functions performatively to enact and communicate horror without attempting to explain it or reduce it. The textual spaces, the gaps, the play of perspective and voice are all strategies that Morrison employs to fulfill her "single gravest responsibility": "not to lie" ("Site of Memory" 113). To try and speak the horror of infanticide and holocaust, to contain overwhelming emotions and experiences in a structured narrative, would be to betray the past. Paradoxically, Morrison can only speak the truth by not speaking it, and the trauma can only be remembered and mourned through the reader's involvement and witnessing.

What *Beloved* demands is the reader's active participation in the process of constructing meaning and memory. Morrison is explicit concerning this narrative strategy and comments in several different interviews and articles about her partnership with the reader. She observes addressing ambiguities in her texts, "These spaces, which I am filling in, and can fill in because they were planned, can conceivably he filled in with other significances. This is planned as well. The point is that into these spaces should fall the ruminations of the reader and his or her invented or recollected or misunderstood knowingness" ("Unspeakable" 29). In *Beloved*, the reader's participation is pivotal in as much as the reader's piecing together of the textual fragments amounts to the piecing together of a damaged past, functions as a way to "evolve a subjective language with which to attach different meanings to slavery outside the ways in which it has become fixed in historiography and myth" (Keenan 55).

Ultimately, what *Beloved* demands is that the reader, like Ella, "listen for the holes" (92), or, as Dori Laub puts it, the listener to trauma "must *listen to and hear the silence*, speaking mutely both in silence and in speech, both from behind and from within speech" (58). This listening for the holes, listening to silence, is an act of "creative listening," one that allows a story to emerge that the teller cannot know in the process of telling. And the listener, by virtue of the listening, becomes implicated in the event: "By extension, the listener to trauma comes to be a participant and a co-owner of the traumatic event: through his very listening, he comes to partially experience trauma in himself" (Laub 57). The reader's active participation in the construction of *Beloved* functions as a witnessing to the historical trauma of slavery and the Middle Passage and, to the extent that *Beloved*'s "breakage of words" functions as performative testimony, moves the reader to feel the "bewilderment, injury, confusion, dread, and conflicts that the trauma victim feels" (Laub 58), one can say in Caruth's terms that the "falling" or "departure" of the text, its impossibility of telling, impacts on the reader—that the "ghost of reference" returns in the very disarticulation of the text itself In the absence of knowing, one is moved by an epitaph that haunts.

Passing On

The ghost therefore presents an impossible task—to attempt to negotiate an unstable past and to speak what cannot he spoken fully. This dilemma is most forcefully imposed by the radical ambiguity of her thrice repeated insistence that the story of Beloved was and to "not a story to pass on" (274–275)—that suggests simultaneously that the story is one that should not be bypassed and that the story is one that should not be communicated. The paradox of speaking the unspeakable remains unresolved and doing justice to the dead, in the sense of redressing past injuries, impossible. What can be done with the aporetic conclusion of a story not to pass on, of a story that is too painful to remember but must he remembered to prevent it from being repeated? Morrison's answer is a "creative listening" and imaginative revisioning that listens to the silences of traumatic history and, rather than trying to fill them in, appreciates the silences as silences.

To move through *Beloved* is to undergo the ordeal of undecidability. Morrison's ghost Beloved gestures toward these gaps and Beloved's story is a "laying alongside" of a different story against the historical record. The injustices done to the dead can never be redressed. However, justice can be done to their memories by remembering their stories in order to open a different future, an always yet-to-come future of justice. And this necessary remembrance is not just the unearthing of facts to fill in gaps in the historical record. Rather, it is an interrogation of the record itself, the constant reminder that one story assumes prominence at the expense of others and that what is necessary to recover these other, forgotten stories is the act of imagining. Truth, Morrison tells us, differs from facts. And justice, Derrida notes, is different from law—and the gap between each is the space in which the ghost returns to open up the possibility of a future-to-come different from what' one can imagine in the present.[10]

Although Morrison writes that "by and by all trace is gone, and what is forgotten is not only the footprints but the water and what is down there," the last word of the text, "Beloved," belies this forgetting for the tombstone of the "crawling already?" baby and its overdetermined epitaph remain. To learn to live with ghosts is neither to reject the past, nor to let it overwhelm the present. Rather to live with ghosts is "to be haunted in the name of a will to heal," which means to "allow the ghost to help you imagine what was lost that never even existed, really" (Gordon 57). And this imagining cannot be done alone. In *Beloved*, it is the community that rallies to expel Beloved, and Paul D who returns Sethe to herself, thus opening for her a chance for a future. The last word of the text, which circles back around to the title and the beginning, reminds one that Beloved belongs to each of us individually and all of us together. *Beloved* demands to be read as an epitaph. The starkness of the title and the unspeakable incommensurability of "ten minutes for seven letters" is crushing. The ethical imperative that it sets forth is for one to recognize the immensity and terrifying reality of loss. *Beloved* structures an encounter with lostness and introduces the necessity of mourning the lost as lost so as to open the possibility of a different future. Finally, what Sethe and Denver learn to do, at the end of it all, is to live. And it is a ghost that teaches them how.

NOTES

1. Scruggs suggests that Sethe's fornication with the stonecutter is not just payment but an act of penance (189), in which case, one may add "guilt" to the list essential terms manifest in the encounter.

2. However, although Sethe clear has not forgotten or repressed the past, she also has not "worked through" the trauma of the loss of her baby girl. Caruth's description of trauma survivors as not possessing but "possessed" ("Introduction" 5) by an event or image is clearly applicable to Sethe who undergoes the "literal return of the event" against her will. Sethe does not remember, but "rememories," relives or experiences as flashbacks.

For her, "rememory" entails "being there," returning to site of trauma. I will argue that this phenomenon of rememory, as *distinct from remembrance*, is connected to a failure of mourning and "working through."

3. Wyatt writes that "the novel withholds judgment on Sethe's act and persuades the reader to do the same" (476). Henderson brings up the question of Sethe's accountability, but concludes that Morrison, within the text, "neither condemns nor condones," but "delivers" her protagonist (82), delivers in the sense of redemption. Morrison herself comments in a 1988 interview with Marsha Darling that "I got to a point where in asking myself who could judge Sethe adequately, since I couldn't and nobody else that knew her could, really, I felt that the only person who could judge her would be the daughter she killed" ("In the Realm" 248). However, Beloved's judgment, one that locks Sethe into a "cycle of impossible atonement and expiation" (Keenan 72) and ultimately necessitates her exorcism from the text, early is not a verdict Morrison supports.

4. Here one should recall Morrison's comment in "The Site of Memory" that journeys to a site of trauma to "see what remains were left behind" (112), to construct what remains unthought or untold through the imagining stimulated traces. The remains themselves cannot be spoken, but openness to the trace as absence yields the possibility of telling a new story.

5. Derrida writes,

> Memory stays with traces, in order to "preserve" them, but traces of a past that has never been present, traces which themselves never occupy the form of presence and always remain, as it were, to come—come from the future, from the to come. Resurrection, which is always the formal element of "truth," a recurrent difference between a present and its presence, does not resuscitate a past which had been present; it engages a future [*Memoires* 58].

In this sense, "memory projects itself toward the future, and it constitutes the presence of the present" (*Memoires* 57). At this point in the text, Derrida also quotes Paul de Man on "this trace of the future as the power of memory." De Man writes, in his reading of Poulet reading Proust, "The power of memory does not reside in its capacity to resurrect a situation or a feeling that actually existed, but is a constitutive act of the mind bound to its own present and oriented toward the future of its elaboration" (*Memoires* 59).

6. As Morgenstern observes, "much of the criticism on *Beloved* celebrates the text as it retells its story as a story of cure" (122, n28).

7. Jessee observes that what slavery and the Middle Passage disrupted were West African conceptions of time and death in which "present" time "encompasses much of the immediate past, including several generations of ancestors" (199). According to Jessee, Beloved is a "forgotten ancestor" (200) who returns to "initiate the collective sharing of memory" (208), which Jessee figures as a process of healing.

8. The absence of linear plot development has also been associated with Morrison's incorporation of aspects of African American oral traditions as well as with African conceptions of time. See Christol, Gorn, Jessee, Sale, and Traoré.

9. Bouson writes concerning this point that, "Deliberately using a fragmented and repetitive narrative structure to convey the disrupted, obsessive world of the trauma victim, Morrison circles around and around the shameful secrets that haunt her characters" (136).

10. Derrida observes the difference between law and justice in "Force of Law."

Works Cited

Benjamin, Walter. "Critique of Violence." *Reflections: Essays, Aphorisms, Autobiographical Writings*, translated by Edmund Jephcott, edited by Peter Demetz. Schocken Books, 1978, pp. 277-301.

———. "Theses on the Philosophy of History" in *Illuminations*, translated by Harry Zohn, edited by Hannah Arendt. Schocken, 1969, pp. 253-264.

Bouson, J. Brooks. *Quiet As It's Kept: Shame, Trauma, and Race in the Novels of Toni Morrison*. SUNY Press, 2000.

Bowers, Susan. "Beloved and the New Apocalypse." *The Journal of Ethnic Studies*, vol. 18, no. 1, 1990, pp. 59–78.

Caruth, Cathy. "Introduction" to *Trauma: Explorations in Memory*, edited by Cathy Caruth. Johns Hopkins University Press, 1995, pp. 3–12.

———. *Unclaimed Experience: Trauma, Narrative, and History*. Johns Hopkins University Press, 1996.

Chase, Cynthia. "Reading Epitaphs" in *Deconstruction is/in America: A New Sense of the Political*, edited by Anselm Haverkamp. New York University Press, 1995, pp. 52–59.

Christol, Helene. "The African-American Concept of the Fantastic as Middle Passage" in *Black Imagination and the Middle Passage*, edited by Maria Diedrich, Henry Louis Gates, Jr., and Carl Pedersen. Oxford University Press, 1999, pp. 164–182.

Cornell, Drucilla. *The Philosophy of the Limit*. Routledge, 1992.

Derrida. Jacques. *Memoires for Paul de Man*. Revised edition, translated by Cecile Lindsay, Jonathan Culler, Eduardo Cadava, and Peggy Kamuf. Columbia University Press, 1989.

———. "Force of Law: the 'Mystical Foundations of Authority'" in *Deconstruction and the Possibility of Justice*, edited by Drucilla Cornell, Michel Rosenfeld and David Gray Carlson. Routledge, 1992, pp. 3–67.

———. *Given Time: 1. Counterfeit Money*, translated by Peggy Kamuf. University of Chicago Press, 1992.

———. *Specters of Marx: The State of Debt, the Work of Mourning, & the New International*, translated by Peggy Kamuf. Routledge, 1994.

Felman, Shoshana, and Dori Laub. *Testimony: Crises of Witnessing in Literature, Psychoanalysis, and History*. Routledge, 1992.

Furman, Jan. *Toni Morrison's Fiction*. University of South Carolina Press, 1996.

Gates, Henry Louis, Jr., and K.A. Appiah, eds. *Toni Morrison: Critical Perspectives Past and Present*, Amistad, 1993.

Gordon, Avery. *Ghostly Matters: Haunting and the Sociological Imagination*. University of Minnesota Press, 1997.

Gorn, Elliott J. "Black Spirits: The Ghostlore of Afro-American Slaves." *American Quarterly*, vol. 36, no. 4, 1984, pp. 549–565.

Henderson, May G. "Toni Morrison's *Beloved*: Re-Membering the Body as Historical Text" in *Comparative American Identities: Race, Sex and Nationality in the Modern Text*, edited by Hortense J. Spillers. Routledge, 1991, pp. 62–86.

Hirsch, Marianne. "Maternity and Rememory: Toni Morrison's *Beloved*" in *Representations of Motherhood*, edited by Donna Bassin, Margaret Honey, and Meryle Mahrer Kaplan. Yale University Press, 1994, pp. 92–110.

Horvitz, Deborah. "Nameless Ghosts: Possession and Dispossesion in *Beloved*." *Studies in American Fiction*, vol. 17, no. 2, 1989, pp. 157–168.

Jessee, Sharon. "'Tell me your earrings': Time and the Marvelous in Toni Morrison's *Beloved*" in *Memory, Narrative and Identity: New Essays in Ethnic American Literatures*, edited by Amritjit Singh, Joseph T. Skerrett, Jr., and Robert E. Hoga. Northeastern University Press, 1994, pp. 198–211.

Keenan, Sally. "Four Hundred Years of Silence" in *Recasting the World: Writing After Colonialism*, edited by Jonathan White. Johns Hopkins University Press, 1993, pp. 45–81.

Krumholz, Linda. "The Ghosts of Slavery: Historical Recovery in Toni Morrison's *Beloved*." *African American Review*, vol. 26, no. 3, 1992, pp. 395–407.

Laub, Dori. "Bearing Witness, or the Vicissitudes of Listening" in *Testimony: Crises of Witnessing in Literature, Psychoanalysis, and History*, by Shoshana Felman and Dori Laub. Routledge, 1992, pp. 57–74.

Lawrence, David. "Fleshly Ghosts and Ghostly Flesh: the Word and the Body in *Beloved*." *Studies in American Fiction*, vol. 19, no. 2, 1991, pp. 199–202.

Mobley, Marilyn Sanders. "A Different Remembering: Memory, History, and Meaning in *Beloved*" in *Toni Morrison: Critical Perspectives Past and Present*, edited by Henry Louis Gates, Jr., and K.A. Appiah. Amistad, 1993, pp. 356–66.

Morgenstern, Naomi. "Mother's Milk and Sisters Blood: Trauma and the Neoslave Narrative." *Differences: A Journal of Feminist Cultural Studies*, vol. 8, no. 2, 1996, pp. 101–126.

Morrison, Toni. *Beloved*. Plume, 1987.

———. "A Conversation: Gloria Naylor and Toni Morrison, 1985" in *Conversations with Toni Morrison*, edited by Danielle Taylor-Guthrie. University of Mississippi Press, 1994, pp. 188–217.

———. "In the Realm of Responsibility: A Conversation with Toni Morrison" in *Conversations with Toni Morrison*, edited by Danielle Taylor-Guthrie. University of Mississippi Press, 1994, pp. 246–254.

———. "Interview with Toni Morrison in *Toni Morrison: Critical Perspectives Past and Present*, edited by Henry Louis Gates, Jr., and K.A. Appiah. Amistad, 1993, pp. 412–420.

———. "The Site of Memory" in *Inventing the Truth: The Art and Craft of Memoir*, edited by William Zinser. Houghton Mifflin, 1987, pp. 103–124.

———. "Unspeakable Things Unspoken: The Afro-American Presence in American Literature." *Michigan Quarterly Review*, vol. 28, no. 1, 1989, pp. 1–34.

Page, Philip. *Dangerous Freedom: Fusion and Fragmentation in Toni Morrison's Novels*. University Press of Mississippi, 1995.

Rody, Caroline. "Toni Morrison's *Beloved*: History, 'Rememory,' and a 'Clamor for a Kiss.'" *American Literary History*, vol. 7, no. 1, 1995, pp. 92–119.

Sale, Maggie. "Call and Response as Critical Method: African-American Oral Traditions and *Beloved*." *African American Review*, vol. 26, no. 1, 1992, pp. 41–50.

Scruggs, Charles. *Sweet Home: Invisible Cities in the Afro-American Novel*. Johns Hopkins University Press, 1993.

Smith, Valerie. "'Circling the Subject': History and Narrative in *Beloved*" in *Toni Morrison: Critical Perspectives Past and Present*, edited by Henry Louis Gates, Jr., and K.A. Appiah. Amistad, 1993, pp. 342–355.

Spillers, Hortense J. "Notes on an Alternative Model: Neither/Nor" in *The Year Left 2: An American Socialist Yearbook*, edited by Mike Davis. Verso, 1987, pp. 176–194.

Taylor-Guthrie, Danielle, ed. *Conversations With Toni Morrison*. University of Mississippi Press, 1994.

Traoré, Ousseynou B. "Mythic Structures of Ethnic Memory in *Beloved*: The Mammy Watta and Middle Passage Paradigms" in "*Beloved, she's mine.*" *Essais sur Beloved de Toni Morrison*, edited by Genevieve Fabre and Claudine Reynaud. Cetanla, 1993, pp. 77–89.

Wyatt, Jean. "Giving Body to the Word: The Maternal Symbolic in Toni Morrison's *Beloved*." *PMLA*, vol. 108, no. 3, 1993, pp. 474–488.

Act II

Vampires

Permit me to start Act II with an interesting little factoid about Bram Stoker's novel *Dracula* (1897). Dracula can and does move about during the day—the character Jonathan Harker sees Dracula, looking younger, out and about in Piccadilly Circus in London during daylight hours. Dracula's weaker during the day, yes, but doesn't go up in flames when exposed to the sun's rays. The idea that sunlight kills vampires doesn't in fact come from Stoker, but rather from one of the first cinematic adaptations of *Dracula*: F.W. Murnau's German Expressionist *Nosferatu: A Symphony of Horror* (*Nosferatu, eine Symphonie des Grauens*, 1922). In Murnau's film, the vampire, having feasted all night on blood of the virtuous Ellen Hutter (Greta Schröder), who has martyred herself to save her town, is caught off guard by the rising sun and disappears in a disappointing little puff of smoke. Or rather, I should say disappointing for contemporary viewers because, in the context of early twentieth-century film, it was a pretty good effect—something called a substitution or stop trick in which the camera shoots a scene, stops filming but stays in place, and a change is made. In this case, the actor disappears from the scene and smoke takes his place. Presto! No more vampire. Since *Nosferatu*, the vampire's "allergy" to sunlight has been exaggerated to the point that vampires now literally burst into flames when exposed to the sun and sometimes even explode! It's very visual and that's the point: the flammable vampire is a cinematic invention that highlights the vampire's shifting relationship to technology—our ideas of vampires have developed together with cinematic special effects.

I introduce the vampire cluster with this piece of trivia both because it's fun and because it helps to frame the four essays that follow, each of which emphasizes the ways vampire narratives in fiction and film have evolved. The first two essays, "American Vampires" from the *Edinburgh Companion to the American Gothic* and "The Cinematic Vampire," which is included in the long-delayed *The Vampire: An Edinburgh Companion*, paint the development of vampire narratives in broad strokes. The two essays that follow, "Circumcising Dracula" from *The Journal of the*

Fantastic in the Arts and "Vampire Suicide" from the edited collection of scholarly essays *Suicide and the Gothic*, then consider associated themes or recurring motifs in vampire narratives—specifically, anti–Semitism and suicide—showing how fantastic narratives can nevertheless come freighted with ideological values. The vampiric body is thus shown to be a vehicle used to insist on particular understandings of the world.

American Vampires

In "Monster Culture (Seven Theses)," Jeffrey Jerome Cohen asserts that monsters of all varieties should be considered as "cultural bodies" (4) that embody specific cultural moments as they give shape to particular times, places and feelings. "The monster's body," writes Cohen, "quite literally incorporates fear, desire, anxiety, and fantasy ... giving them life and an uncanny independence. The monstrous body is pure culture" (4). The vampire clearly serves this purpose, acting as a flexible metaphor condensing widely held yet culturally nuanced anxieties and desires. The vampire has found a congenial home in the United States where the "pure culture" of its overdetermined body has materialized fears and fantasies related to preoccupations with racial, sexual and economic otherness—issues that have haunted the American psyche from the colonization of America by European powers to the present. In keeping with representations of other monsters, the American vampire has also undergone a metamorphosis over time, from something to fear into something to emulate.

This chapter will chart the development of the American vampire narrative in four sections. I will begin by outlining a "prehistory" of the American vampire narrative. Although "actual" vampires as supernatural blood drinkers are rare in pre-twentieth-century American literature, one can nevertheless identify "proto vampires," particularly racialized cannibal blood drinkers and controlling women, which reflect nineteenth-century anxieties about race and gender. Furthermore, the appropriation of European vampire models becomes notable in the later part of the nineteenth century through adaptations for the American stage, providing a more familiar template for twentieth-century literary and cinematic representations. The second section will emphasize the legacy of Bram Stoker's 1897 *Dracula* in American literary and cinematic adaptations of the vampire narrative in the first part of the twentieth century, particularly the continued demonization of female sexuality in silent films of the 1910s and 1920s. Moving to the second half of the twentieth century, the third section will note the proliferation of vampire narratives via their emphasis on the increasing celebration of the vampire as a hero liberated from stultifying social convention and as an embodiment of post–Watergate skepticism of authority. My final section attends to twenty-first-century representations that extend the ironic humanization of the vampire, often in order to contest hegemonic structures of race, gender and sexuality. Lacking a reflection of its own, the vampire as pure culture nevertheless mirrors back culturally specific anxieties and desires.

The Pre-History of the American Vampire

Like Stoker's Renfield anticipating the arrival of Count Dracula, the cultural imaginary of nineteenth-century American literature was haunted by vampires prior to the actual emergence of the literary figure, and the vexed issue of American race relations is at the core of many of these "proto-vampire" accounts. James Fenimore Cooper's *Last of the Mohicans* (1826) is a case in point. Cooper "supernaturalizes" American Indians as spirits of the forest with almost magical abilities to appear, disappear and track their quarry. He then bifurcates this image into the Rousseauan "noble savage," represented by the stoic Mohican Chingachgook and his courageous son Uncas, and the barbaric, conniving Huron Indian Magua. Borrowing elements of the Native American captivity narrative, such as *The Sovereignty and Goodness of God: Being a Narrative of the Captivity and Restoration of Mrs. Mary Rowlandson* (1682), in which Indians are presented as demonic "ravenous beasts" and "hell-hounds" (Rowlandson 308), the plot of *Mohicans* revolves around the kidnapping by Magua and attempted restoration of two white women, Cora and Alice. During a central scene, Indians massacre British soldiers peacefully vacating the surrendered Fort William Henry in the then-province of New York. In Cooper's words, "as the natives became heated and maddened by the sight" of flowing blood that "might be likened to the outbreaking of a torrent," "many among them even kneeled to the earth, and drank freely, exultingly, hellishly, of the crimson tide" (198).

Cooper's portrayal of the vampiric Indian also drew upon and influenced lurid anthologies of anti–Indian propaganda that proliferated across the nineteenth century. With titles such as *Horrid Indian cruelties!* (1799) and *Indian Atrocities! Affecting and Thrilling Anecdotes Respecting the Hardships and Sufferings of Our Brave and Venerable Forefathers, in Their Bloody and Heartrending Skirmishes and Contests with the Ferocious Savages* (1846), these compendiums freely mixed fact with fantasy, often with avowedly genocidal intentions. As Kathryn Derounian-Stodola and James Arthur Levernier note, sensational accounts of murder and torture predominate in such works: "Babies are thrown into cauldrons of boiling water, fried in skillets, eaten by dogs, or dashed against trees or rocks.... The aged are dispatched with tomahawks and scalped. Women are sexually violated, and captives of all ages and both sexes are burnt at the stake, dismembered, and sometimes even devoured in orgiastic rituals said to be almost, but not quite, 'too shocking a nature to be presented to the public'" (33). Robert Montgomery Bird adopts this dim view of Indians in his popular *Nick of the Woods* (1837), written as a direct refutation of Cooper's romantic representation of noble Indians. Symbolically named protagonist Nathan Slaughter is an Indian hater intent on the destruction of his barbaric foes. The cannibalistic propensities of indigenous populations are also at the center of Herman Melville's first novel, *Typee: A Peep at Polynesian Life* (1846), although Melville adopts a more tolerant perspective toward native characters. As in his more famous story *Benito Cereno* (1855), which thematizes a shipboard slave revolt, *Typee* displaces antebellum American racial anxieties to the South Seas as the protagonist Tommo finds himself captive of the cannibalistic Typee tribe on the island of Nuku Hiva in the Marquesas Islands. Provoking the ire of conservative critics, Melville's novel seems to excuse the indigenous cannibalization of enemies slain in battle by comparing this horror in an otherwise pastoral society to Western white men consumed by greed, disease, anxiety, and unfulfilled desire. The native's "savage" practice pales in comparison to how modern existence debilitates and sucks dry "civilized" men. To varying extents works by Cooper, Melville, and Bird represent atavistic savagery as an intrinsic feature of indigenous populations whose racial otherness is then counterpoised against Anglo defenders of enlightened civilization enlisted to combat the hellish creatures of night and forest. While not immortal or literally able to transform, Indians are nevertheless both more and less than human, possessing almost supernatural powers of stealth and observation. They are savage, demonic creatures able to appear and disappear at will, to move silently, to sense and control nature, and to track their quarry across forbidding terrain.

Unlike James Malcolm Rymer's serialized account of Varney in his Victorian "penny dreadful" *Varney the Vampire; or, The Feast of Blood* (1845–7), which influenced Bram Stoker's *Dracula* (1897), there is no known nineteenth-century American literary equivalent of an "actual" vampire. While nineteenth-century American fiction restricts blood drinking as a literal or conscious act to non-white races, it is nonetheless rife with psychic vampires who possess seemingly supernatural powers to drain the vitality of others. Like the fears of racial difference in the above accounts of dark-skinned cannibals, these narratives reflect American anxieties about exploitative power relations and often pivot around issues of sexual difference and control embodied by a vampiric female figure. Not surprisingly, such demonic entities figure in the dark romantic writings of Edgar Allan Poe and Nathaniel Hawthorne, as well as the Gothic fictions of Mary E. Wilkins-Freeman and Ambrose Bierce. In both Poe's "Ligeia" (1838) and "Morella" (1835), for instance, mysterious and powerful females captivate their male companions and appear to defy death. After the demise of the eponymous Ligeia, the melancholic narrator remarries and, depending upon how one interprets the ambiguous conclusion, observes Ligeia's spirit taking possession of his dying second bride. The titular character of "Morella" similarly refuses to succumb to death, despite her apparent dissolution during childbirth. American literary critic Allen Tate has compared the surviving daughter—also named Morella and a doppelgänger of her namesake—to a vampire returning "to wreak upon her 'lover' the vengeance due him" for his lack of passion (385). Tate also considers Lady Madeline of Poe's "The Fall of the House of Usher," "back from the tomb, neither dead nor alive," as someone who suffocates her brother in the vampire's "sexual embrace" (387).

A more obvious case of psychic vampirism is featured in Poe's "The Oval Portrait"—originally titled "Life in Death," an allusion to the vampiric figure in Samuel Taylor Coleridge's *Rime of the Ancient Mariner* (1798)—in which an injured traveler seeking refuge in an abandoned chateau discovers an eerie account of a captivatingly realistic portrait. Providing a template for Oscar Wilde's later *The Picture of Dorian Gray* (1891), the narrative explains how the portrait's eccentric creator grew so obsessed with the artistic process that he neglected his model: his young bride. Upon completing the portrait, he exclaims, "This is indeed Life itself!" followed immediately by his discovery of the death of his bride, her vitality drained and transferred to the portrait. One of many Poe tales about the death of a beautiful woman, "The Oval Portrait" also allegorizes the artistic process as a vampiric one that entails the "murder" of the thing represented. A Gothic painting connected to life and blood similarly takes center stage in Hawthorne's *The House of the Seven Gables* (1851). The stern portrait of Colonel Pyncheon, scion of the Pyncheon family upon whom the curse "God will give him blood to drink" was laid following the unjust appropriation of the land of accused witch Matthew Maule, casts its long shadow over the Pyncheon line. The colonel was indeed served up blood to drink, fittingly choking to death on his own before the events of the novel. Thus, his blood drinking is figured as either supernatural payback or poetic justice for having spilt the blood of a disempowered other. In a more metaphoric sense, both Hawthorne's Roger Chillingworth, the cuckolded husband in *The Scarlet Letter* (1850) who drains the life out of the guilt-ridden the Reverend Dimmesdale, and (with interesting parallels to Poe's "The Oval Portrait") the alchemist Aylmer in Hawthorne's "The Birth-Mark" (1843), who "perfects" his wife only at the cost of her life, feed vampirically on those over whom they exert control.

Two more explicitly supernatural early vampire tales—both of which thematize the grasp of controlling women—are Mary E. Wilkins-Freeman's "Luella Miller" (1902) and Ambrose Bierce's "The Death of Halpin Frayser" (1891). The former presents the account of the delicate eponymous character whose suitors and servants waste away and die. Seemingly incapable of caring for herself, Luella too sickens and dies when the townspeople will no longer approach her. In Bierce's strange tale, a distraught mother returns from the grave, like Poe's Lady Madeline, to wreak vengeance upon the son, Halpin Frayser, who left her. In one surreal scene, Frayser lies down in the woods and dreams of blood "about him everywhere," only to find himself "staring into the sharply drawn face and blank, dead eyes of his own mother, standing white and silent in the garments of the grave!" Frayser then "dreamed he was dead" (Bierce 222), which may or may not be the case. Anticipating contemporary queer vampire stories, both tales associate vampirism with excessive or "unnatural" affective attachment. Luella feeds upon the energy of those drawn to her, while the relationship between Frayser and his mother, who "were not infrequently mistaken for lovers" (Bierce 220), transforms into blood-soaked violence and revenge from beyond the grave. Indeed, Bierce's scenario, in which a revenant plagues its immediate family, is much truer to the folkloric roots of the vampire than most literary accounts.

Blood drinkers also emigrated from Europe and England to the nineteenth-century American stage, which "produced a steady stream of plays about vampires, originating in France and quickly 'cannibalized' by the English and Americans" (Stuart 3). For example, Dion Boucicault's *The Vampire, A Phantasm in Three Dramas*, an adaptation of Alexander Dumas's 1851 *Le Vampire* (itself inspired by Charles Nodier's 1820 play, also titled *Le Vampire*, itself an adaptation of John Polidori's 1819 "The Vampyre"), was first presented in Philadelphia using the title *The Phantom* in 1856. Both as *The Phantom* and in at least one pirated version, *The Grand Legendary Drama, Vampire! or The Spectre of Mount Snowden!*, the play had successful American runs in the late 1850s and early 1860s (see Stuart 145–55).

The First Half of the Twentieth Century

The above cultural crossings set the stage for a key moment in the evolution of the American vampire tale at the turn of the twentieth century:

the 1897 publication of Bram Stoker's *Dracula*, which crystallized the vampire archetype in the popular imagination. Although not explicitly indebted to Stoker, F. Marion Crawford's "For the Blood is the Life" (1905), continuing the American tradition of correlating vampirism with enervating female sexuality, displays the influence of both *Dracula* and Joseph Sheridan Le Fanu's 1872 novella *Carmilla* (Carter 625). At the heart of this story within a story is the tragic tale of a murdered gypsy girl who rises from the grave first to prey upon the young man indifferent to her love and subsequently upon any man who accidentally crosses her path. Unlike stories by Poe, Wilkins-Freeman, and Bierce, in which physical violence is either entirely absent or offstage (but very much in keeping with Stoker), Crawford's story renders vampirism explicitly as the red-lipped revenant Cristina lays kisses upon her paramour Angelo's throat and drains his blood.

Yet with this notable exception and the popular 1927 Broadway adaptation of Hamilton Deane's 1924 British staging of *Dracula*, the early twentieth-century American vampire narrative was primarily a cinematic affair. In keeping with Poe, Wilkins-Freeman, Bierce, and Crawford, the first film vampires were not charismatic male seducers but rather "vamps," predatory women who contravened the "laws of nature." Early vamps such as Helen Gardner, Louise Glaum, Valeska Suratt, and particularly Theda Bara, established a pattern of supernaturalizing feminine sexuality. They neither had fangs nor drank blood, and were not undead, but they still seduced their male victims and drained their vitality. Frank Powell's *A Fool There Was* (1915), for instance, inspired by and quoting Rudyard Kipling's poem "The Vampire" (1897), chronicles the downfall of a man seduced by Theda Bara, named only "The Vampire," who mesmerizes men, drives them to drink, and leaves them forlorn and debilitated as she moves on to her next victim.

The vamp films of the 1910s and 1920s suggest a conservative retrenchment in the face of the late-Victorian New Woman's defiance of traditional gender expectations. Even as they titillated the moviegoing public, representations of the vamp as a chaotic force of social disruption demonized her less inhibited female sexuality. Adaptations of Stoker's novel, which retain the plot of brave men fighting with Dracula over control of women, suggest similar anxieties about women stepping outside of their prescribed roles. Such films reassert women's dependence on men and emphasize the pernicious consequences of giving in to "sinful" desires. In the 1927 Broadway stage adaptation of *Dracula*, Lucy Westenra and Mina Murray were fused into a single character, the chaste and innocent Lucy Seward, daughter of Dr. John Seward, who must be protected from the aristocratic vampire *Dracula*—famously played by Bela Lugosi—by the commanding

Van Helsing (played by Edward Van Sloan). Mina's agency in the novel, her role in combating Dracula, was wholly absent from this stage adaptation—one that then served as the impetus for the 1931 film version. Various early films, most notably F.W. Murnau's 1922 *Nosferatu, eine Symphonie des Grauens* (1922), remain somewhat faithful to Stoker's novel. Dracula did not arrive on the American silver screen, however, until the famous 1931 Universal Pictures film directed by Tod Browning. With its central contest between Dracula and Van Helsing and its greatly truncated conclusion culminating in the offstage staking of Dracula in Carfax Abbey, the film capitalized upon the success of the 1927 play as much as it does Stoker's novel by reprising Lugosi's charismatic stage performance. Lugosi's iconic film Dracula cements the contemporary vampire archetype as a foreign aristocrat in evening wear who preys upon attractive women. This cinematic Dracula gave American audiences both an escape from and a reflection of inchoate anxieties about the Great Depression. The classic 1930s monster films—Universal's *Frankenstein* (1932), *The Mummy* (1932), and *Werewolf of London* (1935), and RKO's *King Kong* (1933)—depicted "average" people afflicted by supernatural threats that, like Dracula, arrive suddenly, but also showed misunderstood monsters cursed by forces beyond their control. These films offered film viewers momentary relief from their concerns but also empathic identification with citizens and monsters victimized by problems not of their own making.

Insofar as American vampire narratives of the nineteenth and early twentieth centuries gave shape to underlying gender and sexual anxieties and desires, they suggest how vampires are inevitably "queer," highlighting as they do the social construction of normative sexuality precisely through their transgressions of social expectations (see Weinstock 7–9). One can see this queerness at play, for example, in the incestuous desire underpinning "Morella," "The Fall of the House of Usher," and "The Death of Halpin Frayser"; in the hyperbolic feminine helplessness of "Luella Miller"; and in the transgression of conventional gender expectations in *A Fool There Was*. Of particular note to film critics interested in queer theory and recovering the traces of homosexual history embedded in film has been Lambert Hillyer's *Dracula's Daughter* (1936), in which the title character, Countess Marya Zaleska (Gloria Holden), enters into psychotherapy with Dr. Jeffrey Garth (Otto Kruger) in order to cure her blood-drinking "obsession." When therapy fails, the Countess, resigned to her vampirism, determines to make Dr. Garth her vampire companion, luring him to her Transylvania castle by kidnapping his assistant/love interest Janet (Marguerite Churchill) only to be shot through the heart by her jilted assistant Sandor (Irving Pichel) whom she had promised to make into a vampire. According to Harry Benshoff in his groundbreaking *Monsters in the Closet*

(1997), Zaleska, who preys upon men but relishes young women, and who seeks assistance to combat her deviant desire, is "the most obviously 'lesbian' monster movie of the classical period" (Benshoff 77). Zaleska is, of course, punished in the end for her transgressions as order is restored and the monstrous potential for alternate sexualities is seemingly foreclosed—but not before cracks have appeared in the edifice of hegemonic heterosexuality as the vampire has led us to contemplate tabooed sexual desire even as the film works to diminish and demonize those same alternative sexual possibilities.

The 1930 implementation of the U.S. Motion Picture Production Code (or Hays Code), whose censorship guidelines were in effect until 1968, ensured that post–1930 representations of sexuality and violence were relatively tame by comparison with films of the preceding two decades. Compensating for this cinematic restraint were American pulp magazines such as *Weird Tales*, *Strange Tales of Mystery and Terror*, *Horror Stories*, and *Terror Tales*, which offered a steady stream of lurid, gruesome vampire narratives from authors including Conan-creator Robert E. Howard, Seabury Quinn, Clark Ashton Smith, Frank Belknap Long, August Derleth and *Psycho* creator Robert Bloch. Among the most interesting are two 1937 stories from *Weird Tales*, H.P. Lovecraft's "The Shunned House" (originally written in 1924) and science fiction great Henry Kuttner's "I, the Vampire." Lovecraft claimed to eschew Gothic clichés, but occasionally introduced supernatural creatures. "The Shunned House" recasts the vampire tale as a quasi-scientific story of horrific discovery in which an unnamed protagonist and his uncle investigate a house haunted with a century-long history of sickness and death. The house's monstrous vitality-sapping resident is ultimately defeated not with holy water and communion wafers but with sulfuric acid. Kuttner's story adopts the playful premise that the actor to appear in a horror film titled *Red Thirst* is himself a vampire. Anticipating Francis Ford Coppola's romantic 1992 cinematic adaptation of Stoker's novel, Kuttner's vampire believes the film's leading lady to be the reincarnation of his lost love, which leads to a rather maudlin conclusion in which the vampire sacrifices himself.

Both stories demonstrate an early twentieth-century metatextual vampire consciousness by re-scripting and extending the vampire's literary and cinematic history. Showcasing the vampire as an embodiment of culturally specific anxieties and desires, Lovecraft's narrative, on the one hand, substitutes a rationalist framework for interpreting the vampire for the conventional supernatural one but, on the other, introduces his characteristic "cosmic fear": the sense that the universe is governed by monstrous forces that render humans insignificant. In Lovecraft's story science displaces religion as a bulwark against the forces of darkness, but ultimately reveals the precariousness of human existence. Kuttner's less innovative updating nevertheless shifts attention from religion to science and technology through its playful emphasis on the movie camera. Anticipating E. Elias Merhige's excellent film *Shadow of the Vampire* (2000), Kuttner's story intimates how film creates legions of the living dead as the camera transfers life from the physical actor to his screen avatar. In this way, Kuttner supernaturalizes technology, suggesting in turn how modern cinema projects an uncanny semblance of life onto the silver screen in the absence of living actors.

The Second Half of the Twentieth Century

In the later twentieth century, a staggering proliferation of American vampire narratives in literature, film and, later, television emphasizes the vampire as a protean metaphor for shifting social anxieties and desires. Richard Matheson's novel *I Am Legend* (1954) functions as a kind of vampiric pivot point by not only rethinking sedimented conventions of the genre, but in a remarkably prescient way foregrounding political and environmental themes that will become central to late twentieth-century culture. Protagonist Robert Neville is apparently the lone survivor of an apocalyptic pandemic that has transformed the world's population into vampires. Seeking answers to what has happened, he conducts research and traces the root of the disease to a strain of bacteria that infects both living and dead hosts. Along the way he draws conclusions as to why various vampire prophylactics are effective and develops increasingly efficient ways to kill his undead antagonists. In the novel's infamous conclusion (spoiler warning!), Neville is stunned to discover that the vampires he has been indiscriminately killing during their daytime dormancy have in fact established a society of their own that fears him as the monster that comes while they sleep. In a world of vampires, the human being is the monster.

Matheson's novel constitutes a prophetic amalgamation of contemporary themes. As a story about the aftermath of a global pandemic, it anticipates the current preoccupation with viruses and zombie apocalypses. By seeking a rational explanation for seemingly supernatural affliction, it speaks to the modern faith in science to unlock the secrets of the universe, but also to science as a double-edged sword by connecting the pandemic to rampant militarism and biological warfare among nations. Most notably, the novel's surprising conclusion undoes the knee-jerk equation of difference with monstrosity through a relativist view of culture exemplified particularly in later films for children, such as *Shrek* (2001) and *Monsters, Inc.* (2001). Matheson's novel thus anticipates a later skepticism toward authority and celebration of the vampire as hero liberated from stultifying social convention.

That monsters should be construed as "cultural bodies," as Cohen puts it, giving shape to particular times, feeling and places, is particularly evident in Stephen King's punningly titled post–Watergate 1975 novel, *'Salem's Lot*. the Nosferatu–styled vampire, Kurt Barlow, is an imperial force of evil who, like Dracula, travels across the ocean to invade fresh territory in the rural Maine town of Jerusalem's Lot, an apparently pastoral refuge from modern life that slowly reveals the banal evils of covetousness, bigotry, lust, and selfishness. The loss of faith in authority, religion, and the clichéd wholesomeness of small-town life is embodied by the alcoholic priest Father Callahan who falls prey to the vampire, who in turn materializes the evil already lurking in the poisoned heart of the town whose inhabitants are gradually transformed into a legion of the walking dead. In King's novel, the traditionally villainous antagonist reflects a postmodern skepticism about authoritative frameworks and metanarratives (see Lyotard) and thus a heightened sense of cultural relativism. This post-1970s re-evaluation of monstrousness then leads to a transformation of the vampire in subsequent works from threatening antagonist to sympathetic protagonist beset by conservative culture intent upon demonizing sexual and racial difference.

Following Fred Saberhagen's sympathetic first-hand retelling of Stoker's novel from the vampire's perspective in *The Dracula Tape* (1975), Anne Rice's *Vampire Chronicles* series exemplifies this shift in the vampire's moral status through its non-judgmental representations of affectively intense same-sex relationships. The series' first three novels in particular—*Interview with the Vampire* (1976), *The Vampire Lestat* (1985) and *Queen of the Damned* (1988)—reinvent vampire culture and mythology by presenting vampires as superheroes (and literally in Lestat as rock stars) endowed with immortality, supernatural strength and speed, and even the ability to fly. No longer subject to God's curse, vampires in Rice's saga are freed from their conventional antagonism to social mores, their fluid sexuality reflecting the natural expression rather than transgression of a more evolved vampiric consciousness. In an ironic reflection of the 1970s gay rights movement, Louis and Lestat even "adopt" a daughter in the form of the child vampire Claudia. Unlike *Dracula's Daughter*, which excises the queer vampire with an arrow through Zaleska's heart, Rice celebrates queer as the new normal with a progressive attitude toward erotic relationships that disregards conventional gender expectations.

Although not told from a first-person perspective, Jewelle Gomez's lesbian feminist vampire novel *The Gilda Stories* (1991) completes the inversion of monstrosity initiated by Rice and others. The eight sections of this episodic work chronicle the life of the eponymous protagonist, from her experience as a young runaway slave rescued in 1850 and introduced into a vampire family of sorts in Louisiana, to a dystopian future 200 years later in which vampires reveal their presence to the world. As Amy Harlib notes, Gomez constructs a form of "benevolent vampirism" that "involves the non-fatal sharing of blood that happens alongside the sharing of dreams and life force to the mutual benefit of both individuals involved in the encounter" (Harlib). *The Gilda Stories* reimagines vampirism as a form of symbiosis benefiting both parties, a model appropriated by Octavia Butler in *Fledgling* (2005), discussed below, while associating true vampirism with the oppressive regimes of slavery and white hetero-patriarchy.

Similarly, the *Blade* (1998, 2002, 2004) and *Underworld* (2003–) film franchises harken back to American proto-vampire narratives, but with an updated message: those who would assert a racialized social hierarchy based on "purity" of blood are mired in the past and are the source of contemporary social strife. Emphasizing the "half-breed" as hero, both series reject an earlier paranoia over contamination of blood by proposing miscegenation as the answer to racism in Western culture. In the *Blade* series' thinly veiled allegory of American race relations, vampires, defined by wealth and power, stand in for whites and humans for minorities. Loosely based on a Marvel Comics character, the films center on the black vampire Blade (Wesley Snipes), who has special abilities because he was born soon after his mother was bitten by a vampire. As a result, he is a "daywalker," a human/vampire hybrid whose powers outstrip those of both races. As a "hybrid," he also possesses the moral compass and empathy for "mortals" that the vampires in the series, believing themselves to be superior to humans, lack. In this racial allegory, rather than one blood type overwhelming the other, the mixing of blood produces a superior race—one that shares the white/vampire thirst for domination but recognizes it as evil and controls it. The fantasy of miscegenation as the solution to contemporary racial anxieties embedded in the *Blade* films is shared and rendered even more explicitly in the *Underworld* films. The fundamental premise informing this series is that aristocratic vampires are at war with their former slaves, lycans (short for lycanthropes). The potential to resolve racial tension resides in the relationship between two "hybrids"—Michael (Scott Speedman) and Selene (Kate Beckinsale)—whose powers ultimately exceed those of either vampires or werewolves alone. Like the *Blade* series, the *Underworld* films feature vampire elders who fight to preserve the status quo and refuse to acknowledge their shared relation with those they consider beneath them. Both series show that this type of thinking is obsolete in the modern world and that racial mixing invigorates rather than enervates bloodlines.

By emphasizing class as well as race, George Romero's *Martin* (1977) is perhaps "the most thoroughgoing, sophisticated re-examination of the vampire figure yet attempted" (Newman 130). Eschewing the conventional vampire formula, Martin (John Amplas) is not sexy, aristocratic, or commanding; he does not speak with a Transylvanian accent or garb himself in evening wear—indeed, there is nothing to confirm Tata Cuda's (Lincoln Maazel) accusations that Martin is an 84-year-old vampire with European origins or Martin's own assertions to a radio talk-show host (Michael Gornick) about his vampirism. Instead, Martin re-scripts the vampire as a white working-class twenty-something going through the motions in an economically depressed post-industrial town, associating dread and desire with the vampire's class location. Martin is thus the exception proving the rule that vampire cinema is undergirded by a racialized discourse about social class in which foreign aristocrats prey upon domestic citizens. As with Browning's *Dracula* or King's *'Salem's Lot*, Romero's *Martin* suggests that the vampire's foreign otherness distracts attention from the fact that vampires are the product of domestic forces such as hopelessness, boredom, and financial stress.

In the same way *Martin* revises entrenched class positions of the vampire cinematic tradition, Joss Whedon's TV series *Buffy the Vampire Slayer* (1997–2003), taking its cue from the 1992 film written by Whedon and directed by Fran Rubel Kuzui, inverts—and thereby reveals the sedimented nature of—the vampire narrative's established gender conventions. A female-empowerment narrative, *Buffy* turns the history of vampire cinema on its head through its central character, Buffy (Sarah Michelle Gellar), a perky blonde, teenage girl who protects the fictional town of Sunnydale, California—and the rest of the world—from the forces of darkness, including vampires.

While more conventional than other narratives discussed in this section, Francis Ford Coppola's lush big-budget *Bram Stoker's Dracula* (1992) nevertheless participates in the twentieth-century undoing of the correlation between vampirism and villainy by superimposing a romantic backstory that transforms Dracula into a melancholic lover. To Stoker's tale Coppola adds a prelude in which Vlad Dracula (Gary Oldman) returns from war against the Turks to discover that his wife, Elisabeta (Winona Ryder), has committed suicide after receiving a false report of her husband's death. The enraged Dracula renounces God, which seemingly gives rise to his vampiric state. When Dracula later emigrates to London, he becomes convinced that Mina Harker (Winona Ryder) is in fact the reincarnation of his lost bride. Sympathetically played by Gary Oldman, Dracula is more tragic than horrific. Coppola's film elicits a contemporary desire to rethink monstrosity by understanding the monster's motivations. Indeed, what Stoker carefully refuses the reader in *Dracula* (apart from a speech to Jonathan Harker about his proud martial lineage) is any real elaboration on Dracula's motives that might allow readers to sympathize with him. What Coppola significantly adds to his *Bram Stoker's Dracula* that is in fact nowhere present in Bram Stoker's *Dracula* is a romantic backstory that promotes the sympathy for the vampire that Stoker precisely rejects. Coppola's Dracula in this way is humanized and softened. His motivations are comprehensible and his actions, if not excusable, are at least understandable. Reflecting a contemporary distrust of authority and emphasis on the free expression of individuality, those who hunt Dracula, in contrast, are presented as increasingly priggish and narrow-minded.

The Twenty-First-Century American Vampire Narrative

The vampire narrative is among the most self-referential of literary and cinematic traditions. Later texts insistently allude to, directly reference and innovate on earlier narratives, especially Stoker's novel as Ur-text, in the process assuming audience familiarity with the tradition and its transformations. Matheson's *I Am Legend* both references and rejects Stoker's ideas about vampires, for example, as protagonist Robert Neville seeks to understand and combat his antagonists. In King's *'Salem's Lot*, the vampire hunters prepare by reading up on the entire vampire tradition, including *Varney* and *Dracula*, and the reader discovers, together with King's unfortunate character Father Callahan, that, contra Stoker, religious icons possess no inherent power to ward off the vampire; rather, their power is an extension of the religious faith of their wielder. Anne Rice's vampires, seeking to understand their own nature, introduce and reject Stoker as well, discovering for themselves an ancient tradition and culture.

While an in-depth analysis of the reasons for this vampiric variant of Harold Bloom's "anxiety of influence" (Bloom) is beyond this chapter's scope, it is clear that twenty-first-century American vampire texts continue to demonstrate a pronounced metatextual element as they play with the conventions of vampire narratives in very conscious ways. A dramatic case in point is E. Elias Merhinge's delightful *The Shadow of the Vampire* (2000), a fictional narrative about the making of another fictional narrative, Murnau's *Nosferatu*, which in the process provocatively asserts the vampiric nature of film itself. Count Orlok, played by Willem Dafoe, is a real vampire masquerading as the human actor Max Schreck. Contemplating a "real" actor playing a vampire playing a human playing a vampire, the film's viewer is interpolated into *Shadow*'s playful structure of meaning—its interrogation of the genre's theatricality and cinema's role in producing the vampires it endlessly pursues and destroys. Throughout the film, Murnau (John Malkovich), the director, is paralleled with Count Orlok, the vampire. Murnau "consumes" his actors, uses them as tools in the production of his art and drains them of life and vitality, just as readily as Orlok drinks their blood. The film then culminates with an inspired effect: when exposed to sunlight, both Count Orlok and the film go up in smoke. At the end of *Nosferatu*, the vampire grabs his chest, raises his arm, and dissipates in a rather disappointing puff of smoke. In *Shadow*, the light obliterates all as the film stock itself seems to melt and burn up. As projections of one another, both vampire and film are uncanny creations of shadow and light that can only survive in the dark.

The twenty-first-century American vampire is an increasingly humanized, even deified figure. In the novels and film adaptations of Stephenie Meyer's *Twilight* series (2005–8), vampires and werewolves are presented as powerful and beautiful. At the series' center is human protagonist Bella (Kristen Stewart in the films) who falls in love with Edward Cullen (Robert Pattinson), who turns out to be a vampire—albeit a "vegetarian" who resists drinking human blood. Although "traditionally" a monster, Edward is more angel than demon: powerful, immortal (barring certain forms of physical violation), handsome, caring, faithful and, except in the case of Bella, capable of reading everyone's mind. He is, in sum, the apotheosis of the modern sensitive man rather than a repellent monster and he offers to Bella love, excitement, protection, and escape from the mundane. HBO's *True Blood* (2008–14), based on *The Southern Vampire Mysteries* series of novels by Charlaine Harris (2001–13), similarly presents vampires as powerful and alluring. In keeping with modern inversions of monstrosity that demonize restrictive social norms and celebrate the outsider's individuality, *True Blood* directly parallels the situation of vampires and homosexuals in Western culture. Following the invention of a synthetic blood substitute that liberates vampires from the necessity of consuming human blood, they have "come out of the coffin" and revealed their existence to humankind. In a parody of conservative Christian homophobia, religious zealots such as the anti-vampire Church of the Sun greet this revelation with dismay. Indeed, each show's opening credits feature a church sign on which the hate slogan "God hates fags" has been altered to read "God hates fangs."

The joke at the center of Tim Burton's 2012 film of the American TV soap opera *Dark Shadows* (1966–71) is that the vampire, Barnabas Collins (Johnny Depp), is more normal than the hyperbolic and absurd 1970s culture into which he awakens, complete with lava lamps, hippie pot circles, and Alice Cooper. Viewed from the perspective of the monster and Burton's audience, particularly those conversant with the history of cinematic horror, this strange and fantastic "real world" serves as the backdrop for the more comprehensible world of witchcraft and vampirism. More darkly, in *Let Me In* (2010), the American remake of Tomas Alfredson's 2008 *Let the Right One In* (*Låt den Rätte Komma In*), the real world is an abusive place. Owen (Kodi Smit-McPhee) is a lonely twelve-year-old boy neglected by his divorcing parents and bullied at school. When a young girl named Abby (Chloe Grace Moretz) and her "father" (Richard Jenkins) move in next door, Owen develops an unusual friendship with Abby—a vampire who has been twelve for a very long time. At the film's climax, Abby becomes a superhero who rescues Owen, who then in turn decides to abandon the life he has known to serve as caretaker for Abby. *Let Me In* insists that the world is a harsh place full of "vampires" who prey upon the weak and different, but who, by understanding what it means to be an outsider, also exemplify the compassion humans lack.

Ostensibly leaving the human world almost entirely behind is Butler's novel *Fledgling*, which introduces vampires as a separate race called Ina who are nocturnal, extremely long-lived and physically and mentally superior to the humans from whom they derive nourishment. With parallels to Gomez's *Gilda Stories*, the vampires in *Fledgling* form symbiotic relationships with humans, who not only experience intense pleasure from the vampire's bite, but derive enhanced immune systems and extended longevity from the bond. With a connection to the *Blade* and *Underworld* film franchises, the protagonist of *Fledgling*, Shori, is dark-skinned, the result of genetic experimentation by the Ina to produce resistance to daylight (and as with Abby in *Let Me In*, Shori appears quite young, despite being much older). As a consequence of her color, Shori is victimized by racist Ina, a predicament that drives much of the novel's plot. Here again, the outsider vampire becomes the central figure in a morality tale pitting the forces of racist exclusionism against those of openness and tolerance.

Ironically, even a contemporary film in which vampires are unambiguously evil still manages to convey tolerance. The conceit at the heart of Timur Bekmambetov's campy *Abraham Lincoln: Vampire Hunter* (2012) is that Lincoln (Benjamin Walker) has sworn vengeance against vampires after the death of his mother at the hands of vampire slave owner Jack Barts (Marton Csokas). Through the film's rather unsubtle parallel between vampirism and slavery (the Confederate troops are vampires), Lincoln thus effects a dual emancipation: liberating African Americans from slavery and the human race from the tyranny of vampires.

Countering the impression that all contemporary American vampire narratives utilize the vampire sympathetically as a thinly veiled metaphor for otherness is Guillermo del Toro and Chuck Hogan's *The Strain Trilogy* (2009–11). Fusing the vampire narrative with contemporary anxieties relating to the prospect of global pandemics and nuclear annihilation, the series borrows freely from sources ranging from Stoker, Rice, and King to Matheson, *Blade*, and even the graphic novel *30 Days of Night* by Steve Niles (adapted for film in 2007 by David Slade). In the first instalment, *The Strain* (2009), the human protagonists confront a vampire "virus" with New York City as the epicenter. In the sequel, *The Fall* (2010), human civilization is taken over by a vampire faction lead by a renegade vampire "Ancient one." In the trilogy's post-apocalyptic conclusion, *The Night Eternal* (2011), the remnants of human resistance make use of nuclear weapons to liberate themselves from vampiric servitude.

While the vampire conventionally possesses the power to morph into a bat, wolf, or mist, its true power of transformation inheres in its ability to give shape to shifting cultural anxieties and desires. Prior to the emergence in American narrative of the vampire as the familiar supernatural blood-drinking character, vampirism already infiltrated American culture through racist characterizations of indigenous populations as bloodthirsty cannibals or misogynistic anxieties concerning the debilitating powers of female sexuality. The vampire paradoxically was already here, anticipating its own arrival. With the importation of European stage plays featuring vampires and then Stoker's *Dracula* at the end of the nineteenth century, vampiric anxieties and discourse were concretized and amplified in the form of the familiar supernatural creature, the vampire as "undead" monster, whose unrestrained sexuality threatens even as it titillates. Twentieth-century American adaptations then took the constellation of themes already associated with the vampire—its racialization, its queerness, its embodiment of exploitative power relations foremost among them—and, with a self-referential eye toward the conventions of the vampire tradition already established, repeatedly redeployed and updated these themes to reflect shifting cultural emphases, notably recasting the vampire not as villain but as hero resisting the stultifying expectation of social conformity. The outsiderdom of the vampire, its queer sexuality, its refusal to respect authority all become causes of celebration rather than castigation—and, in an increasingly secular society, the vampire's association with satanic forces waned, while leaving its longevity and superpowers intact.

From a scourge to be eradicated to a symbol for unjust ostracism, and from a metaphor for threatening female sexuality to an embodiment of post-human promise, the metamorphic power of the vampire showcases the monster as an embodiment of "pure culture." Twenty-first-century American iterations of the vampire in the texts addressed above—as well as other recent texts, such as the television drama *The Vampire Diaries* (2009–) and Jim Jarmusch's film *Only Lovers Left Alive* (2014)—continue to demonstrate the interest the vampire commands, the trend of its humanization and the ways in which vampire narratives are invariably, on some level, precisely about vampire narratives, as new rescriptings anticipate audience awareness of the tradition being utilized and updated. Lacking a reflection of its own, the vampire continues to reflect back to the reader or viewer the anxieties and desires of its cultural moment.

WORKS CITED

Benshoff, Harry. *Monsters in the Closet: Homosexuality and the Horror Film*. Manchester University Press, 1997.
Bierce, Ambrose. "The Death of Halpin Frayser" in *American Gothic: From Salem Witchcraft to H.P. Lovecraft. An Anthology*, 2nd ed., edited by Charles Crow. Blackwell, 2013, pp. 217–26.
Bird, Robert Montgomery. *Nick of the Woods; Or, The Jibbenainosay: A Tale of Kentucky*, edited by C. Dahl. Rowman & Littlefield, 1967.
Bloom, Harold. *The Anxiety of Influence: A Theory of Poetry*. Oxford University Press, 1973.
Butler, Octavia. *Fledgling*. Grand Central Publishing, 2005.
Carter, Margaret L. "The Vampire" in *Icons and the Supernatural: An Encyclopaedia of our Worst Nightmares*, edited by S.T. Joshi. Greenwood Press, 2007, pp. 619–52.
Cohen, Jeffrey Jerome. "Monster Culture (Seven Theses)" in *Monster Theory: Reading Culture*, edited by Jeffrey Jerome Cohen. University of Minnesota Press, 1996, pp. 3–25.
Cooper, James Fenimore. *The Last of the Mohicans*. Bantam, 1982.
Crawford, F. Marion. "For the Blood is the Life" in *Wandering Ghosts*. The Macmillan Company, 1911, pp. 165–94.
Del Toro, Guillermo, and Chuck Hogan. *The Fall*. Harper, 2010.
———. *The Night Eternal*. Harper, 2011.
———. *The Strain*. Harper, 2009.
Derounian-Stodola, Kathryn, and James Arthur Levernier. *The Indian Captivity Narrative, 1550–1900*. Twayne Publishers, 1993.
Gomez, Jewelle. *The Gilda Stories*. Firebrand Books, 1991.
Harlib, Amy. "Review of *The Gilda Stories*." *Queer Cultural Center*, http://www.queerculturalcenter.org/Pages/Gomez/GomezGida.html. Accessed 21 February 2014.
Hawthorne, Nathaniel. "The Birth-Mark" in *The Norton Anthology of American Literature*, 7th ed., edited by Nina Baym, et al. Norton, 2007, pp. 1320–31.
———. *The House of the Seven Gables*, edited by Robert Levine. Norton, 2006.
———. *The Scarlet Letter*, edited by Brian Harding. Oxford University Press, 2009.
King, Stephen. *'Salem's Lot*. Pocket Books, 1999.
Kuttner, Henry. "I, the Vampire" in *Weird Vampire Tales: 30 Blood-Chilling Stories from the Weird Fiction Pulps*, edited by Robert Weinberg, Stefan R. Dziemianowicz, and Martin H. Greenberg. Gramercy Books, 1992, pp. 207–22.
Lovecraft, H.P. "The Shunned House" in *The Dreams in the Witch House and Other Weird Stories*, edited by S.T. Joshi. Penguin, 2004, pp. 90–115.
Lyotard, Jean-François. *The Postmodern Condition: A Report on Knowledge*, translated by Geoffrey Bennington and Brian Massumi. Manchester University Press, 1984.
Matheson, Richard. *I Am Legend*. Tor Books, 2007.
Melville, Herman. *Typee: A Peep at Polynesian Life*. Penguin, 1996.
Newman, Kim. *Nightmare Movies: A Critical Guide to Contemporary Horror Films*. Harmony Books, 1988.

Poe, Edgar Allan. "Ligeia" in *Poe: Poetry, Tales, & Selected Essays*, edited by Patrick Quinn and G.R. Thompson. Library of America, 1996, pp. 262–277.
———. "Morella" in *Poe: Poetry, Tales, & Selected Essays*, edited by Patrick Quinn and G.R. Thompson. Library of America, 1996, pp. 234–239.
———. "The Oval Portrait" in *Poe: Poetry, Tales, & Selected Essays*, edited by Patrick Quinn and G.R. Thompson. Library of America, 1996, pp. 481–484.
Rice, Anne. *Interview with the Vampire*. Alfred A. Knopf, 1976.
———. *The Vampire Lestat*. Alfred A. Knopf, 1985.
———. *Queen of the Damned*. Alfred A. Knopf, 1988.
Rowlandson, Mary. *The Sovereignty and Goodness of God: Being a Narrative of the Captivity and Restoration of Mrs. Mary Rowlandson*, in *Early American Writings*, edited by Carla Mulford. Oxford University Press, 2001, pp. 307–327.
Saberhagen, Fred. *The Dracula Tape*. Warner, 1975.
Stuart, Roxana. *Stage Blood: Vampires of the 19th-Century Stage*. The Popular Press, 1994.
Tate, Allen. "Our Cousin, Mr. Poe" in *Modern Criticism: Theory and Practice*, edited by Walter Sutton and Richard Foster. Western Publishing Company, Inc., 1963, pp. 383–390.
Weinstock, Jeffrey Andrew. *The Vampire Film: Undead Cinema*. Columbia University Press, 2012.
Wilkins-Freeman, Mary E. "Luella Miller" in *American Gothic: From Salem Witchcraft to H.P. Lovecraft. An Anthology*, 2nd ed., edited by Charles L. Crow. Blackwell, 2013, pp. 344–352.

The Vampire Cinema

This chapter on the cinematic vampire updates and extends upon my analysis of vampire movies in *The Vampire Film: Undead Cinema*, a study that takes as its organizing premise the assertion that the vampire—regardless of media of representation—serves as a screen onto which to project a range of culturally specific anxieties and desires. In that study, I focus on the relationship of the cinematic vampire to sex, race, class, and technology, while bearing in mind that, as Jack Halberstam (writing as Judith) observes, "The body that scares and appalls changes over time, as do the individual characteristics that add up to monstrosity, as do the preferred interpretations of that monstrosity" (8). Thus, while vampires may always be to varying extents about sex, racial and social otherness, and the vexed human relationship to technology, what they have to say about these issues and others, and how the vampires themselves are regarded (as villains, heroes, or something less simplistic), shifts according to context.

While also offering a condensed recapitulation of the history of the cinematic vampire, this chapter seeks to illustrate the shifting valences of the cinematic vampire by using as touchstone texts four notable contemporary films not addressed in my 2012 study: Australian filmmakers Peter and Michael Spierig's *Daybreakers* (2010), Russian director Timur Bekmambetov's *Abraham Lincoln: Vampire Hunter* (2012), Irish filmmaker Neil Jordan's *Byzantium* (2012), and American director Jim Jarmusch's *Only Lovers Left Alive* (2014). I turn to these particular films for several reasons: first, the sheer volume of vampire films (and the ranks of the cinematic undead have swelled to truly epic proportions) requires one to narrow things down; second, the movies in question represent a mix of big-budget blockbusters (*Daybreakers*, *Abraham Lincoln*) and art-house pictures by notable independent filmmakers (*Byzantium*, *Only Lovers Left Alive*) and thereby showcase both continued interest in the cinematic vampire and a diversity of approaches to the subject; and, third, the films usefully allow me to foreground the ways in which cinematic vampire films engage long-standing social concerns in culturally specific ways. These films, together with the others introduced in less depth below, thereby illustrate the irony inherent in the cinematic vampire: while presented as immortal, the vampire is nevertheless inevitably a flickering reflection of its historical moment. Indeed, the vampire in this way is much like a film: the timeless preservation and repetition of a specific moment.

An Overview of the Vampire Cinema

This parallel between cinema and vampires has been noted by Stacey Abbott, who in her study of vampire film, *Celluloid Vampires: Life and Death in the Modern World*, observes that "[m]ade up of still images, ghostly shadows of the dead that are reanimated through technological means, film bears striking parallels with vampirism" (43). It is perhaps for this reason that film and vampires have been connected since the origins of the medium at the end of the nineteenth century. Georges Méliès, for example, credited with being the father of horror cinema, included within his fin-de-siècle nineteenth-century repertoire of Gothic devices dancing skeletons, the devil, witches, ghosts, and what has been described as the cinema's first vampire—a devilish fellow in *Le Manoir du Diable* (1896) who is warded off with a large cross. Credited with having pioneered special effects such as time-lapse photography, multiple exposures, dissolves, hand-painted colors, and the "stop trick" (stopping the camera and substituting one object for another, thus making it appear that one object has turned into another), what Méliès explored through his cinematic experimentation is what Lewis Jacobs refers to as the "'supernatural' capacities of the moving picture" (23)—the uncanniness of a medium that conjures phantoms of light and shadow.

This relationship of the vampire to the cinematic medium is foregrounded in two pioneering twentieth-century works of the vampire cinema: F.W. Murnau's iconic *Nosferatu, eine Symphonie des Grauens* (1922) and Carl-Theodor Dreyer's *Vampyr* (1932). Murnau's much-discussed unauthorized adaptation of Bram Stoker's *Dracula* (1897) is perhaps most notable for its expressionistic use of framing and special effects to create atmosphere and to emphasize the supernatural nature of the vampire, Count Orlock (Max Schreck). *Nosferatu*, as both Lotte H. Eisner (100) and David J. Skal (87) have observed, is filled with striking images—the most striking of which are associated with the vampire. Orlock's first appearance as he emerges from darkness to meet Hutter, his staring at Ellen (the film's Mina Harker, played by Greta Schröder) from behind the bars of his window in Wisborg "clinging to a window grid like a spider in a Bauhaus web" (Skal 87), and his clutching his heart before disappearing in a puff of smoke at the end all are triumphs of framing and composition. The film's most memorable image, however, arguably is that of the vampire's shadow creeping up the stairs to Ellen's room, grotesque hands stretching and elongating toward the door. Orlock's shadow, as Abbott notes, is projected like film onto white surfaces, partaking of film's "shadowy nature" (52–53). In *Nosferatu*, the vampire is a purely cinematic creation, a monster birthed by film's uncanny capacities.

Also capitalizing on the seemingly supernatural properties of the still relatively new cinematic medium is Carl-Theodor Dreyer's surreal *Vampyr*. Focused loosely on the young protagonist, Allan Gray (Julian West), who arrives in a French town plagued by a vampire, *Vampyr* is a film that resists summarization for, as David Bordwell has developed at length in his excellent study of Dreyer, the film constantly works to retard conclusions and obfuscate meaning. Rather than plot, what *Vampyr* instead foregrounds is the uncanniness of film itself as detached shadows act independently, space is rendered "fluid, plastic, uncertain" (Bordwell 98), and the camera asserts itself as an "*independent* factor" that "need not be subservient to narrative causality" (Bordwell 105). In this film, as in *Nosferatu*, the vampire is an explicitly cinematic creation, an entity of light and shadow paralleled with the supernatural qualities of film itself.

While both *Nosferatu* and *Vampyr* are landmark contributions to vampire cinema history that reflect a pronounced metatextual element of the tradition, not all vampire films are as self-reflexive. This is certainly true of the two most important Western vampire film cycles, Universal Studios' five Dracula films and Hammer Film Productions' nine Dracula films, as well as of Hammer's "Karnstein Trilogy" of films loosely based on J. Sheridan Le Fanu's novella, *Carmilla* (1871). Undoubtedly best known of all vampire films is Universal Studios' *Dracula* (1931) directed by Tod Browning and famously starring Bela Lugosi as the title character. Indebted as much to Hamilton Deane and John L. Balderston's 1924 stage adaptation of *Dracula* as to Stoker's novel itself, the truncated plot introduces Mina (Helen Chandler) as Dr. Seward's (Herbert Bunston) daughter, omits Arthur Holmwood and Quincy Morris, and centers on a contest of wills between Dracula and the stern and authoritative Van Helsing (Edward Van Sloan). Lugosi's performance in the film has come to define the cinematic vampire; however, he only played Dracula one more time for Universal—in 1948's comic *Abbott and Costello Meet Frankenstein* (Charles Barton).

Rather than a focus on Dracula, 1936's *Dracula's Daughter* (Lambert Hillyer), as per the title, revolves around Dracula's daughter, Countess Zaleska (Gloria Holden), who curiously enters into analysis in the attempt to rid herself of her "addiction." According to Harry Benshoff, Countess

Zaleska, who preys upon both men and women—but seems to relish attractive young women the most—and who seeks assistance from the psychologist Dr. Jeffrey Garth (Otto Kruger) in combating her deviant desire, is "the most obviously 'lesbian' monster movie of the classical period" (77), and the film is one in which lesbianism and vampirism blur together as "evil forces that the heterosexual male must oppose" (195). In this sense, vampire Countess Zaleska reflects what I refer to as the "hyperbolic sexuality" of the cinematic vampire (Weinstock 7)—that is, the vampire as a monster marked by excessive or deviant sexual desire. Less obviously queer is Universal's 1943 *Son of Dracula* (Robert Siodmak), which features Lon Chaney, Jr., in the role of Count Alucard (Dracula spelled backward). Set in New Orleans, the film is notable for showing Dracula transforming into a bat on screen. *House of Dracula* (Erle C. Kenton, 1945) continued the theme introduced in 1944's *House of Frankenstein* (Erle C. Kenton) of combining Universal's three most popular monsters—Dracula (here played by John Carradine), Frankenstein's monster (Glenn Strange), and the Wolf Man (Lon Chaney, Jr.). One of the last of Universal Studios' classic monster films, the plot—in some ways similar to *Dracula's Daughter*—features a vampire initially seeking a cure for his affliction.

The other great cycle of vampire films, Hammer Film Productions' Dracula films, consists of nine movies released between 1958 and 1974, six of which star Christopher Lee in the role of the Count, frequently contending with Peter Cushing's Van Helsing. The first in the series, 1958's *Dracula* (Terence Fisher)—released in the U.S. as *The Horror of Dracula*—revised and updated Dracula as aggressive and forceful rather than suave and sophisticated. Instead of residing in a dilapidated castle, his home is modern and neat and, after his predation upon Lucy Holmwood (Carol Marsh) and her sister-in-law, Mina Holmwood (Melissa Stribling), Dracula is discovered hiding within the Holmwood house itself. Pursued back to his castle by Van Helsing (Peter Cushing) and Arthur Holmwood (Michael Gough), Dracula memorably is pinned in place by a cross formed by Van Helsing out of a pair of candlesticks and then turns to dust when exposed to sunlight.

Hammer's *Dracula* and the other entries in the series exemplify the thesis that the true transformative power of the vampire inheres in its morphing to suit each era's culturally specific anxieties and desires. In 1958's *Dracula*, the vampire is first traced to undertaker J. Marx and then is discovered lurking in the basement of an affluent home and working to convert others to his undead state—a literal "Red Scare." Fifteen years later, in 1973's *The Satanic Rites of Dracula* (Alex Gibson), the conspirators are not communist but corporate. In this penultimate entry into Hammer's Dracula series, Dracula (Christopher Lee in his last Dracula appearance for Hammer) is a reclusive property developer seeking to unleash a virulent strain of bubonic plague upon humanity—a genocidal impulse here is masked by a capitalist front as bacteriological research is essentially militarized.

Some mention of Hammer's "Karnstein Trilogy," indebted increasingly loosely to Le Fanu's *Carmilla*, is also necessary for its promotion of the lesbian vampire theme. A premise that I introduce in my *The Vampire Film* study is that although vampire sex takes a variety of forms—from the decorously heterosexual to the polymorphously perverse—vampires are nonetheless inevitably "queer"; by recklessly transgressing gender expectations and sexual mores, they foreground the social constructedness of gender, as well as the hegemonic devices that attempt to naturalize those constructions. And nowhere is the queer sexuality of the vampire more readily apparent than in the prominence of the lesbian vampire character—a character type that Carol Jenks finds so ubiquitous as to constitute "an entire sub-genre of the horror film in itself" (22). Countess Zaleska of *Dracula's Daughter*, as I note above, has been interpreted as an early cinematic representation of this character type and it is certainly the case that Hammer's "Karnstein" films, particularly the first two, *The Vampire Lovers* (Roy Ward Barker, 1970) and *Lust for a Vampire* (Jimmy Sangster, 1971), fall into this category as well. While *The Vampire Lovers* offers a relatively faithful retelling of Le Fanu's *Carmilla* with Ingrid Pitt's Carmilla preying upon the naïve Laura (Pippa Steel), *Lust for a Vampire* features the revived Mircalla (Yutte Stensgaard) preying upon female schoolmates at her finishing school. The third film in the series, *Twins of Evil* (John Hough, 1971), has the least to do with Le Fanu and emphasizes the lesbian vampire theme far less than the other two.

Sharing with Hammer's Karnstein Trilogy films an emphasis on the transgressive sexuality of the vampire with a pronounced homoerotic element are also Spanish director Jesús Franco's *Vampyros Lesbos* (1971), French director Jean Rollin's *Requiem for a Vampire* (1971), Spanish director José Ramón Larraz Gil's *Vampyres* (1974), and Belgian director Harry Kümel's *Daughters of Darkness* (1971). Of these, *Daughters of Darkness* in particular warrants some discussion here due to its influence on later vampire films. What is most significant about *Daughters of Darkness* is its use of the lesbian vampire theme to critique patriarchal oppression of women. Within the film, a young woman on her honeymoon, Valerie (Danielle Ouimet), finds herself at the center of a contest for her possession by her brutal husband, Stefan (John Karlen), and the glamorous Hungarian vampire countess, Elizabeth Báthory (played in a tour-de-force performance by Delphine Seyrig). Stefan, who beats his bride with a belt and cheats on her with Elizabeth's "secretary" Ilona (Andrea Rau)—whom he then accidentally kills—is shown to be just as much a vampire in his own way as Elizabeth, and Valerie's rejection of him in favor of latter signals her rejection of patriarchal control of women. Lesbianism in *Daughters of Darkness* thus functions as a politicized critique of normative patriarchal heterosexuality and its historic circumscription of women's capacity for self-determination. 1983's *The Hunger* (Tony Scott) starring Catherine Deneuve, Susan Sarandon, and David Bowie, tells a similar story of lesbian seduction but with less politically radical implications as the vampire, Miriam Blaylock (Deneuve), is shown to seduce both men and women who may achieve immortality as a result, but not eternal youth. After prolonged youth, when their bodies begin to rapidly age and deteriorate, she literally boxes them up and puts them away in the attic.

Beginning in the 1970s, vampire films proliferated at a dizzying pace. Space here only permits me to highlight briefly three significant trends in post-1970s vampire film production—remakes, adaptations, and action films—as well as to call attention to a handful of iconic movies. As Nina Auerbach addresses in *Our Vampires, Ourselves*, across the twentieth century (and, one should add, now into the twenty-first), remakes of Stoker's Dracula have been constant—although, as Auerbach points out, Dracula himself keeps changing with the times. "More than our heroes or pundits, our Draculas tell us who we were," writes Auerbach (112)—and of course who we are and imagine ourselves to be as well. Among notable remakes of *Dracula* are John Badham's 1979 version starring Frank Langella in the title role and Francis Ford Coppola's 1992 *Bram Stoker's Dracula*. In Badham's version, as Auerbach puts it, "Stoker's good men are villains; Stoker's vampire is a hero; the women, victims no more, embrace vampirism with rapture as the sole available escape from patriarchy" (140). Coppola's version also presents a softened Count, played by Gary Oldman, and invents a reincarnation subplot conspicuously absent from Stoker's novel that has Dracula seeking to be reunited with his long-lost bride whom he sees reincarnated in Mina (Winona Ryder).

Two other remakes of note are Werner Herzog's beautiful 1979 version of *Nosferatu*, titled *Nosferatu the Vampyre*, starring Klaus Kinski as the vampire, and Tim Burton's lackluster 2012 "reimagining" of the 1960s ABC soap opera, *Dark Shadows*. Herzog stays faithful to the plot of Murnau's silent original film (while incorporating additional aspects of Stoker's novel), yet produces a very different mood emphasizing the isolation of the vampire. "Time is an abyss," says Kinski's Count Dracula, "profound as a thousand nights.... Centuries come and go.... To be unable to grow old is terrible.... Death is not the worst.... Can you imagine enduring centuries, experiencing each day the same futilities...." Burton's light-hearted rendering of *Dark Shadows* plays the vampire's immortality for laughs, creating a garish 1970s America that bewilders his vampiric protagonist Barnabas Collins (Johnny Depp).

Increasingly quick to cash in on best-selling contemporary novels, modern cinema unsurprisingly has turned its attention repeatedly to popular fiction for safe sources of inspiration. Worth mentioning here are the 1994 big-budget adaptation of Anne Rice's *Interview with the Vampire*, directed by Neil Jordan (who also directed *Byzantium*—see below) and starring Tom Cruise, Brad Pitt, and Antonio Banderas, as well as the sequence of five fantasy/romance *Twilight* films begun in 2008 and ending in 2012 derived from the four vampire novels by American author Stephenie Meyer. Comparing *Interview* to the *Twilight* films in terms of sexual politics is instructive in terms both of the hyperbolic sexuality of the vampire and the range of ideological encodings the vampire permits. Both *Interview* and the *Twilight* films feature male actors conventionally regarded as sex symbols. In keeping with Rice's novels, however, *Interview* highlights same-sex eroticism and the transgressive sexuality of the vampire whereas the *Twilight* films are not only rigidly heterosexual in orientation but also adopt a "family values" platform forbidding premarital intercourse between the films' female protagonist Bella Swan (Kristen Stewart) and her vampire paramour, Edward Cullen (Robert Pattinson). Despite the apparent ideological divide, I argue in *The Vampire Film* that the effect is curiously similar: in each case, the hyperbolic sexuality of the vampire renders the vampire "queer." *Interview* outs vampires as gay while *Twilight* shows us that the perfect man can only be perfect by virtue of not being a man at all.

Of interest both as an adaptation of a popular vampire novel and as a film that flirts with tabooed sexuality in its own right is 2008's Swedish *Let the Right One In* (*Låt den Rätte Komma In*), directed by Tomas Alfredson and based on the 2004 novel of the same name by John Ajvide Lindqvist. Within the film, Oskar (Kåre Hedebrant) is a twelve-year-old boy bullied at school and suffering from benign neglect at home who strikes up an unusual friendship with Eli (Lina Leandersson), a vampire who appears to be a young girl about his age (but who is revealed in the book to be a castrati). Oskar harbors fantasies of revenge against those who abuse him and Eli needs an assistant to protect her while she sleeps during the day and to help procure blood. In the end, after Eli literally rips apart the bullies who appear to be intent on drowning Oskar, Oskar becomes Eli's companion/familiar. In provocative ways, *Let the Right One In* deals with the sexuality of children, transsexuality, and pedophilia, as well as school bullying. What the film suggests through Oskar and his murderous desire for revenge is that monsters are not born but made.

One also would be remiss in discussing adaptations to neglect the three versions (so far) of Richard Matheson's 1954 novel, *I Am Legend*:

1964's *The Last Man on Earth* (Ubaldo Regona and Sidney Salkow) starring Vincent Price, 1971's *The Omega Man* (Boris Sagal) starring Charlton Heston, and 2007's *I Am Legend* (Francis Lawrence) starring Will Smith. Each incarnation is true to Matheson's bleak vision of a world ravaged by plague; only the 1964 version, however, retains Matheson's startling conclusion that normativity is relative; in a world in which all are vampires, the "normal" human is the monster.

Probably the most significant trend in post–1970 vampire films is the development of the vampire action film—fast-paced films built around carefully choreographed battles and dazzling special effects. One could include here *30 Days of Night*, David Slade's 2007 adaptation of the comic book miniseries of the same name; Russian director Timur Bekmambetov's *Night Watch* (2004) and *Day Watch* (2007) adaptations of author Sergey Lukyanenko's novels; and Stephen Sommers's unfortunate 2004 *Van Helsing*. The two most visible examples of this trend, however, are the big-budget *Blade* and *Underworld* franchises. Based on the fictional Marvel Comics character of the same name, the Blade films focus on superhero vampire-hunter Blade, played by Wesley Snipes, who was born as a "dhampir," a human with vampire genes. This "mixed blood" lineage allows him all the advantages of the vampire in terms of strength and speed, but also permits him to walk unharmed in daylight. In the first film, *Blade* (Stephen Norrington, 1998), Blade must thwart evil vampire Deacon Frost (Stephen Dorff) from awakening an evil force and gaining godlike powers; in the sequel, *Blade II* (Guillermo del Toro, 2002), Blade forms an uneasy alliance with vampires to fight an event more dangerous enemy, Reaper vampires, who feed on vampires; and in the final installment, *Blade: Trinity* (David S. Goyer, 2004), Blade must pit his resources against Dracula himself, revealed to be the progenitor of all vampires. The *Underworld* film series features four installments, the first three of which (*Underworld* [Len Wiseman, 2003], *Underworld: Evolution* [Len Wiseman, 2006], and *Underworld: Rise of the Lycans* [Patrick Tatopoulos, 2009]) focus on a war between vampires and lycans (werewolves). As I address in *The Vampire Film*, what is striking about both these series is that "contamination" of bloodlines, rather than being the conventional anxiety of the vampire film, is instead presented as the solution. Each series features a set of vampire elders who fight to preserve the status quo and refuse to acknowledge their shared relation with those they consider beneath them. Each series then demonstrates that this type of racist thinking has no place in the modern world and that racial mixing, rather than enervating bloodlines, in fact invigorates them. Marking a significant shift in western thought, purity of blood in these two series is repeatedly associated with megalomaniacal and genocidal intentions and racial mixing is the key to a future of reduced antagonism.

While space limitations prohibit anything approaching a complete overview of the vampire film genre, other cinematic highlights worth mentioning in passing for their innovations on the conventional vampire narrative include George Romero's *Martin* (1978), Kathryn Bigelow's *Near Dark* (1987), and E. Elias Merhige's *Shadow of the Vampire* (2000). Assuming the protagonist of Romero's *Martin* is what he claims to be, *Martin* offers an unusual example of a working-class vampire. Bigelow in *Near Dark* infuses the vampire film with elements of the Western and road movie. And Merhige's self-aware *Shadow of the Vampire* offers a fictionalized account of the making of Murnau's *Nosferatu*, with the twist that the actor playing Count Orlock (Willem Dafoe) is in fact a vampire.

Case Studies

The remainder of this essay will develop the emphasis above on the vampire film as cultural barometer of historical anxieties and desires through a focus on four high-profile twenty-first-century contributions to the vampire film genre: Peter and Michael Spierig's *Daybreakers* (2010), Timur Bekmambetov's *Abraham Lincoln: Vampire Hunter* (2012), Neil Jordan's *Byzantium* (2012), and Jim Jarmusch's *Only Lovers Left Alive* (2014). Both *Daybreakers* and *Only Lovers Left Alive* will be shown to use the vampire motif to address environmental concerns and anxieties related to income inequality, while *Abraham Lincoln: Vampire Hunter* and *Byzantium* will be addressed in relation to their engagement with issues of race and gender.

Daybreakers

Written and directed by Australian filmmakers Michael and Peter Spierig, 2010's *Daybreakers* is a science fiction vampire action film that demonstrates the ways in which the genre shifts to reflect cultural anxieties by fusing contemporary concerns about global pandemics, climate change, transnational capitalism, and economic disparity into one ideologically vexed package. Set in 2019, the world of the film is one in which—as in Richard Matheson's *I Am Legend* and its various cinematic adaptations—a plague has transformed most of the world's population into vampires. As a consequence, amid a desperate shortage of blood, humans are hunted down and their blood harvested in laboratory farms while scientists at the Bromley Marks pharmaceutical company seek to create a synthetic blood substitute. In keeping with the modern vampire convention, sunlight must be avoided at all costs as it causes vampires to catch fire; vampires deprived of blood for extended periods are shown to degenerate into psychotic bat-like creatures called "subsiders."

A chance encounter with a group of humans helps the film's protagonist, vampire hematologist Edward Dalton (Ethan Hawke), develop a "cure" for vampirism consisting of controlled exposure to the sun (subsequently, it is learned that feeding from a former vampire also effects a cure)—even as blood reserves run dry and vampire soldiers are shown destroying subsiders and poor vampires to control the population. The Bromley Marks company, however, has no interest in helping to cure vampirism. The company's owner, Charles Bromley (Sam Neill), enjoys his immortality and reveals that his company has successfully developed a blood substitute and will thus corner the market. Additionally, his company will control remaining reserves of human blood because "there are always people who are willing to pay extra for the real thing." Whether or not the cure can be successfully implemented or if Edward is too late remains an open question in the end.

The vampiric body in the *Daybreakers* arguably gives shape both to contemporary anxieties concerning ecological catastrophe and income inequality. In this, it seems clearly to bear out Halberstam's assertions in *Skin Shows* that Gothic monsters function as "meaning machines" (21) that condense and entangle various cultural anxieties into one supersaturated form and the texts that contain monsters are thus "technologies of monstrosity" that produce the monster as a "remarkably mobile, permeable, and infinitely interpretable body" (21). As concerns global catastrophe, in the age of AIDS, SARS, Swine Flu, Covid, and so on, *Daybreakers* gives us vampirism as a disease brought on by a global pandemic and, in an era of increasingly dire predictions concerning climate change and global warming, the sun in *Daybreakers* kills in spectacular fashion; while the latter emerged as a common trope in twentieth-century vampire films (Dracula, it is worth noting, is able to move about during the day in Stoker's novel and does not burst into flames, explode, or turn to dust), the deadliness of the future sun in *Daybreakers* is repeatedly emphasized both through images of panicked vampires fleeing the sun and catching fire when exposed and through various technologies such as UV-insulated homes and cars driven by using cameras.

As concerns income inequality, as Ken Gelder appreciates, *Daybreakers* is "about resources: blood as a base commodity, like oil, or water" (131). On the one hand, the film literalizes Karl Marx's metaphor of capitalism as vampiric through the Bromley Marks company that farms humans for their blood (keeping them in a state of suspended animation without the solace of a fantasy matrix) and seeks to control flows of blood substitutes as well as real blood; however, on the other hand, if *Daybreakers* indicts the 1 percent for monstrous vampiric greed, it also has deep suspicions about the remaining 99 percent who turn unredeemably feral when deprived of the life's blood they need to subsist. The vampire in *Daybreaks* is thus positioned at the center of an apocalyptic allegory of the consequences of exploitation of both natural and human resources in the era of late capitalism.

Abraham Lincoln: Vampire Hunter

Produced by Tim Burton (whose own vampire film, *Dark Shadows*, also came out in 2012), Timur Bekmambetov's campy *Abraham Lincoln: Vampire Hunter*, based on the mash-up novel of the same name by Seth Grahame-Smith (author of *Pride and Prejudice and Zombies*), offers a revisionist history of the United States that makes vampires central to the debate over slavery and presents a new angle on the connection between vampires and race. As I discuss above, the monstrous vampire as racial other undergoes an interesting reversal in the *Blade* and *Underworld* vampire action series of the 1990s and the first decade of the twenty-first century in which contamination of blood is presented not as a problem, but as the solution to racial animosity. Those who remain wed to the "purity" of bloodlines in the modern vampire film are shown to be racists, often with genocidal intentions, wed to old and discredited ideas. *Abraham Lincoln: Vampire Hunter* advances this narrative by literally equating vampires with slave owners and thereby undercutting racial difference by recasting whites and blacks as allies in the war against vampires. The film indeed opens with a scene in which young Abraham Lincoln (Lux Haney-Jardine), age nine, attempts to come to the aid of a black boy (Curtis Harris) who is being savagely whipped. The confrontation sets in motion a sequence of events leading to the death of Lincoln's mother at the hands of a slave-trading vampire, Jack Barts (Marton Csokas), and the subsequent enlistment of Lincoln (Benjamin Walker) as a vampire hunter by Henry Sturges (Dominic Cooper). In the course of Lincoln's training, it is explained to Lincoln by Henry that, vampires, descended from the first American vampire, Adam (Rufus Sewell), "have been in the new world for centuries. Slaughtering native tribes and early settlers." They now support the slave trade as it provides them with a ready source of sustenance. The conflation of vampires with slaveholders is then elaborated upon across the film until seemingly unstoppable vampire soldiers in Confederate uniforms strike terror into the hearts of Union troops at the battle of Gettysburg.

Abraham Lincoln: Vampire Hunter ultimately finds its organizing premise in Lincoln's recollection of his mother's assertion that, "until every man is free, we are all slaves." Lincoln's emancipatory objective is thus doubled: to eliminate black slavery and to liberate the human race as a whole from the tyranny of vampires—and effecting the latter will go a long way toward achieving the former inasmuch as the vampires are directly implicated in supporting the slave trade. The vampires in *Abraham Lincoln* who slaughtered natives and settlers and now own plantations are literally bloodthirsty invaders corrupting "civilized" society. *Abraham Lincoln: Vampire Hunter* however presents itself as "post racial." The confrontation staged by the film is not, as in Stoker's novel, westerners against debased racial others (see Arata), but rather against infringements upon personal liberty—and, in this fight, blacks, whites, and even vampires (it turns out that Sturges is a member of the undead) must come together as equals to combat tyranny.

Byzantium

The 2012 British-Irish vampire film *Byzantium* is unconventional filmmaker Neil Jordan's second foray into undead territory, having directed 1994's *Interview with the Vampire*. Through allusions to the literary and cinematic vampire traditions—most especially Kümel's *Daughters of Darkness*—the film offers an updated feminist critique both of the vampire tale and of patriarchy more generally.

The film focuses on mother/daughter vampire pair Clara Webb (who initially goes by the name Camilla), played by Geema Arterton, and Eleanor Webb (Saoirse Ronan), who are forced to flee to a dated coastal resort after Clara kills a man who has been pursuing her. There, Clara seduces Noel (Daniel Mays), a socially awkward and lonely man who, upon the death of his mother, has just inherited the Byzantium hotel—a once-thriving business now in disrepair. While Clara turns the hotel into a brothel, Eleanor hesitantly enters into a relationship with a sickly boy named Frank (Caleb Landry Jones), with whom she shares her mother's and her own story: during the Napoleonic Wars, her mother was approached by two Royal Navy officers, the cruel Captain Ruthven (Jonny Lee Miller) and the gentler Midshipman Darvell (Sam Riley). Forced into prostitution by Ruthven, Clara gave birth to a daughter, Eleanor, who she left at an orphanage. Years later, apparently dying of tuberculosis, Clara steals from Ruthven a map leading to an island on which an ancient force transforms individuals willing to die into immortal vampires. Following her transformation, Clara learns of the existence of a secret society of vampires, the Brethren, that refuses to admit women. Clara can have no part in the brotherhood, but must obey their rules. The syphilitic Ruthven, to revenge himself upon Clara, rapes and presumably infects Eleanor, and Clara takes her to the island to see her transformed into a vampire as well—breaking the Brethren's code that women cannot create other vampires. Clara has been shielding Eleanor from the Brethren's "justice" ever since. At the end of the film, Darvell assists Clara in evading the Brethren—decapitating the Brethren's leader, Savella (Uri Gavriel) with the latter's own sword from Byzantium, his "souvenir from the Crusades"—and Eleanor takes Frank to the island to usher in his own transformation.

In keeping with my claim in *The Vampire Film* that vampire films are inevitably intertextual, *Byzantium* is very conscious of itself as a vampire film and plays with the conventions of the genre in ways both obvious and subtle. While Jordan's vampires still subsist on blood and must be invited in to gain entrance to a home, they can move about by day, do not sleep in coffins, are not affected by religious icons, and, in place of fangs, have a fingernail that grows pointed and sharp when they are excited. Further, Clara initially refers to herself as Carmilla, alluding to Le Fanu's story, while Captain Ruthven is an obvious allusion to the vampire antagonist of John Polidori's 1819 tale of seduction, betrayal, and death. At one point in the film, Eleanor is even shown watching a particularly brutal scene from Hammer's 1966 *Dracula: Prince of Darkness* (Terence Fisher) in which a woman vampirized by Dracula and now a vampire herself is staked as she screams and struggles. As in Kümel's *Daughters of Darkness*, *Byzantium* involves the return of a vampire to a seaside town and her inhabitation of an essentially empty hotel—a hotel that also calls to mind the Blaylock's sumptuous residence in Scott's *The Hunger*.

Taken together, these revisions to vampire lore and allusions to vampire narrative culminate in a vigorous critique both of the vampire film tradition and of patriarchy more generally. The existence of the Brethren, the all-male vampire secret society that refuses to admit women and forbids women to serve as makers of other vampires, can be taken as a broader commentary on the genre—one in which women are vampirized (Polidori's "The Vampyre"), turned into Dracula's brides, and staked in sexually sadistic scenes (*Dracula: Prince of Darkness*), but are seldom "master vampires" or makers of other vampires. Clara refuses to play by these rules—choosing to become a vampire herself, embracing her vampiric existence, and facilitating the transformation of her daughter as well.

Beyond the exclusionary Brethren and the sexist vampire narrative tradition, however, *Byzantium*—in many respects in keeping with *Daughters of Darkness*—offers a broader critique of patriarchal disempowerment of and violence toward women. The wheels of the narrative were set in motion by the rape of Clara by Ruthven and her abandonment in a brothel. ("You gave me nothing, Sir. And you took," laments Clara following her defilement. "I've given you your profession. Welcome to your adult life, whore," replies the callous Ruthven, who flips her a coin.) Dishonored and tubercular, Clara chooses the empowerment becoming a vampire affords.

When confronted by the Brethren following her transformation and asked what she will do with her "gift," she replies, "to punish those who prey on the weak, to curb the power of men." Her daughter is then raped and infected by the same man who assaulted her—and Clara, rather than watch her daughter die a slow death, chooses the vampiric existence for her as well. In the end, Eleanor then serves as a creator herself, passing along this "gift" to another. The "gift" of vampirism in *Byzantium* is the gift of autonomy and self-determination.

Only Lovers Left Alive

On the face of it, Jim Jarmusch's moody and relaxed *Only Lovers Left Alive* could not seem more distant from *Daybreakers*—and indeed the rest of the vampire cinema tradition. There are no vampire hunters, there is very little blood, and, as Steven Shaviro notes, "no sense of transgression or damnation." Instead, this "largely ... reflective, actionless" (Shaviro) film focuses on the playfully named vampires Adam (Tom Hiddleston) and Eve (Tilda Swinton) as they grapple with the implications of immortality in a rapidly changing world. Much of the action, such as it is, takes place in a deserted, desolate Detroit where the reclusive Adam sulks in a dilapidated house and records gloomy albums lamenting the state of the modern world—"funeral music," as he describes it. Because of the contamination of human blood supplies—suggested but never explicitly stated as AIDS—vampires such as Adam and Eve must be careful concerning sources of sustenance and Adam purchases blood from an agreeable hospital blood-bank employee, Dr. Watson (Jeffrey Wright)—one of a number of literary allusions within the film. Despondent over the decimation of the planet at the hands of "zombies"—mortals—Adam commissions a special wooden bullet and contemplates suicide. Fearing for Adam's life, his wife Eve flies from Tangiers, where she has been living, to join Adam in Detroit and the two reunited lovers contentedly enjoy each other's company, taking nighttime drives around the empty city, dancing at home, playing chess, and snacking on blood popsicles, until their idyllic seclusion is interrupted by Eve's wild sister, Ava (Mia Wasikowska), who arrives from Los Angeles. Ava's abuse of Adam and Eve's hospitality culminates in her vampirization of Adam's human lackey Ian (Anton

Yelchin). After disposing of Ian's corpse in an industrial waste site, Adam and Eve flee to Tangiers (under the assumed names Stephen Dedalus and Daisy Buchanan), only to discover that Eve's source of uncontaminated blood, the undead sixteenth-century poet Christopher Marlowe (William Hurt), himself has consumed tainted blood and is dying. At the film's end, low on money and in need of blood, Adam and Eve, with fangs bared, confront a pair of young lovers.

Like *Byzantium*, *Only Lovers* contributes in a very self-conscious way to the vampire genre. Adam as gloomy rocker in his Detroit mansion fuses Anne Rice's Lestat with *The Crow*'s Eric Draven (the latter not a vampire but a supernatural creature nevertheless), while his immortal malaise seems inherited from Rice's Louis. The emptiness of Detroit seems to echo the emptiness of New York in Lawrence's *I Am Legend* and, at a number of points, such as an overhead shot of the two lovers in bed or the anxiety the characters feel when their cab rides compete with the rising sun, the film seems to allude consciously to Kümel's *Daughters of Darkness*. But these allusions only serve to highlight *Only Lover*'s departure from established narrative conventions. Unlike Lestat, Adam seeks anonymity and the relationship between Adam and Eve is passionate and blissful, rather than dysfunctional.

Curiously, however, while *Only Lovers* is very much a film about the intimacy shared between two immortals and their complication relationship to the passage of historical time, the film nevertheless shares an underlying problematic with *Daybreakers* as it, too, positions its vampires at the nexus of ecological disaster and capitalist exploitation. At the center of *Only Lovers* is twenty-first-century Detroit—a landscape decimated by economic collapse and a city from which "everybody left" as Adam puts it. As described by Shaviro, "Adam takes Eve on nighttime drives through the deserted ruins of Detroit. They pass through empty neighborhoods, with lights gleaming in the distance. They visit landmarks like the Packard plant, and the old Michigan Theater in downtown Detroit (now used only as a parking garage).... You wouldn't know from the film that *anyone* still lives in Detroit." And few do in the film except the undead. In place of a beating heart for the city, Jarmusch instead substitutes a pit of acid in an abandoned factory. In the film's most vivid scene, Adam and Eve dispose of Ian's body by tumbling it into a vat of industrial waste in an abandoned building, where—exactly like a vampire's body exposed to the sun in a more conventional vampire film—it sizzles and is stripped of its flesh before sinking out of sight. Reflecting the viewer's reaction, the somewhat surprised Eve comments, "That was visual"—and what Jarmusch's *Only Lovers* delivers through its representation of Detroit as a deserted underworld is a viscerally visual reflection on the consequences of the reckless pursuit of wealth. While this is a source of despair for Adam, Eve offers a tempered form of optimism in her prophecy that Detroit will rise again "when the cities in the south are burning"—a very qualified silver lining to global warming.

What attention to *Daybreakers, Abraham Lincoln: Vampire Hunter, Byzantium,* and *Only Lovers Left Alive* demonstrates are both the ever-shifting parameters of the vampire cinema and its self-reflexivity. The vampire, in keeping with monsters in general, is always, as Jeffrey Jerome Cohen puts it, a "cultural body" that embodies "a time, a feeling, and a place" (4). The vampire that in early twentieth-century cinema expressed concerns about miscegeny and unregulated sexual desire today gives shape to anxieties about global warming and capitalist exploitation, as well as the continued disenfranchisement of women—while expressing the hope that past racial injustices can be laid to rest. But even as it again and again revises the familiar narrative, the vampire film carries its past along with it, trading on the viewer's awareness of the conventions of the genre that it both respects and violates.

Works Cited

Abbott, Stacey. *Celluloid Vampires: Life After Death in the Modern World.* University of Texas Press, 2007.
Arata, Stephen D. "The Occidental Tourist: *Dracula* and the Anxiety of Reverse Colonization" in *Dracula by Bram Stoker,* edited by Nina Auerbach and David J. Skal. W.W. Norton & Co., 1997, pp. 462–70.
Auerbach, Nina. *Our Vampires, Ourselves.* University of Chicago Press, 1995.
Bordwell, David. *The Films of Carl-Theodor Dreyer.* University of California Press, 1981.
Cohen, Jeffrey Jerome. "Monster Culture (Seven Theses)" in *Monster Theory: Reading Culture,* edited by Jeffrey Jerome Cohen. University of Minnesota Press, 1996, pp. 3–25.
Eisner, Lotte H. *The Haunted Screen: Expressionism in the German Cinema and the Influence of Max Reinhardt,* translated by Roger Greaves. University of California Press, 1973.
Gelder, Ken. *New Vampire Cinema.* Palgrave Macmillan, 2012.
Halberstam, Judith. *Skin Shows: Gothic Horror and the Technology of Monsters.* Duke University Press, 1995.
Jacobs, Lewis. *The Rise of the American Film: A Critical History.* Teacher's College Press, 1968.
Jenks, Carol. "*Daughters of Darkness*: A Lesbian Vampire Art Film" in *Necronomicon: Book One,* edited by Andy Black. Creation Books, 1996, pp. 22–34.
Skal, David J. *Hollywood Gothic: The Tangled Web of Dracula From Novel to Stage to Screen.* Faber & Faber, 2004.
Shaviro, Steven. "Only Lovers Left Alive." *The Pinocchio Theory,* 10 April 2014, http://www.shaviro.com/Blog/?p=1205.
Weinstock, Jeffrey Andrew. *The Vampire Film: Undead Cinema.* Columbia University Press, 2012.

Circumcising Dracula

A young, attractive woman, in a small Eastern European town, develops a mysterious illness. She seems to be "wasting away" inexplicably. Because the family is rich, a series of famous doctors is called in to examine the woman, bringing with them the latest medical treatments, modern technology, and "enlightened philosophy," yet their efforts are in vain; the young lady's condition grows worse and the physicians are at a loss. They consider all variety of explanations. However, they consistently overlook the two pinprick marks on the pale woman's neck.

The local clergyman, a devout, simple man, a native of the region, has his own theory concerning the illness which he is reluctant to share, yet his conscience compels him to do so: "Nosferatu," he explains, "the vampire." As expected, the educated doctors are patronizing and condescending. The clergyman leaves and the doctors burst into laughter over the simple and superstitious nature of the priest and the country folk he represents. "Vampires!" they scoff.

The priest returns to his spartan quarters dejected and with a growing fear in his heart. He takes certain precautions: he brings garlic flowers into his room, places wolfsbane around his window, and, as he climbs into bed, he does so with a large silver crucifix around his neck. During the night, a noise awakens the priest. The moonlight streaming through the window reveals the embodiment of his worst nightmare: the red eyes, the pallid skin, the long and sharp incisors of the vampire! The priest leaps from the bed and, with a terrified yet defiant flourish, brandishes the cross around his neck with outstretched arm at the vampire. The vampire, unperturbed, coolly surveys the crucifix with one eyebrow raised and chuckles at the priest, "*S'vet aykh gornisht helfn.*" Rough translation from the Yiddish: "It's not going to help"![1]

The Lore of Vampirism

Regardless of whether one finds the story funny or not, it is most likely intelligible to those who have never read Bram Stoker's *Dracula*, and even to the minority that has never seen a single vampire film. As James Twitchell indicates, the vampire myth is pervasive in American culture. Concerning the continuing popularity of vampire stories and references, Twitchell observes that

> It is one thing to explain why even "modern" writers, such as Henry James, Oscar Wilde or D.H. Lawrence used the analogy of the vampire to describe the inner and outer lives of their characters; it is quite another to explain why there is a vampire puppet on Sesame Street, "Count Count," who teaches numbers to our children ... or ... why any child would want to eat a "vitamin enriched" breakfast cereal named "Count Chocula" [109].[2]

Twitchell continues, "Any twelve-year-old schoolboy can describe the vampire, and that of course is precisely why it is so important" (110).

The Yiddish-speaking vampire joke is intelligible because all the familiar, clichéd elements are present: the small European town; the inexplicably waning young, beautiful woman; the marks on the neck. This is sufficient evidence for the listener to hypothesize a vampire because the story is familiar. The tension between the earnest yet provincial clergyman and the haughty yet baffled doctors serves only to confirm the suspicion that the priest is correct in his assumption, because, after all, it is the superstitious villagers who are always correct from the outset and the educated, sophisticated elite who scoff—even as they fall prey to the insidious vampire. As Van Helsing, the synthesis figure uniting the dichotomized realms of science and religion, folklore and fact, informs the public in the 1931 film version of Stoker's classic tale, "the strength of the vampire is that people will not believe in him."[3]

When the priest begins his evening preparations, we know precisely what he is doing. There is no mystery in the significance of the garlic, and certainly not in that of the crucifix, the talisman against evil. The priest knows the myths, believes in Evil (with a capital E), and turns to his faith to protect him. As Ken Gelder points out in *Reading the Vampire*, vampire fiction is peculiar in that "it depends upon the recollection and acting out of certain quite specific 'lores' for its resolution" (35), lore such as that the vampire is averse to crosses and garlic, must sleep in its own earth, can be destroyed by sunlight or a stake through the heart, etc. The joke is that the priest's faith won't protect him and the efficacy of his cross is thwarted because the vampire is derived from another faith—a "faithless faith," one that rejects Jesus as the son of God and his concomitant presence in the crucifix and communion wafer. The punch line of the joke is the Yiddish, the foreign tongue. The deviation from the expected progression of the story, the surprising element that perhaps makes it funny, is that the vampire must be Jewish and who ever heard of a Jewish vampire?[4]

The traditional vampire lore makes no reference to Jewish vampires. Yet, I will argue that vampires and Judaism historically have been intricately connected, and I do not think that I will be overstating the case excessively by proposing that the native earth in which the vampire is condemned to rest is the dirt of anti–Semitism. There is another system of "lore" at work in the construction of the vampire myth-lore that connects vampirism and Judaism. I shall focus primarily upon the accusation circulated by medieval clergy that Jews murder Christians, especially Christian children, and drink their blood, which explicitly characterizes the Jew as vampiric, and then consider the connection between two other libels: that Jews poison Christians and that Jews kidnap the communion wafer that is transubstantiated into the body of Jesus and torture it. Finally, I shall also briefly observe the conjunction of Judaism and usury and the familiar derogatory metaphor of the "bloodsucking" money-lending Jew to propose that contemporary conceptions of the vampire are connected to and still resonate on specific levels with virulent anti–Semitic mythologies. The claim here is neither that existing folk belief in vampires led Jews to be understood in terms of an already established category of monstrousness, nor that vampirism is a form of monstrousness derived from anti–Semitic sentiment. Rather, my argument is that the categories of vampirism and anti–Semitism must be considered as having developed together, symbiotically. Figuring Jews as vampires and affording to vampires anti–Semitic Jewish stereotypes establishes a bond between vampire and Jew that functions mutually to inflect constructions and understandings of both vampirism and Judaism.

The Lore of Anti-Semitism

The particular irony of the blood libel, also known as ritual murder, is that it associates vampirism with the first nation in history to outlaw human sacrifice (Genesis 22 and Deuteronomy 18:10), and the only people in the ancient Near East to prohibit the consumption of any blood (Leviticus 3:17, 7:26, 17:10–14, Deuteronomy 12:15–16, 12:23–25). According to Leon Poliakov, the first accusation of ritual murder against the Jews was made in Norwich, England, in 1144 (58). Poliakov explains that after the discovery of the body of a young apprentice on Good Friday eve in a woods near Norwich, the rumor spread that the boy had been murdered by Jews to mock the Passion of the Savoir. He details that

> The accusers specified that the murder had been planned far in advance: a meeting of rabbis, convening at Narbonne, supposedly had designated Norwich as the place for the annual sacrifice. The authorities put no faith in the

accusation, and the sheriff of the city attempted to protect the Jews. There were riots, however, and one of the prominent Jews of the district was murdered by an impecunious knight who happened to be his debtor [58].

Mortimer Ostow, citing historian G.I. Langmuir, provides a somewhat different account of the event. Ostow explains that the family of the unfortunate boy accused the Jews of the murder based on a dream reported by the child's aunt. Two weeks prior to the event, she claims to have dreamed that she was in the marketplace and was attacked by Jews. After the murder, she and the inhabitants of Norwich interpreted the dream as proof of Jewish guilt. Ostow comments that "doubtless the readiness of the family and neighbors to attribute the murder to the Jews in the absence of any real evidence, suggests that this readiness preexisted the murder" (66). Ostow goes on to reveal that the event might have attracted very little notice had not a monk, Thomas of Monmouth, heard the story in 1150, and concluded that not only had the Jews murdered the boy, but also crucified him. He arranged to have the body transferred to the cathedral and managed also to have the tomb become recognized as a source of miraculous healing (66). Although the charges against the Jews in Norwich were dropped as a result of lack of evidence, as Dennis Prager and Joseph Telushkin note, the long-term effects of this accusation have been devastating. They observe that "between the twelfth and the twentieth centuries, Jews and often entire Jewish communities were put on trial on over 150 occasions for engaging in ritual murder. In almost every instance Jews were tortured and put to death" (Prager 98). A particularly inflammatory case was that of Hugh of Lincoln. Nineteen Jews visiting Lincoln, England, in 1255 to attend a wedding were hanged without trial after the body of a Christian child named Hugh, who had been missing for three weeks, was found in a cesspool into which he had apparently fallen. The chronicler of the event, Matthew Paris, proposes that "the child was first fattened for ten days with white bread and milk, and then ... almost all the Jews of England were invited to the crucifixion" (Trachtenberg 131). Later, under torture, a Jew named Copin confessed that the Jews had crucified the boy "in the manner that the Jews had once crucified Jesus" (Telushkin 464). The case of Hugh of Lincoln had a profound impact on the popular image of Jews in England and throughout the Western world. Roth notes that "the legend [of Hugh] entered into the folklore of the English people: it was cited and imitated by Chaucer in his *Canterbury Tales*: it formed the inspiration of many ballads, in English, in French, and in Scots, which were handed down for centuries in the mouth of the peasantry" (57).

By the fourteenth century, the ritual murder charge had become associated with the Jewish holiday of Passover and had acquired a peculiar vampiric twist. Christians accused Jews of using Christian blood in their unleavened bread (matzoh) and in their wine. The claim was made in Savoy in 1329 that Jews "Compound out of the entrails of murdered Christian children a salve of food called *aharance* (*haroseth*), which they eat every Passover in place of a sacrifice" (Prager 100). Trachtenberg allows that "one of the important causes adduced for the expulsion of the Jews from Spain was the constantly repeated accusation that they drank Christian blood" (134). A sixteenth-century document explains that the murder of Christian children and the distribution of their blood among Jews is "a token of their eternal enmity towards Christianity," for, "if they had Christ today, they would crucify Him as their fathers did, but since they do not have Christ, they martyr in His stead an innocent Christian child" (Prager 100). Jews here are characterized explicitly as demonic enemies of Christ who drink the blood of Christian children.

Accusations of ritual murder with its vampiric associations followed the Jews throughout Europe. Historian Haim Hillel Ben-Sasson writes that "generation after generation of Jews in Europe was tortured and Jewish communities were massacred or dispersed and broken up because of this libel" (247). And the blood libel in fact persists into the twentieth-century. Historian James Parkes reports that "in Central Europe, among both Roman Catholics and Eastern Orthodox Christians ... there are almost more examples of the accusation in the years between 1880 and 1945 than in the whole of the middle ages" (*Foundations* 19). Malcolm Hay ascribes much of the continued popularity of the blood libel in modem times to a virulently anti-Semitic faction of the Vatican in the late nineteenth century. He cites a series of articles in the semi-official Vatican journal, *La Cruila Cattolica*, including the March 4, 1882, issue which remarks, "Every practicing Hebrew worthy of that name is obliged even now, in conscience, to use in food, drink, in circumcision, and in various other rites of his religious and civil life the fresh or dried blood of a Christian child ... all this is still true and faithfully observed in the present century" (Hay 311-12).

In the 1930s, the Nazis renewed the libel with vigor, devoting the entire May 1, 1934, issue of the newspaper *Der Strumer* to Jewish ritual murder and routinely including illustrations of rabbis sucking the blood of German children in this same publication (Prager 100). Trachtenberg, writing in 1943, observes that "anthropologists have uncovered places in Germany and the Balkans where it is still believed that Jews consume human flesh [and that] they wash down these ... repasts with the blood they suck at night from the Christian serving girls who work for them!" (139). In the 1960s and 70s, Dennis Prager and Joseph Telushkin report that the blood libel was spread by the leading financial figure of the Arab world, King Faisal of Saudi Arabia, who informed newspaper interviewers that the Jews annually celebrated Passover by murdering a non-Jew and consuming his blood (Prager 101).

The blood libel thus explicitly and non-metaphorically identifies Jews as vampiric—Jews consume the blood of Christians. Other well-known libels, such as the plot to poison Christians and the desecration of the host, ascribe characteristics to the Jews that are also ascribed to the vampire—specifically those of plague-carrier and enemy of Christ—thus placing the Jew and the vampire into the same categories and forging further associations.

Parkes observes that "if a king had a Jewish physician and did not actually die on the battlefield ... there is nothing surprising in his unfortunate doctor being accused of poisoning him" (*Medieval* 50). He cites several instances of Jewish royal physicians being executed after a king's death. According to Prager and Telushkin, almost every medieval Jewish doctor was endangered. Trachtenberg notes that in 1161 in Bohemia, eighty-six Jews were burned as punishment for an alleged plot of Jewish physicians to poison the populace (97). The suspicion that the Jews were plotting to poison the Christian world had particularly horrific results during the plague period of 1348–49. The plague, which killed about one third of Europe's population, was blamed on the Jews, despite the fact that it also killed Jews. Jews were first tortured into confessing to knowingly and maliciously spreading the plague in September of 1348 in Switzerland. According to an extracted confession, a rabbi had instructed the Jews to poison wells and cisterns. In October, the verdict was handed down, "all Jews from the age of seven, cannot excuse themselves from this crime, since all of them in their totality were cognizant and are guilty of the above actions" (Prager 102). Jewish children under the age of seven were then baptized and raised as Christians after their families had been executed. Ostow observes that between 1348 and 1350, thousands of Jews were massacred and hundreds of Jewish communities destroyed based on the suspicion that the Jews were responsible for the Black Death (108).

The association of plague with the Jews is another manner in which Judaism is linked to the figure of the vampire because what the vampire does is to spread its terrible and unholy disease. As my opening story reiterates, victims of the vampire inexplicably sicken and die. In addition, part of the vampire lore is the fact that vampirism is notoriously contagious. The exchange of bodily fluids that occurs during the vampirism condemns the victim to an unholy existence as a member of the living dead. Christopher Bentley observes in reference to *Dracula* that "although vampirism is ostensibly presented as a supernatural phenomenon of evil ... it is in actuality treated as a shameful and terrible disease" (30). The most powerful contemporary conjunction of vampirism, disease, and anti–Semitism appears in Franz Murnau's famous 1922 film *Nosferatu*, in which the vampire, Count Orlock, featuring exaggerated stereotypical Jewish features, such as his disproportionately large, hooked nose and heavy eyebrows, arrives in the German city of Bremen along with the Plague. Ken Gelder notes of *Nosferatu* that it is "difficult not to see this German film as anti–Semitic" (96). Gelder cites the appearance of Nosferatu and his relationship to the hunched, obsessive Renfield character, who, in this retelling of the vampire myth, is Jonathan Harker's employer. Renfield, the city official and apparent financier who helps the vampire purchase property in Bremen, encourages Harker to deal with the vampire, promising Harker wealth and advancement. Later in the film, Renfield, strongly resemblant of the vampire himself, is chased across town by a crowd of angry townspeople.

In a significant reworking of Stoker's tale, the Van Helsing character in *Nosferatu* is rescripted as Jewish and his importance in the film is diminished almost to the point of nonexistence. Clad in his yarmulke, Van Helsing, the Jewish professor representative of the learned elite of the city, is insufficient to deal with the problem of the vampire. He is rather a minor character who arrives too late to intervene. There are no elderly wisdom figures in *Nosferatu*; in fact, all of the older population, if not actually complicit with the foreign invasive entity, is at best incompetent to deal with the problem. The salvation of the German people is left to the young pure German woman Ellen.

One finds in *Nosferatu* compellingly anti–Semitic undertones: the deformed "property-acquiring Jew-vampire" (Gelder 96), with the help of the complicit city fathers, invades the German borders and spreads plague and death in its wake. It certainly is not difficult to believe that a 1922 German monster movie could manifest anti–Semitic tendencies which would link the Jew to the vampire. In the economic chaos of Post-World War I Germany, anti–Semitic scapegoating was already on the rise, and along with it came the prominent revival of several ancient libels against the Jews, including, as previously noted, the charge of ritual murder.

In making a case for the connection between the evolution of notions of the vampire and anti–Semitism, one should also note the charge that Jews desecrate the host, which, in some ways, is the most insidious charge against the Jews. In 1215, the Fourth Lateran Council accepted the doctrine of transubstantiation as official Church dogma. This dogma asserted that the wafer used at the Mass was miraculously transformed into the body of Jesus. The wafer was to be regarded not as a symbolic representation of Jesus, but as his actual body. In 1243, twenty-eight years after the Council declaration, the first accusation of "host desecration" occurred in Berlitz, near Berlin (Prager 103). The city's entire Jewish population was burned alive for allegedly torturing a wafer. In Prague in 1389, the Jewish community was collectively accused of attacking a monk carrying a wafer.

Prager and Telushkin observe that "large mobs of Christians surrounded the Jewish neighborhood and offered the Jews the choice of baptism or death. Refusing to be baptized, three thousand Jews were murdered" (Prager 103). A charge of host desecration was reported in Romania as late as 1836.

The charge of "host desecration" is particularly insidious because it most clearly designates the Jews as satanic. After all, animal crackers aside, as Prager and Telushkin comment, "Clearly, no one, not even a Jew, tortures cookies. If a person tortures one, it could mean only one thing: he, too, recognizes that it is the body of Jesus, and wishes to make him suffer. Who but the people of the Devil recognize the divinity of Jesus but wish to destroy him?" (103). Trachtenberg writes that

> The two inexorable enemies of Jesus, then, in Christian legend, were the devil and the Jew, and it was inevitable that the legend should establish a causal relation between them. ...the devil and the Jew joined forces, in Christian belief, not only in the war against Jesus during his life on earth but also in the contemporaneous war against the Church and its civilization [20–21].

Trachtenberg examines multiple ways in which the Jew and the Devil were linked in the medieval mind-from the popular notion that Jews had horns and a distinctive and unpleasant odor (which Christian blood supposedly could mask),[5] to the association of the Jew with black magic, satanic ritual, and ultimately with the Antichrist. Thus, the Jew and the vampire merge in serving the same master—the devil.[6]

Before concluding this survey, it is necessary to note briefly two other categories—both of which have to do with circulation and which in various ways redeploy the plague association—which seem further to conjoin the idea of the Jew with the idea of the vampire: the Jew as invasive force lacking a homeland, and the relationship of the Jew to capital and capitalism. Critical analyses of Bram Stoker's *Dracula* frequently situate the text within a Victorian xenophobic historical context. Several studies conclude that Stoker's 1897 text, written at the apogee of British Colonialism, manifests a paranoia of reverse colonialism.[7] Dracula, the exotic foreigner, is an external invading force more imperialistic than the imperialists. From the superstitious backwaters of Transylvania, Dracula penetrates the cosmopolitan center of England. Furthermore, Dracula is portrayed as a hoarder of money and gold. At one point, the captive Jonathan Harker enters a forbidden room of Dracula's Transylvanian castle and writes in his journal, "The only thing I found was a great heap of gold in one corner—gold of all kinds, Roman, and British, and Austrian, and Hungarian, and Greek, and Turkish money" (47). Gelder remarks that "Dracula's money is an indication of his mobility: his trade traverses national boundaries, without allegiance to any one nation" (14). Jules Zanger, in "A Sympathetic Vibration: Dracula and the Jews," places these representations of the vampire in the context of Jewish immigration into England in the 1890s and anti–Semitism in Europe—stereotypes which cast the Jews as both rich and nomadic, difficult to monitor and a threat because they "drained capital by moving it elsewhere" (Gelder 14). The classic anti–Semitic conception of the Jew as greedy usurer unfortunately remains all common.[8]

Daniel Pick in his 1989 study *Faces of Degeneration* comments on the "perceived 'alien invasion' of Jews from the East who, in the view of many alarmists, were 'feeding off' and 'poisoning' the blood of the Londoner" (173), and notes that it is an "unscrupulous Jew," Immanuel Hildesheim, in Stoker's words, "a Hebrew of the rather Adelphi type, with a nose like a sheep, and a fez" (349), who facilitates Dracula's escape from England. David Englander, in his "Booth's Jews: The Presentation of Jews and Judaism in Life and Labour of the People in London," observes popularized stereotypes of Jews in Victorian England, including the perception of them as rich, unscrupulous, and devoid of nationalist loyalties (556 and *passim*), and notes that, in terms of overall population, Jews were second only to the Irish in England during the 1890s (551). Gelder concludes that "the anti–Semitic mythology of the Eastern European Jew folded in to what became—through Stoker's novel—the 'Dracula myth'" (16).[9] Thus, the Jew as the Christian Other, as the anti–Christian, invasive, nomadic figure who metaphorically sucks the capital out of a region, becomes recast by Stoker as the monster that literally drains away the life's blood of the victim and the community.

The threefold connection Jew/capital/vampire is also vigorously reinforced by Karl Marx himself. Marx, in *Capital* and elsewhere, repeatedly characterizes capital as vampiric. He writes for instance in a famous quotation from *Capital*, "Capital is dead labour which, vampire-like, lives only by sucking living labour, and lives the more, the more labour it sucks" (342). Taking this striking description of the vampiric qualities of capital as a starting point for his analysis of *Dracula*, Franco Moretti characterizes Dracula precisely as a monopoly capitalist, driven by the urge to accumulate, who drains others to feed his monstrous hunger: "Like capital, Dracula is impelled towards a continuous growth, an unlimited expansion of his domain: accumulation is inherent in his nature" (91). Gelder, noting Marx's repeated references to capital as vampiric, writes that

> The representation of capital or the capitalist as a vampire, was, then, common both to Marx and to popular fiction in the mid-nineteenth century. It would not be an exaggeration to say that this representation mobilized vampire fiction at this time, to produce a striking figure defined by excess and unrestrained appetite-whose strength increased, the more victims he consumed [22].

What is important here is that the Jew was identified by Marx and in the popular imagination in exactly the same terms: as a figure who epitomized the excesses of capitalism and "its appetite, its accumulative powers, its mobility, its increasing internationalization" (Gelder 22). Marx himself represents the Jew in this manner in his notorious essay, "On the Jewish Question" (1843), in which he paints the Jew as a figure reducing every relation to "commerce" and worshiping capital. It is through the Jew, writes Marx, the figure with only a "chimerical nationality," that money had become globalized, "a world power." To emancipate society from these conditions—from capitalism itself—means to "make the Jew impossible" (qtd. in Gelder 22). "His religious consciousness would evaporate like some insipid vapour in the real, life-giving air of society" (qtd. in Gelder 22). While Marx does not explicitly make the connection between Jew and vampire, the relation of both the vampire and the Jew to capital establishes a connection between them by association. The emancipation from capitalism therefore would be the stake through the Jewish vampire's heart.[10]

The Jewish Vampire

From the medieval accusations of ritual murder, poison, and host-desecration, and associations with disease, black magic, and the devil, to the more contemporary rhetoric that associates Jews with capital and capitalism on the one hand and then relates capitalism to vampirism on the other, it is apparent that the concepts of Judaism and vampirism merge. One cannot consider the idea of the vampire without reflecting on a different but convergent set of lore—traditions of anti-Semitism. On both literal and metaphorical levels, the Jew is explicitly identified as a vampire, as a monster that must be resisted and destroyed.

Figuring Jews as vampires functions as a clear-cut example of anti-Semitism and is easy to decry. However, the opposite movement of figuring vampires as Jews is more subtle, but perhaps just as pernicious. Here one is again reminded of King's *'Salem's Lot*, in which a Christian child is sacrificed and his blood drained as a prelude to the vampire's arrival. One must also wonder to what extent the exoticism of Bela Lugosi's Dracula, with his Eastern European intonation, is, on a certain level, associated with the stereotype of the Eastern European Jewish immigrant. To the extent that the vampire remains the enemy of Christ and the Christian religion and engages in practices that suggest historical libels against the Jews, even in contemporary retellings, anti-Semitism remains operative, if implicit, within the figure and field of the vampire.

Notes

1. A variant on it is presented in Roman Polanski's 1967 *The Fearless Vampire Killers* in which the Yiddish punchline is translated to "Boy, have you got the wrong vampire!"

2. Frank Grady, in his essay "Vampire Culture," makes a similar observation about the pervasiveness of vampire thematics in American culture. Noting both Count Chocula and Count Count, Grady observes that "the relentless march of commodification has not spared the realm of the supernatural, or the figure of the vampire" (225).

3. That the villagers (or in other circumstances, children), are always correct in the assumption of the vampire's presence reveals the underside of progress narratives. The vampire emerges precisely during those moments during which the past, tradition, and specifically Christian belief are in danger of being forgotten. Thus, the vampire, although an enemy of God, emerges as the supernatural manifestation of God's power, chastening a hubristic culture. It is the provincial (villagers) and the simple (children) who still retain faith in a world of science.

However, certain modem vampire adaptations recast the vampire not as a supernatural entity, but as a scientifically explicable phenomenon, a separate species. See, for example, Charnas's *The Vampire Tapestry* and Scott's 1983 film *The Hunger*. It is also notable that the Van Helsing character in Murnau's *Nosferatu* makes a similar comparison between vampires and "naturally-vampiric" entities, such as venus flytraps. However, the ending of the film belies a scientific explanation.

4. Much recent vampire fiction trades on the reader's familiarity with this lore, recapitulating it and, just as often, frustrating it. The fiction now uses the lore as a point of reference, taking it seriously and even exaggerating its use and effect, as in the Hammer Studio productions of the 60s and 70s, parodying it, as does my initial story/joke, or modifying it, as does Anne Rice in her series of immensely popular vampire novels.

The reader conversant with the vampire lore frequently is allied with the intrepid vampire hunter who can battle the vampire precisely because he or she knows and accepts this lore, which often includes direct references to other works within the vampire genre. Vampire texts and especially contemporary vampire retellings are notable in that they engage in a conscious dialogue with other texts and frequently foreground the constructedness of the text itself by incorporating explicit references to other texts. Thus, Stoker's text quotes Coleridge, Rice's vampires scoff at Stoker, and Stephen King's vampire hunters in *'Salem's Lot* bone-up on everything from Stoker's *Dracula* and Rymer's serial *Varney the Vampire* to the soft-porn comic *Vampirella* as preparation for doing battle with the forces of Evil. King's text abounds with references to other texts and it is the reader's and the characters' knowledge of these other texts that permits the divergences from the vampire tradition to be recognized as King's innovations. King's innovations cannot be recognized as such, without the ground of lore upon which the tale rests.

The vampire movie tradition, if possible, is even more self-referential than the fiction, trading on the viewer's knowledge of both the written and cinematic vampire traditions and demonstrating how new elements become incorporated into the tradition itself. One example of this is the Van Helsing/Dracula contest of wills, prominent in 1931 Bela Lugosi film, but absent from Stoker's text. After surmising that Dracula himself is within the confines of Dr. Seward's sanatorium, Van Helsing is left alone while the rest of the party dashes off to confront the Count. Dracula appears in the room and a tense but deliberate battle of the wills begins. In a line that will be repeated many times in future retellings, Lugosi intones, "For one who has not lived even a single lifetime, you are a wise man, Van Helsing." Then the fiendish aristocrat attempts to hypnotize Van Helsing. Van Helsing successfully resists and, as the foiled Count flees, he exits acknowledging Van Helsing's triumph, observing, "your will is strong, Van Helsing." This sequence, established in the Lugosi version, has become a mainstay of the Dracula tale, repeated almost word-for-word for example in the 1979 Frank Langella version, a version in which we disturbingly find ourselves rooting for the attractive, cultured Count to prevail over the feeble, priggish opposition, and a version in which the aging Van Helsing, played by Laurence Olivier, is staked in the final sequence by Dracula!

5. It should be noted that the unpleasant odor is a reoccurring vampire motif as well.

6. The ambiguous origin of the vampire in Stoker's *Dracula* is traced to black magic and Satanic dealings. The same Voivode Dracula who is revealed by Van Helsing to have once fought in the name of Christ against the Turkish Infidel, is revealed to be derived from a lineage held to "have had dealings with the Evil One" (Stoker 241). In King's 1975 retelling of the vampire story, Matthew Burke, the elderly schoolteacher Van Helsing character comments matter-of-factly, "There were certain rites to be performed, in propitiation of the Dark Father. Even Barlow has his Master, you see" (319). The rites in question are the sacrifice and draining of the blood of a Christian child by the vampire's bald lackey.

7. Cf. Hindle's introduction to the Penguin Classic version of Stoker's *Dracula*, Moretti's *Signs Taken for Wonders*, Gelder's *Reading the Vampire*, and Grady's "Vampire Culture."

8. Zanger also focuses on the character of Svengali in George du Maurier's popular and extremely anti-Semitic *Trilby*, with whom he connects Stoker's Dracula. The hypnotic Svengali, like Dracula, is from the "poisonous East." He is "of Jewish aspect, well featured but sinister" (Zanger 35). It is worth remarking that Dracula does not in fact have to be Jewish to exhibit stereotypically anti-Semitic characteristics. As one reviewer of this essay remarked, Jewishness as a generalizable category of monstrosity allowed for negative qualities associated with Jews to be extrapolated and applied to non-Jews in order to denigrate or denounce them. Part of what is so monstrous about Dracula is precisely that he exhibits stereotypically anti-Semitic Jewish characteristics.

9. Gelder also notes in this context the anti-Semitic representation of Hungarian Jews provided in Major E.C. Johnson's *On the Track of the Crescent*, a source upon which Stoker drew for Dracula (Gelder 15).

10. Even today, the association of Jews with money lending and the derogatory epithet of "bloodsucker" for such activity unfortunately remain all too common.

Works Cited

Ben-Sasson, Haim Hillel. *Trial and Achievement: Currents in Jewish History*. Keter Publishing House, 1974.
Bentley, Christopher. "Sexual Symbolism in Dracula" in *Dracula: The Vampire and the Critics*, edited by Margaret L. Carter. U.M.I. Research Press, 1988, pp. 25–34.
Chamas, Suzy McKee. *The Vampire Tapestry*. Tom Doherty Associates, 1980.
Englander, David. "Booth's Jews: The Presentation of Jews and Judaism in Life and Labour of the People of London." *Victorian Studies*, vol. 32, no. 4, 1989, pp. 551–71.
Gelder, Ken. *Reading the Vampire*. Routledge, 1994.
Grady, Frank. "Vampire Culture" in *Monster Theory Reading Culture*, edited by Jeffrey Jerome Cohen. University of Minnesota Press, 1996, pp. 225–243.
Hay, Malcolm. *Europe and the Jews*. Beacon Press, 1961.
Hindle, Maurice. "Introduction" to *Dracula* by Bram Stoker. Penguin, 1993, pp. vii-xxx.
King, Stephen. *'Salem's Lot*. New American Library, 1975.
Marx, Karl. *Capital: A Critique of Political Economy, Volume 1*, translated by Ben Fowkes. Penguin, 1976.
Moretti, Franco. *Signs Taken for Wonders: Essays in the Sociology of Literary Form*. Verso, 1988.
Ostow, Mortimer. *Myth and Madness: The Psychodynamics of Anti-Semitism*. Transaction Publishers, 1996.
Parkes, James. *The Foundations of Judaism and Christianity*. Quadrangle Books, 1960.
———. *The Jew in the Medieval Community*. 2nd ed. Hermon Press, 1976.
Pick, Daniel. *Faces of Degeneration: A European Disorder, c.1848–c.1918*. Cambridge University Press, 1989.
Poliakov, Leon. *The History of Anti-Semitism: From the Time of Christ to the Court Jews*, translated by Richard Howard. Schocken Books, 1965.
Prager, Dennis, and Joseph Telushkin. *Why the Jews? The Reason for Anti-Semitism*. Simon & Schuster, 1983.

Roth, Cecil. *A History of the Jews in England*. Oxford University Press, 1941.
Stoker, Bram. *Dracula*. Oxford University Press, 1983.
Telushkin, Joseph. *Jewish Literacy: The Most Important Things to Know About the Jewish Religion, Its People, and Its History*. Morrow, 1991.
Trachtenberg, Joshua. *The Devil and the Jews: The Medieval Conception of the Jew and Its Relation to Modern Anti-Semitism*. 2nd ed. The Jewish Publication Society, 1983.
Twitchell, James. "The Vampire Myth" in *Dracula: The Vampire and the Critics*, edited by Margaret L. Carter. U.M.I. Research Press, 1988, pp. 109–116.
Zanger, Jules. "A Sympathetic Vibration: Dracula and the Jews." *English Literature in Translation 1880–1920*, vol. 34, no. 1, 1991, pp. 33–44.

Vampire Suicide

> "You will make what haste you can," said the stranger, "from the mountain, inasmuch as it is covered with sulphurous vapours, inimical to human life, and when you reach the city you will cause to be published an account of my proceedings, and what I say. You will say that you accompanied Varney the Vampyre to the crater of Mount Vesuvius, and that, tired and disgusted with a life of horror, he flung himself in to prevent the possibility of a reanimation of his remains."
>
> Before then the guide could utter anything but a shriek, Varney took one tremendous leap, and disappeared into the burning mouth of the mountain.
> —James Malcolm Rymer,
> *Varney the Vampire; or, the Feast of Blood* (759)

So ends the inglorious career of terror practiced for over two centuries by the antagonist of James Malcolm Rymer's sprawling 666,000-word penny dreadful, *Varney the Vampire; or, the Feast of Blood*, published serially from 1845 to 1847. And while Bram Stoker's *Dracula*, published fifty years later is generally considered to have established the "ground rules" for how vampires act, Varney can take credit for one of the more curious recurring tropes of vampire narrative: vampire suicide. From Rymer's undead omnibus, considered the first full-length work of vampire fiction, to modern vampire narratives including films such as *Blacula* (William Crain, 1972), *Thirst* (Park Chan-wook, 2009), and *Only Lovers Left Alive* (Jim Jarmusch, 2014); television programs including *True Blood* (based on the Southern Vampire Mystery series by author Charlaine Harris) and *Angel* (the *Buffy the Vampire Slayer* spin-off); and the literary works of authors such as Anne Rice and Kim Newman, vampires attempt suicide with relative frequency—and with a fair amount of success. This raises questions about why the immortal un-dead seek to be dead-dead, and what this tells us about the human creators that imagine them into being in the first place—because, as Jeffrey Jerome Cohen has famously asserted, monsters of all stripes are "pure culture" (4), inventions of the human imagination that reflect human anxieties and desires. Looking to the extensive body of vampire fiction and film that has developed since the early part of the nineteenth century, it becomes clear that vampires commit suicide for a variety of reasons that mostly fall into three broad categories: remorse, ennui, and heroism. Taken together, the attempted or accomplished suicides of vampires function ideologically to bolster anthropocentrism, reaffirm conventional Judeo-Christian morality, and undercut the appeal of immortality, particularly as the religious stigmatization of vampires as inherently evil wanes. While it can often seem as a narrative representation of human "sour grapes," vampire suicide frequently functions to affirm that immortality is as much a curse as a gift. Put differently, vampire suicide is a lesson for the living as such narratives convey the message to envious humans to be careful what you wish for.

Interestingly, vampire suicidal tendencies can also be construed as representing a half-hearted attempt to recuperate the vampire genre from charges of immorality through a strategy of inversion. In folklore and in some popular culture texts, the punishment for the mortal sin of suicide is precisely to become a vampire. The consequence of the sin of hubristic unmaking is to become the embodiment of sin. Vampire suicide, particularly in instances of guilt or martyrdom then, is a curious type of cleansing—purification achieved through the preferred means of self-slaughter: suicide by sunlight. As the creature of darkness waits for dawn or steps out into the midday sun, "evil" transforms into a small pile of ashes. The second suicide then is the antidote for the first (or for the other sins that led to the transformation into a vampire). Narratives of vampire ennui are somewhat more complicated than those of vampiric regret; however, they nevertheless convey the message that the presumed pleasures of immortality and great power wear thin over the years as the world changes around the static vampire. In this way, narratives of vampire suicide are presented as cautionary tales: Evil (with a capital "E") will be punished, life is a gift to be respected, the prospect of death gives life meaning, be satisfied with your lot, and so on. This insistent reassertion of conventional anthropocentric morality (common to the Gothic overall) thereby functions as an alibi, allowing consumers of vampire narratives to "have their cake and eat it too"—that is, to take pleasure in and even identify with monstrous creatures that prey on human life while disavowing them in the end. Vampire suicide thus arguably becomes emblematic of the Gothic genre in general as the lewd and lurid middle gives way to the tidy conclusion and reassertion of conventional morality. We enjoy the bloody mayhem, and then the sun rises, the penitent monster turns to ash, and order is restored.

Vampiric Remorse

Literary narratives of vampire suicide as a consequence of remorse for crimes committed against humans and associated self-disgust originate with Varney and constitute the variant of the vampire suicide trope that most clearly depicts vampiric immortality as a curse rather than a gift. For a vampire to attempt suicide as a result of overwhelming guilt and regret requires several conditions: First and foremost, the vampire must come to consider feeding on humans as a transgression rather than a natural or permissible act; this entails both that the vampire subscribe to or retain a moral framework that distinguishes right from wrong and good from evil, and that the vampire construe vampiric predation upon humans as the latter. The vampire thus experiences a form of cognitive dissonance as the requirements for its survival conflict with its own ethical principles. The vampire must either empathize or sympathize with its prey and retain a conscience that causes it to feel guilty. More succinctly, the vampire must at some point recognize its actions as *evil* and regret them, but be unable to stop because its continued existence depends upon feeding on humans. It must come to appreciate its very nature as both evil and unchangeable—or at least conclude that its guilt is impossible to expiate in any other way.

Rymer's Varney, as a handful of commentators have observed, starts off monstrous and predatory, but becomes more conflicted and sympathetic as the narrative progresses. Bette B. Roberts explains that Varney "indulges in repeated moments of self-pity for his loathsome, outcast experience" (3), and notes Varney's weary questioning in volume II, "How long is this hated life to last?" (Rymer qtd. in Roberts, 3). We learn in volume III, prior to Varney's first unsuccessful suicide attempt, that Varney "would gladly have been more human, and lived and died as those lived and died whom he saw around him. But being compelled to fulfil the order of his being, he never had the courage absolutely to take measures for his own destruction, a destruction that should be final in consequence of depriving himself of all opportunity of resuscitation" (650). Varney then tries to drown himself in the ocean, but is revived in keeping with the series' premise by moonlight. The "Varney" entry on the *Victorian Gothic* site characterizes this as Varney's "existential crisis," asserting that it is in the third volume that Varney "develops into an increasingly reflexive, tormented character" ("Varney"). In an extended overview of the series, the *Skull in the Stars* site similarly observes that,

> Varney the vampire is a creature who does many evil acts, but is simultaneously haunted by those same acts and tormented by his own existence. As the epic progresses, Varney vacillates increasingly rapidly from monster and criminal to victim and even altruist, and one never quite knows what one will get

from him! This sympathetic depiction of vampires is unmatched in other contemporary tales of vampirism and would not be reexplored until Anne Rice's Interview with the Vampire (1976) ["James Malcolm Rymer"].

Roberts concludes that, at the end, the Varney we see "is worn out and conscience-stricken, hardly the rebellious and indestructible symbol of evil" (4).

Although Rymer's narrative is inconsistent concerning Varney's origins, one account offered by Varney is that his vampirism is divine punishment for having murdered his son, resulting "in his rebirth as a vampire; a wretched, unending existence as a parasite and a pariah" ("Varney the Vampire"). He considers his appetite "horrible" and his repast "terrible and disgusting" (Rymer 627), and wonders when his "weary pilgrimage" will end (681). Varney's existential crisis, initial suicide attempt, and final completion of the act that culminates the series thus undercut the allure of eternal life by characterizing the cost as unendurable. In doing so, *Varney* establishes a recurring trope—the benefits of being a vampire aren't worth the ethical price that must be paid. Envy not the vampire, mortal readers (or viewers), for immortality is not worth the cost to one's conscience.

While Varney's suicide is an early example of the remorseful vampire taking his own life, the trope finds its fullest expression in late twentieth- and twenty-first-century vampire narratives. In some cases, vampire suicide as a refusal to accept the moral transgression of vampirism is relegated to minor characters who make clear that the option exists for the protagonist. This is the case, for example, in the Swedish film *Let the Right One In* (Tomas Alfredson, 2008) in which the character Virginia (Ika Nord) survives the attack by the vampire Eli (Lina Leanderssun) after the predation is interrupted by another character (Lacke, played by Peter Carlberg) and is taken to the hospital. Aware of what she is becoming, Virginia asks an orderly to open the blinds to her room and—vampires having become remarkably flammable in the intervening century and a half—she bursts into flames. This is similarly the case in Michael and Peter Spierig's science fiction horror film *Daybreakers* (2009) in which the character Alison (Isabel Lucas) is forcibly turned into a vampire, but refuses to drink blood (apart from her own) and degenerates into a monstrous creature called a "subsider" who is then put to death by being exposed to the sun. Alison's refusal to drink others' blood is a conscious one that she knows will lead to hear death.

The moral cost of being a vampire and the place of vampires within some kind of divine plan are questions frequently contemplated by Anne Rice's reflective vampires who often meditate and sometimes commit suicide. While, as I discuss below, this is most frequently because their extended lifetime takes its tool and they can no longer adjust to a changing world, it is also occasionally due to guilt and regret. This is the case for Rice's melancholic Louis de Pointe du Lac, a central character within the Vampire Chronicles. Although deeply conflicted about his vampiric existence—indeed, the first book in the series, *Interview with the Vampire* (1976) is essentially about Louis trying to come to terms with his new identity—Louis's suicide attempt doesn't come until *Merrick* (2000), the seventh book in the series. Here, unable to resist the seductions of the eponymous Merrick, a powerful and attractive witch, he repeats the mistake he believes he made with Claudia—a young girl vampirized by Lestat and "turned" by Louis in *Interview*—and transforms Merrick into a vampire. Having been manipulated by Merrick into betraying his principles, such as they are, Louis's intense guilt prompts him to expose himself to the sun at dawn, leaving him a charred and desiccated husk. Only the ministrations of David Talbot, a powerful vampire whose existence is linked to Lestat, prevent Louis from being successful in ending his existence.

While Louis's suicide attempt derives from his guilt over his implication in the creation and destruction of Claudia and then the transformation

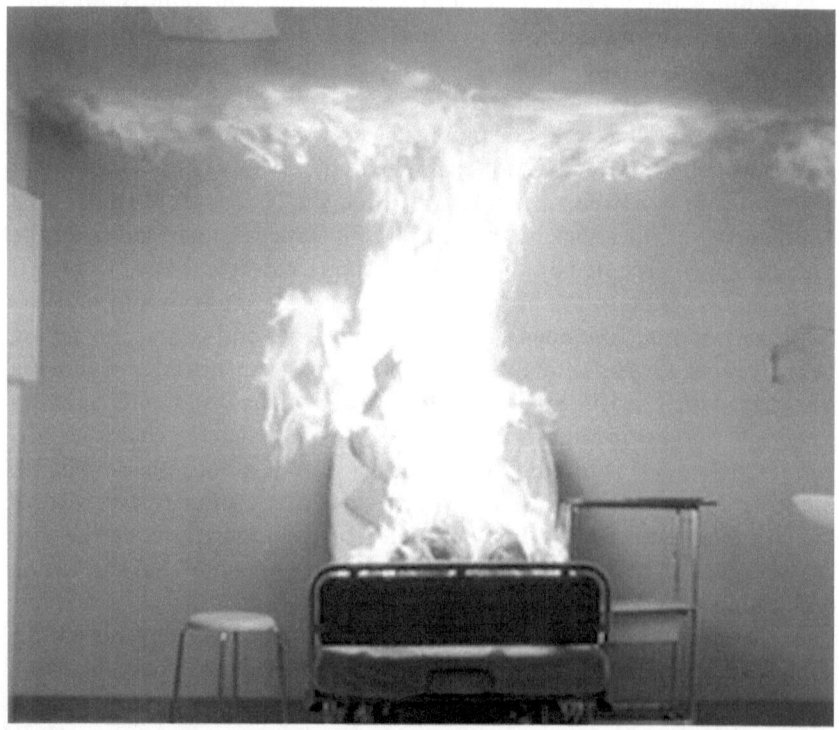

The combustible vampire 1: Virginia from **Let the Right One In.**

The combustible vampire 2: Alison from **Daybreakers.**

of Merrick, Rice's vampire Armand attempts suicide after a religious epiphany, making him in some ways similar to Varney. In *Memnoch the Devil* (1995), the fifth installment in Rice's Vampire Chronicles series, Armand is filled with religious fervor after hearing of Lestat's own religious revelation. Believing that Lestat has retrieved the mythical Veil of Veronica imprinted with the face of Christ, which seems to confirm the truths of the Christian Bible, Armand—now believing himself evil—makes an impassioned decision: "'I will bear witness. I will stand here with my arms outstretched' ... 'and when the sun rises, my death shall confirm the miracle,'" he cries to his auditors (297). "Bear witness, this sinner dies for Him!" (297). As with Louis in *Merrick*, Armand's attempt is unsuccessful (and, indeed, there is a good deal of doubt surrounding Lestat's visions). Nevertheless, the suicide attempt comes as a consequence of accepting a vision of the universe at least temporarily, that places humanity at the center of a cosmic contest between good and evil with vampires aligned with the latter.

Perhaps the most striking iteration of the trope of the remorseful vampire committing suicide is Park Chan-wook's 2009 film, *Thirst*. As with Rice's melancholic Louis, the protagonist of Chan-wook's *Thirst*, Sang-hyun (Song Kang-ho), does not seek to become a vampire, nor is his vampirism a consequence of divine retribution. Instead, Sang-hyun (whose name either by design or chance resonates with the English word "sanguine," a blood-red color) is a Catholic priest who ironically becomes a vampire not as a result of evil action or reckless deed, but rather as a consequence of his selflessness—he has participated as a human guinea pig in a failed medical experiment seeking to develop a vaccine against a fatal disease. Although infected with a deadly virus, Sang-hyun appears to make a miraculous recovery. He has not, however, been cured entirely and returned to "normal" health; instead, he has become a vampire and the virus in his system is only kept in check through the consumption of human blood—a condition that precipitates a moral crisis for Sang-hyun. Although endowed with super strength, dexterity, and almost complete invulnerability, he nevertheless initially attempts to kill himself after finding himself unable to resist drinking blood from a comatose hospital patient.

Sang-hyun's transgressions, however, do not end with blood drinking as he finds himself attracted to Tae-ju (Kim Ok-bin), the wife of his childhood friend Kang-woo (Shin Ha-kyn). Feeling liberated from social constraints and doubting the religious faith to which he had previously subscribed, Sang-hyan begins an adulterous affair with Tae-ju that culminates in the murder of her husband Kang-woo and the transformation of Tae-ju into a vampire. Tae-ju, to borrow from Rice's Vampire Chronicles, becomes the Claudia to Sang-hyun's Louis. Whereas Sang-hyun, conflicted about his vampirism and still retaining remnants of his human ethical code, has attempted to keep his vampirism in check and to avoid killing, Tae-ju transforms into a remorseless monster who revels in her supernatural abilities. Tae-ju not only takes pleasure in the kill, but sadistically enjoys scaring her victims. In what is the film's goriest and most disturbing scene, Tae-ju viciously turns on three prior friends who have discovered her and Sang-Hyun's involvement in her husband's disappearance, stalking them through her apartment-turned-bunker. One friend survives only as a consequence of Sang-hyan's merciful deceit of Tae-ju, leading her to believe that he has killed the friend.

It is the massacre in the apartment that appears to convince Sang-hyun that vampiric existence is unethical to the point of being unbearable. Persuading Tae-ju that they must flee, the two (together with Tae-ju's almost entirely paralyzed mother) drive through the night, arriving much to Tae-ju's dismay at the edge of a cliff looking out over the ocean as dawn approaches. Sang-hyun has taken them to the end of the road—both literally and figuratively. With no apparent cover, Tae-ju attempts to hide from the sun in the car's boot and then beneath the vehicle, but each time is dragged out by Sang-hyun. Resigned to her fate, she then sits with Sang-hyun on the roof of the car, looking at over the sea. As the sun rises, their skin bubbles, smokes, and burns and then, as they embrace in agony, they are reduced to blackened cinders—for them, sunrise is sunset.

In each of these works, the suicide of the remorseful vampire is the solution to an existence construed as evil—and what is striking is that vampiric "life" remains evil even in the absence of a conventional religious framework with God at the center. The characters in the nineteenth-century *Varney* believe in the goodness of God, and Varney acts more or less within the context of traditional Christian framework—his vampirism is a consequence of mortal sin and divine punishment. Having acted monstrously in life, he is punished by God and transformed into a monster (which then curiously preys on the innocent). Accursed, he performs the role of evil predator apparently assigned to him—even relishes it—until he can bear it no longer and, pricked by compunction, immolates himself in Mt. Vesuvius. The logic, of course, defies close scrutiny—why would God punish someone by denying him death and presumably eternal damnation? Why would God transform a sinner into an almost indestructible monster who preys on the innocent? And why then would God allow that same monster to end his existence through suicide under particular conditions? Despite these vexing theological questions however, the narrative framework constructs a familiar moral universe with God as arbiter

The sole remains at the end of Thirst.

of right and wrong, good and evil. The vampire is an abomination, a crime against nature, and the vampire's growing acceptance of this ultimately precipitates his self-destruction. God seems to demand—or at least sanction—the vampire's suicide.

Rice's Louis, in contrast, spends a lot of time fretting about God's apparent absence; indeed, a central scene in *Interview with the Vampire* has Louis attacking a priest at the altar. Holding the priest fast and compelling him to look at his vampiric face, Louis states rather than asks, "Why, if God exists, does He suffer me to exist!" "He was cursing me, calling on God at the altar," recalls Louis. "And then I grabbed him on the very steps to the Communion rail and pulled him down to face me there and sank my teeth into his neck" (114). Louis, transformed into a vampire by Lestat without his consent and searching for meaning, finds none in the church and is not punished for his heretical act. Although later installments of the Vampire Chronicles series call into question pronouncements concerning God's demise, the series, particularly in the first three books, nevertheless has vampires suffering existential crises and developing moral codes of conduct precisely in the absence of the specter of divine reward and punishment. Louis's qualms about vampiric existence derive from a respect for human life. For a time, he will only feed on animals (so a vampire "vegetarian" in the language of Stephenie Meyer's *Twilight* franchise) and later restricts his feeding to human evildoers. Nevertheless, he frequently meditates and at one point attempts to end an existence he perceives as cursed.

The situation for Sang-hyun in *Thirst* is the most ironic of all because he begins the narrative as a Catholic priest who selflessly volunteers himself for a dangerous medical drug trial. What kind of a God, one could reasonably ask, would punish someone so devout and altruistic with vampirism? As in Rice's Vampire Chronicles, there is no sense in *Thirst* that vampirism is a divine punishment or that religious iconography holds any intrinsic power over the vampire. God is absent from the tale and there is nothing to inhibit Sang-hyun or Tae-ju except their own residual moral scruples. In the end, Sang-hyun's suicide/murder—locked in an agonized embrace with Tae-ju looking out across a sublime vista as the sun rises—constitutes a refusal to embrace a kind of feral post-human ethics that license bloodshed. Since God will not punish them, they must punish themselves—and their punishment confirms that human ethics remain the yardstick against which their actions must be measured. They are monstrous because they prey upon humans and suicide does not so much redeem them as relieve them (or at least delivers Sang-hyun) of the burden of vampirism, which acts as a blot on the human conscience in his vampire body. Put differently, when one transforms from human to vampire, the human superego goes along for the ride.

Thirst and the importance of sunscreen.

Vampiric Ennui

Varney and Sang-hyun successfully commit suicide—and Louis attempts it—because of the weight of the guilt they bear. They increasingly feel the burden of having transgressed against God, turned against friends and loved ones, and/or committed bloody and despicable acts, and reach a point where they can no longer "live" with their bloody undead selves. While there are some vampires who assert that vampires are a superior species and should prey on humans without compunction—that humans are to vampires as animals are to humans—vampire narratives in large measure reject such thinking as evil, casting those vampires as antagonists, and focusing instead on vampire protagonists who acknowledge the sanctity of human life. Perhaps if cows and chickens wrote novels, they might invent similarly conflicted human protagonists. The point of course is that such works function ideologically to reconfirm the human as the center of the universe—they are "pro-life." And they need to be because in many contemporary vampire narratives, vampires *are* the superior species: virtually immortal, able to fly or read minds, beautiful, strong, super intelligent, and so forth. Particularly in the absence of any God as arbiter of absolute morality, what would prevent mere mortals from envying and aspiring toward vampirism if not for quibbles about taking life? As vampires increasingly approximate superheroes, we can note a corresponding increase in suicidal vampires who cannot stomach the precondition for their continued immortal existence: the killing of humans. This is in some cases because God has commanded that Thou Shalt Not Kill and the vampires become religious converts; in other's cases, it is because, even in the absence of God (or, from an existentialist perspective, perhaps precisely because of it), they still acknowledge the sanctity of human life. Conventional morality reasserts itself in the end, even as the lascivious middle licenses libidinal transgressions of all sorts. When the vampire commits suicide, it reminds us that the vampire is a monster and nice people don't wish to be monsters.

Although the vampire as murdering monster offers a compelling rationale for not aspiring to become one, modern vampire narratives introduce an additional drawback: ennui. Immortality, it turns out, may become burdensome because vampires-née-humans are creatures of the world—and the world keeps on turning. Indeed, the passage of time confronts vampires with two challenges: to remain connected to an ever-changing world and to stay "lively." When literary and cinematic vampires as a consequence of longevity can no longer recognize the world through which they stalk, or when they can no longer find sources of excitement or interest, they begin to contemplate ending their existence.

This challenge faced by immortal creatures attempting to live a temporal existence is one developed extensively by Rice in her Vampire Chronicles. While Rice introduces a number of ancient vampires in her series, most vampires do not achieve great age, often because they can't adjust to the changing conditions of a world they find increasingly bewildering. The *Vampire Chronicles* wiki explains that "during their immortality, vampires will sometimes go into a kind of hibernation, either because they have become mentally unbalanced from knowing what they have become or because their surroundings have changed too much for them to cope with. ... Many vampires commit suicide if they continually exist in the world, leading to Marius [an ancient vampire] telling Lestat that he should live out one lifetime pretending to be human and watching the world change" ("Vampire"). Lestat's maker, Magnus, in *The Vampire Lestat* (1985), fails to heed this lesson and is presented as having been driven mad over the centuries by his vampiric nature and immortality. Having turned Lestat and imparted the rudiments of vampiric existence, he prepares to immolate himself. "It's only mercy I ask," he says to Lestat, "that I go now to find hell, if there is a hell, or sweet oblivion which surely I do not deserve. If there is a Prince of Darkness, then I shall set eyes upon him at last. I shall spit in his face" (69). He then leaps into the fire.

Perhaps the most beatific representation of a vampire committing suicide as a consequence of the burden of extreme longevity appears in the HBO series *True Blood*. Introduced in the second season, the character Godric, played by Allan Hyde, is an ancient and powerful vampire who sired central *True Blood* characters Eric Northman (Alexander Skarsgård) and Nora Gainesborough (Lucy Griffiths). As revealed in the series and summarized on the *True Blood* wiki, Godric is over 2,000 years old. For his first millennium, he was a "violent, bloodthirsty savage with no regard for human life" and he passed along to his progeny his nihilistic view that "there was no right or wrong, only survival, or death" ("Godric"). Then, finding that "senseless killing had only left him feeling detached and empty" ("Godric"), he had a change of heart, becoming gracious and compassionate toward humans.

At the end of season 2, episode 9—in what may well be the series' most poignant moment—Godric chooses to "meet the sun." "Two thousand years is enough," he tells his offspring Eric, who is pleading for Godric to change his mind. "Our existence is insanity. We don't belong here," he explains ("I Will Rise Up"). Commanding Eric to depart (a convention of *True Blood* is that vampires are subject to the commands of their makers), Godric turns to face the sun, accompanied by series protagonist Sookie Stackhouse. "A human with me at the end, and human tears," he observes. "Two thousand years, and I can still be surprised. In this, I see God," Godric concludes ("I Will Rise Up"). Then the sun rises and Godric burns. Christlike, Godric hopes that his suicide will in some way inspire compassion in the radical members of both the human and vampire communities, each of which views the other with contempt.

Godric's suicide is presented as the culmination of a two-millennia-long process of self-scrutiny leading to enlightenment, which conveys two conclusions: Compassion is preferable to nihilism, and immortality is more

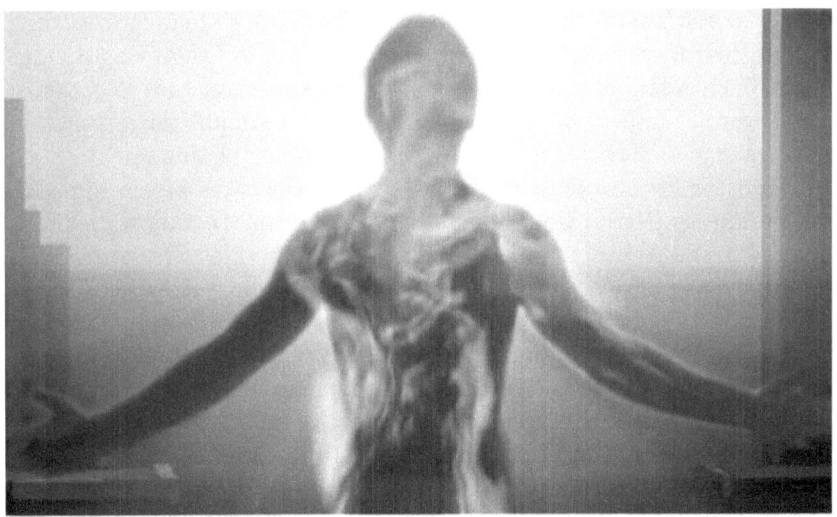

Godric meets the sun.

appealing in theory than in fact. Godric initially shared with Rice's Lestat a conception of the world as what Lestat calls throughout the series a "savage garden," a place of beauty and danger without deeper meaning or divine guidance. Having been victimized himself and feeling unhindered by internal inhibition or external constraint, Godric allowed hatred and resentment to drive him, hunting humans for sport and "passing on his disdain for the living to his progenies," Eric and Nora ("Godric"). Godric, however, ultimately rejected this nihilistic philosophy in favor of one founded on compassion, acknowledging his implication in the human hatred of vampires. The suggestion here is a kind of evolution of conscience that causes the reflective vampire to acknowledge the sanctity of human life and to reject his own existence—when your own existence is "insanity," suicide becomes the logical resolution. Unlike Varney or Rice's Armand however, Godric seems less guilt-ridden than simply tired. Despite his immense power, he concludes that his existence has run its course. To shuffle off his immortal coil and meet the sun is for him an act of purification that he hopes will inspire others to overcome prejudice and antagonism.

Less Christ-like than Godric and even more melancholic than Rice's Louis (if that's possible) is Adam (Tom Hiddleston) in Jim Jarmusch's 2013 art-house vampire film, *Only Lovers Left Alive*. Married for centuries to Eve (Tilda Swinton), but living on his own in his crumbling mansion in a desolate, depopulated Detroit, Michigan, Adam spends his time recording moody goth songs he calls "funeral music" on outdated studio equipment, collecting vintage musical instruments, and lamenting the state of a world presided over by thoughtless human beings (which he refers to as "zombies"). "I'm sick of it—these zombies, what they've done to the world, their fear of their own imaginations," bemoans Adam to Eve during a video chat. When Adam dispatches his lackey Ian (Anton Yelchin) to commission a wooden bullet, the familiar conventions of vampire narrative allow the viewer to understand that he is a vampire contemplating suicide.

Sensing his despondency long distance, Eve travels from Morocco to join him in Detroit where the bulk of the minimal action takes place. Soon after she arrives, while Adam is out procuring blood (Adam's favorite, O-negative, which they get from an obliging doctor), Eve discovers the newly made wooden bullet and a small revolver. Confronting Adam on his return, Eve—who we understand is even older than Adam—berates him for his selfish introspection and despondency when the wonders of the world surround them and they have each other: "How can you have lived for so long and still not get it? This self-obsession, it's a waste of living that could be spent on surviving things, appreciating nature, nurturing kindness and friendship. And dancing." "You've been pretty lucky in love, though, if I may say so," she adds wryly.

A morose Adam holds a pistol to his heart in Only Lovers Left Alive.

Hell for Adam is not immortality but, to borrow from Sartre, other zombies. Adam despairs over what human beings are doing to their world, and the ways in which they have polluted their own blood. Adrift in an impoverished city that reflects and amplifies his sense of despondency, Adam feels cursed to be a bystander as human beings wreck the world and kill themselves in a kind of slow-motion (although rapidly accelerating) suicide of their own. Eve, in contrast, takes the long view, prognosticating that Detroit will rise again because it is situated by water, which will become a valuable commodity "when the cities in the South are burning"—presumably a reference to climate change. But she also reminds Adam of the beauties and pleasures that the world holds for them. They are presented as lovers of art, culture, and the natural world who have had centuries to hone and indulge their tastes. Eve loves literature and her closest friend is Christopher Marlowe, revealed by the film to be both a vampire and the author of Shakespeare's works. Both are lovers of music who appreciate all forms from classical to R&B to alt rocker Jack White. And while Eve possesses encyclopedic knowledge of plant and animal life, marveling at mushrooms and urban coyotes (and using their Latin names), Adam seems possess an intuitive knowledge of physics, having perfected a kind of dynamo that generates power from the atmosphere and explaining to Eve sub-atomic "spooky action at a distance" (a notion concerning "entwined particles" that reflects the pair's relationship).

Unlike Godric, Adam thus does not end up committing suicide. Instead, Eve's arrival lifts his spirits (as much as possible for the constitutionally morose Adam) as the two lovers comfort each other, dance to vintage R&B, enjoy frozen blood popsicles, and tour Detroit at night in Adam's classic 1982 Jaguar XJ-S. As with human beings, for vampires to overcome ennui and enjoy existence requires companionship and a conscious effort at engagement with the world and its beauties. The irony of *Only Lovers Left Alive* is that the vampiric undead are the liveliest among us—from drug dealers in Tangiers to abandoned factories in Detroit, the slow suicide of the human race is a consequence of rapacious appetite and blunted sensitivity. In *Only Lovers*, the zombie human race is every bit as monstrous, bloodthirsty, destructive, and suicidal as the vampires we create.

Vampire Martyrdom

The inversion of conventional roles in contemporary monster narratives that cast monsters as sympathetic protagonists, and human society writ large—intolerant of difference, exploitative of the natural world—as the antagonist plays into one final category of vampire suicide: vampire martyrdom. These are narratives in which vampires perform heroic acts of selflessness in order to protect those they love or the world in general. In some cases, the vampires are action heroes who put their lives on the line, so to speak, to protect an unsuspecting public from insidious danger; in other cases, the vampires are monsters who surprisingly discover residual goodness lurking in their black souls.

There are a number of vampire superheroes who are prepared to martyr themselves in the service of protecting either humans or those they love from predatory monsters. The two most obvious as a consequence of the big-budget film franchises in which they star are probably Blade

Vampire Suicide

from the Blade series and Selene from the Underworld films. Neither, I should point out, consciously attempts suicide; however, both repeatedly jeopardize their leather-clad existence by confronting powerful forces that threaten the world. In the Blade films, the half-vampire, half-human (or *dhampir*) Blade (Wesley Snipes) is a vampire hunter who attempts to keep the vampire threat to the human race in check. In the Underworld franchise, Selene (Kate Beckinsale) is a "Death Dealer" who hunts werewolves (Lycans). Neither feeds on innocent humans; both repeatedly are ready to martyr themselves for their noble causes.

More immediately connected to heroic vampire suicide are Eben in the American horror film *30 Days of Night* and Darla on the *Buffy the Vampire Slayer* spin-off *Angel*. The plot to David Slade's 2007 American horror movie *30 Days of Night*, based on the comic book miniseries of the same name, has an elegant simplicity to it: What better place for vampires than Barrow, Alaska—located above the Polar circle—where the sun doesn't rise for thirty days straight? When vampires converge on Barrow for the month-long polar night feeding frenzy, the residents of the isolated town are forced into survival mode. Sheriff Eben Oleson (Josh Hartnett) and his estranged wife, Stella (Melissa George) almost last the month, but when the vampires begin burning down the town to destroy the evidence of the carnage that has transpired, Eben concludes that they can't win without his making the ultimate sacrifice. Determining that in order to protect Stella he must fight fire with fire, Eben injects himself with tainted vampire blood and changes into a vampire. This gives him the strength and dexterity to confront the vampiric threat, and after Eben kills the lead

Eben bakes and flakes at the end of 30 Days of Night.

vampire, Marlow (Danny Huston), the others disperse. Eben and Stella then watch the sun rise and share one last kiss before Eben's body turns to ashes in Stella's arms. His has been a double suicide—first undead, then dead-dead.

The recurring character Darla (Julie Benz) on Joss Whedon's *Angel* meets her end not by sacrificing her life for her lover, but rather for her unborn child. Unlike Eben, whose purpose in *30 Days of Night* is that of a protector from the start, Darla's role on *Angel* is essentially to be an antagonist to the eponymous Angel (David Boreanaz), a vampire with a soul who in the spinoff series is dedicated to helping the helpless. After a sexual rendezvous with Angel (a strategic attempt to deprive Angel of his soul), Darla finds herself in the curious situation of being pregnant—vampires normally cannot conceive children through sexual intercourse and cannot give birth naturally to live offspring. Her pregnancy precipitates a reconsideration of her purpose as she begins to experience a new range of emotions, including love for the developing fetus, and, at the end of episode 9 of season 3 ("Lullaby"), she stakes herself, sacrificing herself for her baby who remains as she turns to dust—a "final act of redemption to ensure the life of their son, Connor" ("Darla"). Akin to Bella Swan in Stephenie Meyer's fourth *Twilight* installment, *Breaking Dawn* (2008), who risks her vampiric life to bring a child into the world, Darla—with all the politically charged implications—concludes that the life of her child is more important than her own.

Conclusion: Immortality Hangs Heavy Over the Heads of the Undead

Narratives of vampire suicide clearly depict how monsters function to limn the human and naturalize a specific set of ideological values. When vampires attempt or commit suicide as a consequence of remorse, they comprehend themselves and convey to readers and viewers their own immorality. This may be as a consequence of accepting God's divine decree, or coming to appreciate the intrinsic value of human existence. These are ironically "pro-life" narratives in which the suicide of the undead ensures the safety of the living and reaffirms a conventional good/evil dichotomy with human life at its center: that which benefits humans is good; that which harms them is bad. No matter how superior or powerful vampires may be, human life is represented as sacrosanct.

Narratives of vampire suicide as a consequence of ennui amplify the message that immortality is a curse rather than a gift. Far from being something to covet or aspire toward, immortality instead drains meaning from existence. Life is for the living, such narratives seem to say—and human beings have an obligation to cultivate an attitude receptive to the wonders of the world and to facilitate harmonious coexistence. Otherwise, we are committing a kind of suicide ourselves and are as good as dead already.

Narratives of vampire martyrs and vampire heroes prepared to sacrifice themselves for the good of others make the ideological "stakes" of the vampire suicide narrative most immediately apparent as they clearly affirm altruism over self-interest. To give one's life for others when one can never die takes the "ultimate sacrifice" one step further. However, while one might perhaps be unlikely to question the nobility of a vampire soldier fighting on behalf of humanity or a vampire lover giving his life so that his wife may survive, what of the message that vampire women should be prepared to die so that their pregnancies can be carried to term? The unstated values informing such decisions make clear what is implicit in all narratives of vampire suicide—that the decision of the immortal creature to end its existence helps naturalize a set of values that foreground specifically human concerns.

WORKS CITED

Cohen, Jeffrey Jerome. "Monster Culture (Seven Theses)" in *Monster Theory: Reading Culture*, edited by Jeffrey Jerome Cohen. University of Minnesota Press, 1996, pp. 3–25.

"Darla." *Buffy the Vampire Slayer: 20 Years of Slaying* Wiki. N.d., http://buffy.wikia.com/wiki/Darla.

"Godric." *True Blood Wiki*. N.d., http://trueblood.wikia.com/wiki/Godric.

"James Malcolm Rymer's Varney the Vampire." *Skull in the Stars*. 24 Sept. 2008. https://skullsinthestars.com/2008/09/24/james-malcolm-rymers-varney-the-vampire/

Rice, Anne. *Interview With the Vampire*. New York, Knopf, 1976.

———. *Memnoch the Devil*. New York: Knopf, 1995

———. *Merrick*. New York: Knopf, 2000.

———. *The Vampire Lestat*. New York: Knopf, 1985.

Roberts, Bette B. "*Varney, the Vampire*, or, Rather, Varney, the Victim." *Gothic*, vol. 2, 1987, pp. 1–5.

Rymer, James Malcolm. *Varney the Vampire. Or, The Feast of Blood*. Crestline, CA: Zittaw Press, 2008.

"Vampire." *The Vampire Chronicles Wiki*. N.d. http://vampirechronicles.wikia.com/wiki/Vampire.

"Varney the Vampire; or, The Feast of Blood." *Victorian Gothic*. 1 March 2012. http://www.victoriangothic.org/varney-the-vampire-or-the-feast-of-blood/.

Act III

Monsters

There's an argument to be made that Act III of this anthology film, the cluster of essays on monsters, should come first. After all, ghosts and vampires are subsets of monsters (and I *do* consider ghosts to be monsters). There's also an argument to be made that the more specific readings in the earlier clusters set the stage for this cluster, which offers some larger pronouncements about monsters—and this is the argument I'm going to run with, particularly because the final two essays in this cluster target our modern moment more fully than the others in this collection.

As with the other clusters, the monsters one consists of four essays and begins with a general overview of the subject in relation to American literature and culture. "American Monsters," which appeared in Charles L. Crow's excellent *A Companion to the American Gothic* collection, groups monsters in American literature into different categories reflecting different kinds of anxieties. The piece that follows it, "Introduction: A Genealogy of Monster Theory," then takes a step back from considerations of particular monsters and instead focuses on different ways that monsters and monstrosity have been theorized and understood from antiquity forward. (One could reasonably argue this piece should open the cluster, but it would interrupt the nice "American Ghosts," "American Vampires," "American Monsters" symmetry of the book!) I conceive of the two essays that follow, "Invisible Monsters: Vision, Horror, and Contemporary Culture" from *The Ashgate Research Companion to Monsters and the Monstrous* and "What Is IT? Ambient Dread and Modern Paranoia in *It* (2017), *It Follows* (2014), and *It Comes at Night* (2017)" from the scholarly journal *Horror Studies*, as working in tandem. Both of them consider how twenty-first-century monsters reflect a contemporary mindset in which monsters are marked by invisibility. Where once upon a time we knew a monster when we saw one, today appearance has been decoupled from monstrosity. Instead of reading books by their covers, in the era of terrorists and global pandemics, "stranger danger" and surveillance our concern is instead that anyone could be a monster and danger could be anywhere. I outline this proposition in "Invisible Monsters" and then it receives fuller elaboration in "What Is IT?" through a focus on three films that that fill us with dread over the possibility that the monster can take on many forms and appear at any time. These final two essays in particular showcase how our monsters change together with cultural shifts.

American Monsters

American author Stephen Crane's 1898 novella, *The Monster*, offers a clear demonstration of the making of a monster. Within the story, African American coachman Henry Johnson is horribly disfigured after he rushes into a house fire to save his employer's son. Johnson is not simply burned; during the rescue attempt, caustic chemicals from Dr. Trescott's laboratory eat away his face. Assuming that he cannot live, the town mourns Henry as a hero. Despite being urged to let Henry die, Dr. Trescott—out of a sense of obligation to the man who saved his son as well as to his occupation—applies his art and preserves Henry's life, but Henry emerges deeply scarred, both physically and psychically. The subsequent trouble he causes, however, is not of his own making. The members of the town who were willing to hail dead Henry Johnson as a hero are unable to accept living and disfigured Henry Johnson as human. At the end of the story, even Jimmie—the boy he saved from the fire—mocks him and dares his friends to approach the sad man now regarded as a monster. What *The Monster* demonstrates is that monsters are not born but made. Although like Frankenstein's monster Henry's form is created in a laboratory, he is not a monster until the town—based on his divergence from established physical and behavioral norms—labels him as one.

The English word "monster" derives from the Latin *monstrum*, which itself is related to the verbs *monstrare* (to show or reveal) and *monere* (to warn or portend). The monster is thus a kind of omen that gives shape to moral vice, reveals the will of the gods, and forecasts the future. As is indicated by *The Monster*, however, monsters "reveal" in another sense because, as Douglas E. Cowan points out in his discussion of what he calls "sociophobics," "what we fear, how we fear, and the ways in which we react to fear are profoundly shaped by the cultures in which we live" (Cowan 171). Monsters thus embody culturally specific anxieties and tabooed desires. In Jeffrey Jerome Cohen's formulation, "[t]he monstrous body is pure culture" (4)—the product of a particular time, place, and feeling. What this means is that human beings invariably give life to monsters;

they are a kind of "cultural category" (Asma 13) we use to describe that which threatens, that which tempts, and that which confounds our framework for making sense. Our monsters therefore tell us a great deal about ourselves—they tell us who we imagine we are, what we hope we're not, and what we are afraid we might ourselves become.

The messiness of monsters, however, is that they are also inevitably "overdetermined"—that is, like any element in a dream or nightmare, they have multiple origins. Monsters resist any simplistic one-to-one analogy. While it would be convenient to be able to interpret the zombies of the comic book-based AMC series *The Walking Dead* that premiered in 2010, for example, as symbolizing cultural anxieties about dying and death in a secular age, they nevertheless also express simultaneously other fears and desires—among them, concerns about viral contagion, media saturation, mob mentality, and human hubris, and desires to overcome death, to see human arrogance upbraided, and perhaps even the deeply transgressive craving to taste human flesh. This density of the monster is reflected in Jack Halberstam's (writing as Judith) characterization of them as "meaning machines" (21) that can represent gender, race, nationality, class, sexuality, politics, and so forth all at once in one hypersaturated body that disrupts categories and violates boundaries (27).

Bearing in mind the messiness of monsters, this chapter will hazard nonetheless a concise and unavoidably reductive survey of the monsters that have shambled through the pages of the U.S. historical narrative since the colonial period. Rather than moving chronologically, the discussion will instead be organized thematically and will address four insistently recurring—and inevitably overlapping—subcategories of monstrosity that define the American experience: the monster as cultural other, the numinous monster, the monster as human invention, and the natural monster. The intention here is to provide an overview of the many forms that the monster has taken in the American Gothic and the uses to which the concept of monster has been put.

Monsters Are Other People: The American Monster as Cultural Other

A convenient first step in running roughshod over someone is always to label that person or group as a monster. As Cohen observes, any kind of somatic or social difference can be exaggerated into monstrous aberration (7) and the discourse of monstrosity functions politically to facilitate or retard particular cultural agendas. In early American history, the monsterizing of indigenous peoples helped bolster Puritan exceptionalism and the "powerful political machine of Manifest Destiny" (Cohen 8). The presumed monstrosity of Africans and persons of African descent helped justify the institution of slavery. In the nineteenth and twentieth centuries, freak shows thrilled audiences with spectacles of monstrous somatic difference that reified the unmarked white able body as ideal—a belief that helped legitimate the persecution of those deviating from the norm. In the twenty-first century, the practice of "racial profiling" continues to assert a connection between appearance and monstrosity, even as cultural anxieties about two other monsters—the serial killer and the terrorist—call this link into question.

Cowan observes that, when Christopher Columbus arrived in the "New World," he brought with him a rich European heritage of legend and speculation about monsters (28) and, in the indigenous inhabitants of North America, Europeans found the monsters they conjectured. The earliest writings of American colonizers, including John Smith, John Winthrop, and William Bradford, imagine the struggle for survival in the wilds of the New World as a contest with nature and with the "savage and brutish men" (Bradford 25), the Indians, who inhabit the forest. Cotton Mather famously figures the American wildness as the "devil's territories" (308) in *The Wonders of the Invisible World* (1693), reinforcing the characterization of Native Americans as diabolic agents repeatedly made in Native American captivity narratives such as Mary Rowlandson's popular *A Narrative of the Captivity and Restoration of Mrs. Mary Rowlandson* (1682) published eleven years before.

Although the representation of the American Indian bifurcates in the work of later American authors into the twin images of the debased heathen and the "noble savage," these formulations remain mutually constitutive, one reinforcing the other, and both participate in the exoticization of cultural difference. Thus, in *Edgar Huntly* (1799), the fourth novel from America's earliest Gothic novelist, Charles Brockden Brown, Indians are presented as "projection[s] of natural evil and the id; his red men are therefore treated essentially as animals, living extensions of the threat of the wilderness" (Christophersen 156). James Fenimore Cooper plays both images off of each other, contrasting his noble Chingachgook and Uncas in *Last of the Mohicans* (1826), for example, to the savage Magua and the Hurons who attack Fort William Henry and who become so excited by the carnage and flow of blood that "many among them even kneeled to the earth, and drank freely, exultingly, hellishly, of the crimson tide" (208). Robert Montgomery Bird accentuates solely the negative in his 1837 *Nick of the Woods*, which depicts early Kentucky settlers in conflict with "ignorant, violent, debased, brutal" Indians (32) and celebrates the aptly named Philadelphia Quaker turned "Injun" killer, Nathan Slaughter.

It was of course much easier to express outrage at the inhuman cruelty of indigenous people than to defend a policy of separating them from their land. Similarly, asserting the monstrosity of those of African descent helped to legitimate slavery and, as the nineteenth century cascaded toward the Civil War, the rhetoric of monstrosity was repeatedly employed by proslavery apologists to make their case (Poole 46). Pseudo-scientific anthropological theories asserted the inferiority of Africans, often paralleling them with apes or "Oran-ootans," and insisting that "[t]he African was a monster in the most basic sense, outside the limits of the rest of humanity" (Poole 48). As was the case with representations of Native Americans, Africans and their American descendants were imaged either as bestial and dangerous or as childlike and simple—images that combined especially following the 1831 Nat Turner Revolt in Virginia to suggest to Americans (especially Southern slaveholders) that blood-thirsty animals lurked just beneath the surfaces of cheerful household domestics and field workers.

Edgar Allan Poe sought to capitalize on American anxieties toward the potential monstrosity of persons of African descent in his one novel, *The Narrative of Arthur Gordon Pym of Nantucket* (1838), in which a previously undiscovered tribe of primitive, black-skinned people near the South Pole turns out to be especially devious and malicious. The anxiety that beneath kindly dark complexions lurk savage beasts is similarly conveyed by Herman Melville in his 1855 *Benito Cereno*, in which the paternalistic attitude and racist beliefs of Captain Delano blind him almost to the end to the duplicity and malevolence of the monstrous Babo, the orchestrator of a slave revolt and subsequent masquerade to conceal it.

The American cultural practice of equating monstrosity with deviation from a white, able-bodied physical ideal was demonstrated clearly by the late nineteenth- and early twentieth-century freak show. In 1842, P.T. Barnum presented "The Fijee Mermaid"—a taxidermied monkey/fish hybrid—to the world and, in the process, popularized displays of human abnormalities. By the late nineteenth century, circuses and carnivals regularly included freak shows freely mingling conjoined twins, unusually large or small humans, and individuals with rare genetic mutations or diseases with races considered exotic. African Americans were presented as savage tribal Africans, Hispanics pretended to be Polynesian cannibals, and so forth. Poole notes that such displays "allowed customers to react in horror to what conservative, middle-class American culture viewed as the outcome of miscegenation and racial blending" (90). *Freaks*, the 1932 Tod Browning film about sideshow entertainers, took the unusual steps of casting actual carnival performers, including conjoined twins Daisy and

Violet Hilton and Prince Randian "the living torso" (a man without arms or legs), and adopting a sympathetic attitude toward its subject by illustrating the moral bankruptcy of those who seek to exploit the performers.

The practice of equating physical difference with monstrosity emerged as an explicit topic of debate following World War II and the revelation of Hitler's horrific extension of eugenics. While the racist American tendency to associate monstrosity with those who deviate from the white, able-bodied norm continues in the twenty-first century—witness contemporary debates over the controversial law enforcement practice known as "racial profiling" that uses an individual's physical characteristics as a primary factor in determining whether to engage in enforcement (to make a traffic stop, to pull someone aside at airport security for additional screening, etc.)—the tendency in much contemporary media has been to dissociate appearance from monstrosity. In revisions to monster narratives—most especially those for children (e.g., the *Shrek* films, *Monsters, Inc.*) and those centered on vampires (Anne Rice's *Vampire Chronicles*, the HBO series *True Blood*, the *Twilight* franchise, etc.)—the traditional monster becomes the protagonist and often it is society itself with its stultifying insistence on conformity that is portrayed as the antagonist.

Concomitant with this decoupling of monstrosity from appearance is the pervasive anxiety that modern monsters are no longer visible to the naked eye. This is particularly true in relation to two ubiquitous contemporary monsters, the serial killer and the terrorist. As Philip L. Simpson develops, the serial killer horror/crime story subgenre dates from the late 1970s or early 1980s (although there are of course earlier representations of psychopaths in literature and film, such as Norman Bates in Hitchcock's 1960 *Psycho*) and is defined by a horrific monster who "appears human" (10). Indeed, the "everydayness" of the serial killer's appearance is precisely the point of the Showtime series *Dexter*, based on the novels by Jeff Lindsay, in which the normal façade of forensic blood-spatter expert Dexter Morgan (played by Michael C. Hall) conceals a monstrous serial killer who channels his murderous desire into preying upon criminals who have escaped the legal system. Terrorist narratives, too—such as the television series *24* that ran from 2001 to 2010—emphasize that terrorists (who are essentially serial killers with more political motivations) are virtually indistinguishable to the naked, untrained eye from the rank and file of humanity. As a consequence of the disconnection of appearance and monstrosity, a contemporary anxiety exists, as expressed in one slogan for the popular 1990s television series *The X-Files*, "Trust No One," that anyone could be a monster.

The Numinous American Monster

"The voice of the monster," writes Timothy K. Beal, "is the audacious voice of theodicy" (3). In Beal's analysis of the monster's relation to religion, he observes that "whether demonized or deified or something in between, monsters bring on a limit experience that is akin in many respects to religious ... drawn toward and repulsed by a *monstrum tremendum*" (195). For Beal, the existence of monsters inevitably raises thorny questions about God, religion, and the existence of evil in the world, and that is certainly the case with "numinous" American monsters—those monsters having a strong religious or spiritual quality. This encompasses God himself, both great and terrible; his demonic adversaries or flunkies (depending on one's point of view); and those "somethings" in between, supernatural creatures such as witches, ghosts, and vampires that partake of the spiritual in fearful and fascinating ways.

As alarming and monstrous as the Indians were to the New England Puritans, far more awesome and dreadful was God himself, who acted in the world in inscrutable ways and whose wrath was terrible indeed. The Puritan impulse was to interpret natural events as signs of the divine will—Puritan poet Anne Bradstreet, for example, rationalizes the burning down of her house in 1666 as God's reminder to her that material objects are of no consequence when compared to salvation ("Upon the Burning of Our House—July 10th 1666," *c*. 1666), and poet Edward Taylor comes to terms with the deaths of his children in "Upon Wedlock, and Death of Children" by consoling himself with the reflection that "Christ would in Glory have a Flowre, Choice, Prime, / And having Choice, chose this my branch forth brought" (lines 27–29, *c*. 1684; Taylor 303). Both these poets attempt to answer that most vexing of questions—why do bad things happen to good people? For Bradstreet, God acts as a divine arsonist to remove a stumbling block on her way to salvation, while Taylor, Job-like, can only resign himself to faith in the ultimate benevolence of God's plan to which he is not privy.

This benevolence, however, is hard to rely on given that God in Puritan theology chastises not only those he loves, but seemingly everyone else, too. God hates sin and, in Jonathan Edwards's stunning and thoroughly Gothicized 1741 sermon, "Sinners in the Hands of an Angry God," seems monstrous indeed as he holds unrepentant sinners in the utmost contempt, dangling them over the fires of perdition "much as one holds a spider, or some loathsome insect over the fire" (680). "Natural men"— those who have not yet been born again—are in extreme peril because, Edward tells us in another arresting image, "The bow of God's wrath is bent, and the arrow made ready on the string, and justice bends the arrow at your heart, and strains the bow, and it is nothing but the mere pleasure of God, and that of an angry God, without any promise or obligation at all, that keeps the arrow one moment from being made drunk with your blood" (680). This terrifying God who hates sinners and not only drowned the world in the deluge but leveled Sodom and Gomorrah is the same one who in some strands of contemporary evangelical Christian discourse creates plagues such as AIDS and Covid and sends earthquakes and other natural disasters to punish vice.

In keeping with Western religious preoccupations more generally, America has well-established traditions of Faustian pacts with the devil and demonic possessions and harassment. Depending on how one reads Nathaniel Hawthorne's "Young Goodman Brown" (1835), the eponymous protagonist may have been enlightened concerning the mixed moral nature of mankind as a result of a walk in the woods with the devil. Satan—not the actual Satan but his nephew—plays a central role in Mark Twain's *The Mysterious Stranger* (1916), a posthumously published work that conveys Twain's belief in the hypocrisy of organized religion, and Mr. Dark, the leader of a traveling carnival in Ray Bradbury's *Something Wicked This Way Comes* (1962), is certainly devilish, if not the devil himself. Always a bit of a showman, Satan is right at home in cinema and makes guest appearances in numerous films including Roman Polanski's *Rosemary's Baby* (1968), Alan Parker's *Angel Heart* (1987), Taylor Hackford's *The Devil's Advocate* (1997), and Francis Lawrence's *Constantine* (2005).

While the devil never sleeps, sometimes he allows his emissaries to act on his behalf. Witches and demons—at times working in concert—accordingly have vexed Americans since the New England Puritans regarded Indian captivity as capture by diabolic agents and Cotton Mather asserted that Satan had sent demons to tempt and persecute Christians. Given the status of the Salem witch hunts as a foundational American trauma, it is unsurprising that Salem and witches more generally possess a special hold on the American imagination. In Hawthorne's "Young Goodman Brown," Brown may or may not have set out from Salem and joined the devil and various esteemed townspeople at a witches' sabbat in the forest. Written over a century later, Arthur Miller's 1952 play *The Crucible* dramatizes the events at Salem as an allegory of McCarthyism. Witches play a central role in director Tim Burton's reimagining of Washington Irving's "The Legend of Sleepy Hollow" (*Sleepy Hollow*, 1999), and witches are among the variety of supernatural creatures included in Joss Whedon's *Buffy the Vampire Slayer* television program. A softened version of the witch is presented in the romantic comedy *Bell, Book and Candle* (Richard Quine, 1958), as well as on the TV sitcoms *Bewitched*, which ran from 1964 until 1972, and *Sabrina the Teenage Witch*, which ran from 1996 until 2003.

Also partaking of the numinous are supernatural monsters, both disembodied and embodied, that violate binary thinking requiring a clear delineation between the living and the dead. American culture has its own narrative traditions of ghosts, vampires, and other "undead" nasties like werewolves and mummies that get put to work patrolling the boundaries of the possible and permissible. In the writing of Washington Irving, ghosts get conscripted into the service of nation building as Irving seeks to populate the American landscape with specifically U.S. ghosts. In "The Legend of Sleepy Hollow" (1820), the putative spirit haunting this soporific region of New York state is the ghost of a German Hessian—a paid mercenary fighting on behalf of the British who lost his head to a cannonball during "some nameless battle" of the Revolutionary War (273). He is in essence the first U.S. ghost, given that he comes into being coincident with the country establishing its independence. Here, Irving puts the supernatural to work to establish a kind of mythology for a newly established country, populating the landscape with invented spirits of white, European America.

Spirits in the works of those inheriting the mantle of American authorship from Irving tend to be less comical and far less benign. In the Gothic of Edgar Allan Poe, ghosts insistently figure the threat of the irrational and tend to be coded as feminine. Thus, the monstrous wills of both Ligeia and Morella seem to resist the oblivion of death in the eponymous tales (1838 and 1835 respectively), as does Eleonora's more benevolent spirit (1842). In "Berenice" (1835) and "The Fall of the House of Usher" (1839), seemingly dead women refuse to stay buried, while it is the uncanny duplicate of the stygian cat Pluto that shrieks for the silenced wife in "The Black Cat" (1843). In "The Man of the Crowd" (1840), the inscrutable old man who provokes the narrator to follow him around London is arguably a projection of the narrator and ominously undermines all claims to epistemological certainty. Similarly, the phantasmatic "other" William Wilson in the story of the same name (1839) suggests the very Imp of the Perverse—the mind that irrationally acts purely because it knows it should not and turns back upon itself—detailed in both Poe's "The Imp of the Perverse" (1845) and "The Black Cat." The ghost stories of Henry James offer a similarly psychological reflection on the mind itself as a type of haunted house.

Even nastier and more immediately threatening are those ghosts that stalk through the pages of Ambrose Bierce and, later, Stephen King. In Bierce's "The Death of Halpin Frayser" (1893), the titular Halpin is seemingly murdered by the animate corpse of his own mother, while in "The Middle Toe of the Right Foot" (1891), the murderer Manton receives his just deserts from the vengeful ghost of his dead wife. Updating the haunted house tradition is Stephen King, who in *The Shining* (1977; first adapted for screen by Stanley Kubrick in 1980) and the TV mini-series *Rose Red* (2002) creates a haunted hotel and haunted mansion respectively every bit as terrifying as the haunted castles of the late eighteenth-century Gothic novel.

In the hands of female authors, the ghost story genre became a powerful tool of critique, highlighting the various forms of disenfranchisement suffered by women in American culture. Such stories use the supernatural to highlight the terrors of the known, including abuse by fathers and husbands, economic dependency, the demands of motherhood, and circumscribed possibilities for self-actualization. Particularly notable here are the late nineteenth- and early twentieth-century ghostly narratives of Mary E. Wilkins-Freeman and Edith Wharton. In Freeman's stories, such as "The Lost Ghost" (1903) and "The Wind in the Rose-bush" (1903), the ghosts of children and women bear testimony to deprivation and abuse, while Wharton's tales such as "Kerfol" (1916), "Afterwards" (1937), and "Pomegranate Seed" (1931) dramatize the insecure positions of wives whose husbands exercise varying forms of violence on and control over them. Shirley Jackson's 1959 novel *The Haunting of Hill House* deserves mention as an homage to James's *The Turn of the Screw* (and obvious influence on King's *Rose Red*), in which the reader is forced to determine whether the house is actually haunted or if the ghosts are all in the mind of protagonist Eleanor Vance.

In the same way that supernatural themes were utilized by white American women as a form of social critique, as Kathleen Brogan (1998) details, ghosts have played significant roles in the writing of American women of color, including Toni Morrison and Louise Erdrich, who use them as political interventions to address fragmented histories and lost cultural identities. In Morrison's *Beloved* (1987), the ghost of Sethe's "crawling-already" baby simultaneously figures one lost child and all those lost during the Middle Passage from Africa to America, while in Erdrich's *Tracks* (1988), the supernatural foregrounds the tension between traditional Anishinaabe culture and beliefs and those of white, Christian America.

Made in America: Monsters Made by Man

As Stephen Crane's *The Monster* introduced at the start of this chapter makes clear, monstrosity is an anthropocentric concept; that is, human beings define that which is monstrous in relation to themselves. The monster is the other, the inhuman, the "not me." This certainly applies to the monsterization of other races, as well as to the imagined machinations of the devil, demons, and other supernatural entities that bedevil man. All monsters, therefore, can be considered human inventions. Some monsters, however, are more directly human creations than others. This section will survey monsters in American Gothic tradition that are both the explicit results and inadvertent byproducts of ill-advised experimentation. Such monsters created by mad scientists and myopic capitalists encode deep-seated fears of technology, violation of the "natural order," and human hubris.

The prototypical mad scientist is, of course, Mary Shelley's Victor Frankenstein, who made his first appearance in Shelley's 1818 novel. In 1844, Nathaniel Hawthorne appropriated the mad scientist theme in his short story, "Rappaccini's Daughter." Within the story, the young student Giovanni becomes enraptured with the beautiful Beatrice whom he spies from his window among the exotic flowers and plants of Dr. Rappaccini's garden. Entering the garden, Giovanni discovers that not only are the plants poisonous, but so too is Beatrice herself, who has been raised among them. He further determines that, as a result of spending time with Beatrice, he himself is becoming noxious. When an antidote is administered by a rival scientist, Giovanni is cured, but Beatrice dies.

As is the case with most stories of mad scientists, "Rappaccini's Daughter" has two monsters: the poisonous creation alienated from society through no fault of her own and the vastly more culpable scientist who has sinned against creation. The willingness of Dr. Rappaccini to use his daughter as a guinea pig in his experiment and to alter her nature is similar to the quest of another of Hawthorne's characters, the natural philosopher Ayler in "The Birth-Mark" (1843), to perfect his wife Georgiana by removing her only blemish, a small hand-shaped birthmark on her face. Unfortunately, the cost of its removal is her life. Both "Rappaccini's Daughter" and "The Birth-Mark" present cautionary rales concerning human myopia and the manipulation of the natural world. In keeping with the theme that Hawthorne develops in "Young Goodman Brown," "The Minister's Black Veil" (1836), *The Scarlet Letter* (1850), and elsewhere, imperfection is the inevitable mortal condition and the preoccupation with sin turns one distrustful and desperate, alienating one from family, friends, and community.

Roughly a century later, atomic-age anxieties about the dangers of unorthodox or unholy experimentation found expression through narratives of irradiated creatures on the rampage. While the Japanese Godzilla—a dinosaur-like creature awoken/mutated by atomic radiation—is clearly the most famous example of this category of monstrosity, Americans found much to fear in *Them!* (1954) about gigantic, mutated ants, *Attack of the Crab Monsters* (1957) featuring giant mutated crustaceans,

Tarantula (1955) about a giant mutated arachnid, *Attack of the Giant Leeches* (1959), and so forth. The "over-reacher" plot concerning the scientist whose monomaniacal pursuit of technological advancement violates the natural order is also at the heart of many twentieth- and twenty-first-century horror narratives that emphasize anxieties related to genetic engineering. The classic version of this story is encapsulated by the 1957 short story "The Fly," by George Langelaan, about a scientist whose DNA mixes together with that of a fly resulting in a monstrous hybrid. This anxiety concerning monsters created as a consequence of unethical or ill-advised scientific experimentation is also at the center of the *Jurassic Park* franchise, consisting of the novels by Michael Crichton and films directed by Steven Spielberg and Joe Johnston, in which dinosaurs are revived and, despite numerous safety measures and precautions, inevitably still manage to wreak havoc.

A variant on the over-reacher plot and a staple of science fiction encoding technophobic fears is the monstrous robot or cyborg that turns against its makers. This premise underlies the *Terminator* and *Matrix* franchises, as well as Alex Proyas's *I, Robot* (2004), loosely based on Isaac Asimov's collection of stories of the same name published in 1950. Philip K. Dick's *Do Androids Dream of Electric Sheep?* (1968), adapted for film as *Blade Runner* in 1982 (Ridley Scott), offers a particularly sophisticated variant of this plot, in which Rick Deckard (played by Harrison Ford in the film), a bounty hunter of fugitive androids, starts to question human morality and, indeed, his own humanity.

Beginning with George Romero's *Night of the Living Dead* (1968), zombie narratives frequently have tended either to use the unintended consequences of modern technology plot or the virus plot (see below) to explain the origins of the ranks of shambling undead. In such works, mankind reaps the apocalyptic harvest it has sown. In *Night*, radiation from a returning NASA space probe is proposed as the culprit behind the reanimation and cannibalistic acts of the recently deceased. In Stephen King's 2006 novel *Cell*, "the pulse," a global electromagnetic surge, turns the world's cell-phone users into zombie-like maniacs. While neither quite vampires nor zombies, the monsters in Francis Lawrence's 2007 remake of Richard Matheson's *I Am Legend* (1954) result from the mutation of a man-made virus originally created to cure cancer.

Finally, one could add to this category of man-made monsters the entries within the relatively recent eco-disaster genre. In such works, "mother nature" transforms into monster nature as human despoilment of the environment precipitates cataclysmic consequences. Clearly giving shape to the kind of inchoate anxiety produced by the apocalyptic rhetoric surrounding global warming, these narratives depict the ramifications of altering the natural environment on a massive scale and are particularly unsettling because—unlike the reanimated dead or sentient machines—nature's onslaught cannot be resisted, only survived. This is the premise of Roland Emmerich's *The Day After Tomorrow* (2004), in which global warming results in a series of extreme weather events that usher in global cooling leading to a new ice age. In M. Night Shyamalan's 2008 *The Happening*, an epidemic of mass suicide apparently caused by a vegetation-generated neurotoxin makes clear the theme that, as a result of failing to care for the natural world, we are literally killing ourselves.

Natural Monsters

In contrast to monsters produced through human hubris and tampering with the order of things are naturally existing creatures that are deemed monstrous due to their appearance and/or perceived threat to human beings. Into this category fall extraterrestrials, cryptids, dangerous animals, and plagues. Such creatures and events prick mankind's humanist pretensions toward being the center of the universe while also in some cases offering a romantic representation of a world—or indeed a universe—full of mysteries to be explored and wonders still to be discovered (and all too often conquered as well).

The American Gothic tradition in both literature and film is packed with monstrous aliens—bizarre but not supernatural—that arguably can be filtered into two master narratives. In the first, monstrous extraterrestrials must be defeated or destroyed in the name of preserving "the American way." In the second, extraterrestrials initially perceived as monstrous—often due to their appearance—end up teaching human beings (readers or viewers if not characters within the texts) a lesson on what it means to be "human." The preservation of the American way of life sf masterplot is an extension of the "monsters as cultural others" category beyond terrestrial groups. In place of subhuman Native Americans, deceitful persons of color, or dangerous jihadists, American adaptations of H.G. Wells's classic 1898 *The War of the Worlds* give us immunodeficient Martians (Orson Welles on the radio in 1938; George Pal's production for Paramount Pictures in 1953) or more generic aliens (Steven Spielberg's adaptation, 2005); the *Star Trek* franchise gives us, among many others, Klingons, Romulans, and the Borg who wish to subdue or assimilate human beings; the 1996 film *Independence Day* (Roland Emmerich) features savage aliens blowing up the White House and the U.S. Capitol; M. Night Shyamalan's *Signs* (2002) seems to suggest that God is an American as horrifying aliens with terrible foresight are vanquished by baptism by tap water; and, in what I have referred to elsewhere as "deep-space multiculturalism," franchises such as the *Star Wars* and *Men in Black* films displace the terrestrial freak show into orbit and parade for the viewer's amusement an almost endless stream of imaginative monsters that in many cases closely mirror caricatured stereotypes of terrestrial ethnicities (see Weinstock, "Freaks in Space").

In sf texts that fall into the "preserve the American way" category, the monstrous others are alien races that threaten either to impose an alternative way of life on Americans or to wipe out life altogether. In such narratives—even ones in which human beings work together with aliens to confront more aggressive alien species—it is generally up to white American men (or Will Smith) to save the planet and prevent extinction. An interesting variation on this theme is presented in the films that make up the *Alien* franchise. Within these films, the double-mouthed, goo-dripping, acid-for-blood H.R. Giger-designed alien is undeniably monstrous, but equally insidious—if not more so—is the Weyland-Yutani Corporation that seeks to return a living specimen of the alien to earth, an objective in the service of which human lives are of little consequence. In this instance, the monster is bad, but corporations are worse.

In contrast to sf monster narratives in which Americans come together to defend themselves, their country, and the planet are monster narratives in which the alien other turns out to be "more human than human" and thereby critique "inhuman" qualities such as greed, violence, and xenophobia. Examples of this narrative include Orson Scott Card's 1985 novel *Ender's Game*, in which the eponymous Ender is trained from a young age to fight an aggressive alien race called the Formics (derogatorily referred to as the "Buggers"). Thinking he is engaged in a simulation, Ender launches a "molecular disruption device" that destroys not just the entire Bugger fleet, but their planet as well. Only after the fact does he learn that (spoiler!) this was no simulation and he has committed xenocide, apparently wiping out an entire species. Subsequent events reveal that the wars between the Formics and humans were based on each misunderstanding the nature of the other. Also released in 1985 was Wolfgang Petersen's film *Enemy Mine*, based on a story of the same name by Barry B. Longyear (1979), in which two enemies—a human being (Dennis Quaid) and a reptilian "Drac" (Louis Gossett, Jr.)—learn to overcome their differences and understand one another. And if Mary Rowlandson in her captivity narrative had "gone native" and assisted her captors in resisting the encroachments of white colonists, the result would be something along the lines of James Cameron's *Avatar* (2009), in which paraplegic former marine Jake Sully (Sam Worthington), after watching the exploitation of the noble indigenous ten-feet-call, blue-skinned Na'vi on planet Pandora, switches allegiances.

Deflating human pretensions to the fullest are the monstrous extraterrestrials of H.P. Lovecraft's canon of "comic horror." Although sometimes referred to as gods or deities, Lovecraft's "Great Old Ones," including the monstrous squid-faced Cthulhu, are actually extraterrestrial entities of such enormous power that mankind is not even a blip on their radar. The "cosmic horror" associated with them is the realization of mankind's utter insignificance and precarious position in a universe populated by monstrous powers and forces. Jonathan Edwards's wrathful God at least cares enough about sinners to loathe them. Lovecraft's extraterrestrial monstrosities for the most part do not even condescend to notice, much less be angry about, human beings—and that, Lovecraft leads us to believe, is entirely for the best!

While the cosmos is seemingly inhabited by a breathtaking range of alien life forms, one need not leave planet Earth, however, to encounter natural monsters. "Cryptids" are monsters like the Loch Ness Monster whose existence is maintained by some but not yet proven. Among North American cryptids that have found their way into Gothic fiction and film, the most famous include Bigfoot, the Jersey Devil, and the Chupacabra.

Bigfoot (also referred to as Sasquatch) is a hairy hominid sighted across the United States and Canada who, since the 1970s, has also had an occasional career in cinema, TV, and literature. He is probably best known for his role in *Harry and the Hendersons* (William Dear, 1987) and perhaps for lacking a sense of humor in the series of "Messin" with "Sasquatch" commercials for a beef jerky product. The Jersey Devil is proposed as a hominid with an equine head, cloven hooves, bat wings, and a serpent tail that haunts the New Jersey Pine Barrens. It is the object of a *Blair Witch*-style documentary expedition in *The Last Broadcast* (Stefan Avalos and Lance Weller, 1998) and was the focus of a season one episode of *The X-Files* (1993). The word "chupacabra" literally translates to "goat-sucker" in English and is derived from this monster's predilection for the blood of livestock and other animals. Descriptions of this creature, which allegedly roams the desert Southwest of the United States, as well as Latin and South America, vary greatly, with some reports ascribing reptilian features to it and others comparing it to an oversized Mexican hairless dog. This "bigfoot of Latino culture" stars in any number of B-horror movies, including Brennon Jones's *Chupacabra: The Island of Terror* (1997).

In addition to these more famous pop culture phenomena postulated to stalk the American landscape, Gothic authors and filmmakers have imagined an impressive array of animals rendered monstrous as a consequence of unusual features, gigantic size, great numbers, and/or unexpected intelligence. King Kong in both the classic 1933 film (Merian C. Cooper) and subsequent remakes, including the 2005 version by Peter

Jackson, is an enormous ape discovered on an isolated island also containing dinosaurs. The *Jaws* franchise, based on the 1974 book by Peter Benchley, focuses on a gigantic—and surprisingly intelligent—great white shark with a taste for human flesh. The snakes in *Venom* (Piers Haggard, 1981) and *Anaconda* (Luis Llosa, 1997) and its sequels are impressively large, and while the rabid St. Bernard in Stephen King's *Cujo* (1981; adapted for film in 1983 by Louis Teague) isn't larger than usual, he nevertheless is an intimidating presence.

Animals can also become monstrous in great numbers. The strangest and most viscerally affecting example of this is undoubtedly Alfred Hitchcock's 1963 *The Birds*. Adapted from a 1952 novel by Daphne du Maurier, the movie focuses on large flocks of birds that begin attacking humans for no apparent reason. No rationale for the attacks is offered by the film, leaving viewers and critics to arrive at their own explanations. Swarming ants are the focus of *The Naked Jungle* (Byron Haskin, 1954), snakes are the problem in 2006's *Snakes on a Plane* (David R. Ellis), "Africanized" bees are the threat in *The Swarm* (Irwin Allen, 1978), aggressive swarming spiders are central to *Kingdom of the Spiders* (John Cardos, 1977) and *Arachnophobia* (Frank Marshall, 1990), while rats are the problem in Daniel Mann's *Willard* (1971) and its sequel *Ben* (Phil Karlson, 1972).

And then there are natural monsters too small for the human eye to see but that have the potential in American Gothic tales to create cataclysmic effects: viruses. As Priscilla Wald discusses, "outbreak" narratives tell a "contradictory but compelling story of the perils of human interdependence and the triumph of human connection and cooperation, scientific authority and the evolutionary advantages of the microbe, ecological balance and impending disaster" (2)—and in the wake of contemporary AIDS, swine flu, SARS, bird flu, Covid, and other epidemic panics, it is no surprise that Gothic tales have increasingly focused on the virus as monster. In some narratives of contagion such as *The Andromeda Strain* (Michael Crichton novel 1969, Robert Wise film 1971) and *Outbreak* (Wolfgang Petersen, 1995), the pathogen possesses the potential to destroy or actually devastates human life. In others, such as the *Resident Evil* films, *Zombieland* (Ruben Fleischer, 2009), and the trilogy of vampire novels by Guillermo del Toro and Chuck Hogan introduced in 2009 with *The Strain*, the virus is responsible for zombifying the living or reviving the dead.

What the recent emphasis in contemporary American Gothic narratives on viruses demonstrates is the adaptability of monsters. The forms that future monsters will take are uncertain, but we can be sure that they will mirror and give shape to future American anxieties and tabooed desires.

Works Cited

Asma, Stephen T. *On Monsters: An Unnatural History of Our Own Worst Fears*. Oxford University Press, 2009.

Beal, Timothy K. *Religion and Its Monsters*. Rutledge, 2002.

Bird, Robert Montgomery. *Nick of the Woods; Or, The Jibbenainesay: A Tale of Kentucky*. Rowman & Littlefield, 1967.

Bradford, William. *Of Plymouth Plantation 1620-1647*, edited by Samuel Eliot Morison. Alfred A. Knopf, 1953.

Brogan, Kathleen. *Cultural Hauntings: Ghosts and Ethnicity in Recent American Literature*. University Press of Virginia, 1998.

Christophersen, Bill. *The Apparition in the Glass: Charles Brockden Brown's American Gothic*. University of Georgia Press, 1993.

Cohen, Jeffrey Jerome. "Monster Culture (Seven Theses)" in *Monster Theory: Reading Culture*, edited by Jeffrey Jerome Cohen. University of Minnesota Press, 1996, pp. 3–25.

Cooper, James Fenimore. *The Last of the Mohicans*. Signet, 1980.

Cowan, Douglas. E. *Sacred Terror: Religion and Horror on the Silver Screen*. Baylor University Press, 2008.

Edwards, Jonathan. "Sinners in the Hands of an Angry God" in *Early American Writings*, edited Carla Mulford, et al. Oxford University Press, 2002, pp. 676–683.

Halberstam, Judith. *Skin Shows: Gothic Horror and the Technology of Monsters*. Duke University Press, 1995.

Irving, Washington. "The Legend of Sleepy Hollow" in *The Sketch Book of Geoffrey Crayon, Gent*. Penguin, 1978, pp. 272–297.

Mather, Cotton. *The Wonders of the Invisible World* in *The Norton Anthology of American Literature*, 7th ed., edited by Nina Baym, et al. W.W. Norton, 1998, vol. A., pp. 308–313.

Poole, W. Scott. *Monsters in America: Our Historical Obsession with the Hideous and the Haunting*. Baylor University Press, 2011.

Simpson, Phillip L. *Psycho Paths: Tracking the Serial Killer Through Contemporary American Film and Fiction*. Southern Illinois University Press, 2000.

Taylor, Edward. "Upon Wedlock, and the Death of Children" in *Early American Writings*, edited by Carla Mulford, et al. Oxford University Press, 2002, p. 303.

Wald, Patricia. *Contagious: Cultures, Carriers, and the Outbreak Narrative*. Duke University Press, 2008.

Weinstock, Jeffrey Andrew. "Freaks in Space: 'Extraterrestrialism' and 'Deep-Space Multiculturalism'" in *Freakery: Cultural Spectacles of the Extraordinary Body*, edited by Rosemary Garland Thomson. New York University Press, 1996, pp. 327–337.

Introduction: A Genealogy of Monster Theory

Jeffrey Jerome Cohen's 1996 essay "Monster Culture (Seven Theses)," from his edited collection, *Monster Theory: Reading Culture*, holds a prominent position in *The Monster Theory Reader* as the introduction to a volume that named a field—and the naming of a field or subdiscipline can exert a powerful gravitational effect, allowing dispersed scholarship to coalesce around its banner and start to form into something coherent. In this sense, to name a field is a type of performative speech act, bringing something into being that did not previously exist: "I dub thee monster theory." *Presto!* And then, having been named, the larger a field grows, the stronger its gravity becomes as scholarship begets scholarship and scholars acknowledge affiliations with one another. Once there is monster theory, there can be monster theory scholars, monster theory journals, monster theory organizations, monster theory conferences, and so on.

One difficulty confronting monster theory researchers, however, has been the dispersed nature of the scholarship—a difficulty exacerbated by the transnational and transdisciplinary nature of the investigation. Like the monsters it theorizes, monster theory transgresses categorical boundaries, spreading out into different disciplines. What monsters are, where they come from, what they mean, and the cultural work they do are questions that have preoccupied philosophers, theologians, psychologists, physicians, and cultural critics. Because all cultures have their own monsters, monster theory is by necessity an international endeavor—and one that, bearing in mind shifting cultural norms and expectations, must tread carefully when it comes to broad generalizations (the same monster resonates differently in different times and places). And because monsters and monstrosity appear in contexts ranging from art to medicine and religion to sociology and beyond, the theorization of monsters and their meanings has followed suit, with historians and anthropologists, queer theorists, and even computer scientists all attempting to think through what monstrosity is and how it functions. [...]

Because the study of monsters, including theorization about what they are, where they come from, and what they mean, goes back many thousands of years—as does the understanding of how anxieties concerning monsters, as well as the tabooed desires they reflect, can be strategically deployed to prohibit or enable particular behaviors—it may be useful before turning to the contemporary perspectives that compose this volume to take a step back and consider a kind of monster theory genealogy, thereby acknowledging that, although newly named, monster theory is in fact a very old endeavor.

Definitions

The place to begin, even before turning our attention to genealogy, is with the question of definition: just what constitutes a "monster" in the first place? Etymology is suggestive here, although it is of limited overall utility. Timothy Beal tells us in *Religion and Its Monsters* (one of many places where this derivation is rehearsed) that "'monster' derives from the Latin *monstrum*, which is related to the verbs *monstrare* ('show' or 'reveal') and *monere* ('warn' or 'portend')" (Beal 6–7). The *monstrum*, then, at least for the ancients, had a portentous quality, as it was "a message that breaks into this world from the realm of the divine" (Beal 7). Stephen Asma, too, notes the Latin connotation of *monstrum* as a kind of omen, a sign from the gods indicating their displeasure, before elaborating that the monster is "a kind of *cultural category*" employed in various domains ranging from religion to biology (Asma 13). Such discussions do help us understand where the term *monster* came from and begin to help us think about their functions; however, they are not particularly useful in delimiting what does or does not qualify as a monster. Are monsters purely imaginary, like Minotaurs and manticores and zombies? Does monstrosity inhere in substantial deviation from established physical or behavioral norms for a species—like begetting *un*like? Are serial killers and other human beings who engage in depraved acts monsters? Must a monster be physically threatening?

Synthesizing the work of Beal, Noël Carroll, Massimo Leone, and others, Asa Mittman seeks to answer these questions by proposing that the monster is that which unsettles or challenges established cognitive categories and interpretive strategies: "Above all, the monstrous is that which creates [a] sense of vertigo, that which calls into question our (their, anyone's) epistemological world-view, highlights its fragmentary and inadequate nature, and thereby asks us ... to acknowledge the failures of our systems of categorization" (Mittman 8). Mittman thus highlights here the relativity of monstrosity: the monster is the thing that, from a particular perspective in a given context, shouldn't be, but is. The monster is that which threatens understandings of the world, the self, and the relations between the two—and these are understandings that vary depending upon time and place. Mittman also shifts the emphasis from object to subject, from the intrinsic qualities of the thing considered monstrous to the subject doing the considering. The monster, suggests Mittman, comes into being at the moment affective vertigo is translated into the catch-all conceptual category for things that don't fit; that is (like a disciplinary field), the monster comes into being the moment it is called a monster.

Mittman's formulation is broad—given human idiosyncrasies and phobias, on the level of the individual, it could encompass almost anything. And it does raise some questions. For one thing, is something still a monster if one believes in its existence and has a category to define it? Is a troll, for example, still a monster to someone who has grown up believing trolls are part of their world—in which case, they might be scary but presumably would not provoke a sense of epistemological crisis or vertigo? For another, when does something transition from being unsettling or uncanny to vertigo inducing? How profound must epistemological vertigo be for something to be construed as monstrous (assuming there are degrees of vertigo)? Despite these questions, however, Mittman's emphasis on monstrosity being "rooted in the vertigo of redefining one's understanding of the world" is useful for thinking about why the same thing can be regarded differently by different individuals and groups and at different times. It also helps to explain the anxiety that monsters provoke above and beyond any physical threat they present and the hyperbolic response that that which is considered monstrous provokes. The "intolerable ambiguity" of the monster, to reference the title of Elizabeth Grosz's inclusion in this volume, compels two types of responses: to understand it and find a category to contain it—that is, to assimilate it into an existing or altered epistemological framework—or to stamp it out of existence.

To understand monsters or to eradicate them is a succinct formulation of the difference between what we may refer to as the scholarly and political approaches to monstrosity, with philosophers, theologians, and academics seeking to explain monsters—what they are, where they come from, what they mean—and those in or aspiring to positions of power deploying the rhetoric of monstrosity as a tool to manipulate opinion and promote specific political agendas.

Focusing first on the scholarly approach to monstrosity, theorization of monstrosity from antiquity to today has tended to divide along three tracks: *teratology*, the study of "monstrous" births; *mythology*, the consideration of fantastical creatures; and *psychology*, the exploration of how human beings come to act in monstrous or inhuman ways. Teratology and psychology are more immediately connected to what we may think of as the "real world" than mythology, which often has to do with fantasy or dream; however, all three divisions find their grounding in the human experience of overlaying meaning upon existence. Whether the monstrous comes to us or we conjure it up, monstrosity is a loose and flexible epistemological category that allows us a space to define that which complicates or seems to resist definition.

Teratology

Ambroise Paré (circa 1510–90) thought seriously about monsters. This French surgeon and scholar—who tended to Kings Henry II, Francis II, Charles IX, and Henry III; invented surgical instruments; and is considered one of the fathers of modern forensic pathology—wrote about monstrous births in his 1573 *On Monsters and Marvels (Des Monstres Tant Terrestres que Marines avec Leurs Portraits*, part of his *Deux Livres de Chirurgie)*. As Bates observes, *On Monsters and Marvels* is the best-known attempt from the early modern period to theorize monstrous births, and, in its opening chapter, Paré offers a list of "several things that cause Monsters" (Bates 74):

> The first is the glory of God.
> The second, His wrath.
> The third, too great a quantity of semen.
> The fourth, too small a quantity.
> The fifth, imagination.
> The sixth, the narrowness or smallness of the womb.
> The seventh, the unbecoming sitting position of the mother, who, while pregnant, remains seated too long with her thighs crossed or pressed against her stomach.
> The eighth, by a fall or blows struck against the stomach of the mother during pregnancy.
> The ninth, by hereditary or accidental illnesses.
> The tenth, by the rotting or corruption of the semen.
> The eleventh, by the mingling or mixture of seed.
> The twelfth, by the artifice of wandering beggars.
> The thirteenth, by Demons or Devils [Paré 3–4].

Paré's list, which collects causes for monstrous births generally accepted in his time, is fascinating for the way it intermingles superstition with science, as it covers what we could consider the five most important teratological theories: supernatural intervention, hybridization, maternal impression, accident, and what we today would call genetics. We will begin our survey with the supernatural explanations (causes 1, 2, and 13), which themselves can be divided into three subcategories—portents, punishments, and intercourse with diabolic forces—before giving some consideration to the natural causes.

Supernatural Theories

Although the term *teratology*, referring to the study of abnormal gestational development, wasn't introduced until the nineteenth century,[1] human beings have always been interested in understanding the causes and potential meanings of "monstrous births"—animals and human beings demonstrating physiological and/or mental abnormalities. In keeping with the etymology of the word *monster*, there is a long history of monstrous births being regarded as divine portents of things to come. Babylonian priests kept careful records of congenital malformations on clay tablets for purposes of divination—the "appearance of malformations of the ears, nose, mouth, sex organs, and digits," Warkany writes, "had meaning for the future of the king, the land, and the parents" (Warkany 24). The Babylonians' "extensive system of monster interpretation based on emblematic symbolism" (Smith 47), in which particular deformations were interpreted as mapping onto future events or reflecting divine will, was then inherited by the Greeks and Romans (Barrow 18).

Among the Romans, Livy (59 BCE to 17 CE), Tacitus (circa 56–120 CE), and the mysterious fourth-century CE Julius Obsequens discuss monstrous births as supernatural expressions of divine displeasure and as signs of calamitous things to come. Smith explains that "of a hundred or so portentous events in Livy's history, at least fifteen are frightening monsters, such as 'a pig born with a human face' (IIVII.iv.14–5) and a boy with the head of an elephant (XXVII. xi.4–6)" (Smith, "Portent Lore" 48). Tacitus's *Histories*, continues Smith, "is a dark and bloody chronicle of the coups and usurpations of first-century Rome, and among the divine portents of these disasters are animals that 'give birth to strange young' (I.lxxvi)" (Smith 48). And Julius's fourth-century CE *Liber Prodigiorum* (Book of prodigies)—not published until 1508—found its basis in Livy and presents an account of Roman wonders and portents from 249 to 12 BCE. For the Greeks and Romans, as for the Babylonians, monstrous births—both animal and human—were not chance events but meaningful, and they required interpretation to ferret out their occult significance.

Early Christian thinkers as well were inclined to consider monstrous births as messages from God. While Smith notes that both Tertullian (160–220 CE) and Eusebius (263–339 CE) discuss the portentous quality of monstrous births, it is St. Augustine (354–430 CE) who established in the fifth century "a definitive Christian doctrine of the monstrous" (Smith 50). For Augustine, all natural processes are directed by God—nothing in the world happens without God's permission, and God is able to act without constraint. Thus, Augustine writes in book X of *City of God* that "monstrous births" are "arranged and appointed by Divine Providence" (Saint Augustine, 321). When a human woman or animal gives birth to something "monstrous"—something physiologically abnormal—it is God sending us a message, although what exactly it portends is always a matter of debate and conjecture.

The view of monstrous births as supernatural omens persisted through the Middle Ages and Renaissance; however, as Surekha Davies explains, a shift began in the late fifteenth century such that monstrous births were regarded less as "portents of general misfortune" and more as "signs of particular crimes and impending divine retribution for a range of failings indicating wrongful political and religious allegiances" (Davies 52). Martin Luther's influential pamphlet from 1523, for example, composed together with Philipp Melanchthon, explained the manifestations of the "Papal Ass"—a creature allegedly appearing on the banks of the Tiber in 1495 with the head of an ass, a woman's breasts and belly, an elephant's trunk in place of one arm, one cloven foot, and one birdlike foot, and with scales covering its neck, arms, and legs—and the "Monk Calf," a malformed calf born in Saxony in 1522 with a fold of skin over its head shaped like a cowl, as emblems of the corruption of the Roman Catholic Church and signs of God's displeasure. Thirty-five years later, Conradus Lycosthenes wrote in his *Prodigiorum ac Ostentorum Chronicon*, a year-by-year chronicle starting with what Lycosthenes proposed as the year of creation (3959 BCE), of "God's marvelous warnings and portents—monsters, comets, earthquakes, rains of blood or frogs or stones, heavenly visions, and so on" (Smith, "Potent Lore" 57).

While monstrous births could be interpreted as portents of catastrophes to come that would afflict an entire community or region, in some cases, they were construed as signs of divine disapproval for more personal actions already taken—that is, as punishments for moral lapses, often specifically sexual ones, including sodomy, bestiality, adultery, incest, and "impure thoughts" and "unnatural desire" writ large. Overlapping with hybridity theory, to be discussed shortly, the bull-headed Minotaur of Greek mythology, for example, was divine punishment for Queen Pasiphaë of Crete after her coupling with a bull (through the machinations of

Der Bapstesel zu Rom

The Papal Ass.

Poseidon, who inflamed her desire for it). And Peggy McCracken observes in *The Curse of Eve* that some medieval romances took their cue from the biblical passage 2 Esdras 5, interpreted as saying that intercourse with a woman during menstruation will beget monsters, to suggest monstrous births were divine punishment for "impure" copulation.[2] Monstrous births could also be interpreted as signs of God's displeasure outside of specifically sexual immortality. Some seventeenth-century North American Puritans, for example, construed the abnormal offspring of Mary Dyer and Anne Hutchinson as signs of divine disapprobation.[3]

In addition to divine portents and punishments, monstrous births could also reflect the other side of the theological divide: not God's will but diabolical intervention. At the end of Paré's list, he includes "by Demons or Devils," and a final supernatural explanation for monstrous births was found in direct copulation—wittingly or not—with demons, succubi, incubi, witches, the devil himself, and other assorted magical creatures that many used to believe (and some still do) roamed the world, or through the influence of such creatures in the form of a spell, curse, or possession. Narratives of sexual congress with demonic entities can be traced back to ancient Sumeria—the demons Ardat lili and Irdu lili would beget children from sleeping men and women, respectively. St. Augustine believed in the existence of succubi and incubi (Saint Augustine, *City of God*, 15:23) as did Thomas Aquinas, although the latter doubted whether such creatures could themselves sire children, proposing instead that they stole semen from sleeping men and transported it to sleeping women.[4] In literature, the sorcerer Merlin is revealed by Geoffrey of Monmouth to be the son of an incubus and a king's daughter.

Interestingly, while the idea of demonic entities copulating with humans and siring monstrous children is generally given little credence today, the idea still finds considerable purchase in contemporary popular culture—consider, for example, *Rosemary's Baby* (Polanski, 1968), the *Omen* films, and the ending of *The Witches of Eastwick* (Miller, 1987), in which the devil has sired children with three human witches. Half-human, half-monstrous hybrids like the *dhampir*—a half-human, half-vampire synthesis—also stalk through the pages of contemporary fantasy and gaming narratives.

Hybridization

Theorization of part-human, part-animal offspring as the consequence of bestiality or copulation with a supernatural creature points us toward a second prominent teratological explanation: hybridization or the "mingling or mixing of seed" of different species, which can function as an explanation for monstrous birth even outside of the frameworks of divine punishment and moral disapprobation. Warkany, Barrow, and others note that belief in the possibility of monstrous hybrids was widespread and deeply entrenched up until the nineteenth century—when it then migrated from presumed scientific fact into literary fantasy.

The idea of human-animal hybridization flourished in the ancient world, where Egyptian gods and Greco-Roman monsters often combined human and animal aspects, and monstrous races of people with dogs' heads or covered in hair or with horns were reported to live at the ends of the earth. Warkany proposes as well that belief in reincarnation and the transmigration of souls from human to animal in India and Egypt fostered an attitude of, if not reverence, at least acceptance of the idea of human-animal hybridity in those regions (Warkany, "History of Teratology," 27). Mosaic and Christian law, however, didn't mince words when it came to the idea of human-animal sexual congress: "And if a man lie with a beast, he shall surely be put to death: and ye shall slay the beast. And if a woman approach unto any beast, and lie down thereto, thou shalt kill the woman, and the beast: they shall surely be put to death; their blood [shall be] upon them" (Leviticus 20:15, 16). Bestiality was an abomination punishable by death, and any offspring of such congress would be accursed as well.

The idea that bestiality could produce offspring was not universally accepted—Aristotle, for example, rejected the prospect of interspecies copulation yielding hybrid progeny; however, this skeptical position was the exception rather than the rule, as its possibility was taken as an article of faith by most until at least the nineteenth century. Paré, for example, writes, "There are monsters that are born with a form that is half-animal and the other [half] human, or retaining every-thing [about them] from animals, which are produced by sodomists and atheists who 'join together' and break out of their bounds—unnaturally—with animals, and from this are born several hideous monsters that bring great shame on those who look at them or speak to them" (Paré, *On Monsters and Marvels*, 67. Brackets in original). Paré then goes on to give a list of examples of such monstrous births.[5]

Monstrosity in general, it should be noted, is frequently correlated with hybridity perceived to be unnatural. Cohen's third thesis from "Monster Culture" is that the monster "is the harbinger of category crisis": "This refusal to participate in the classificatory 'order of things' is true to monsters generally," writes Cohen. "[T]hey are disturbing hybrids whose externally incoherent bodies resist attempts to include them in any systematic structuration" (Cohen 6). Because of their "ontological liminality" (Cohen

6), disturbing hybrids possess the potential to evoke the kind of epistemological vertigo proposed by Mittman and are frequently met with a violent response out of all proportion to the actual physical threat they present as a result. The widespread acceptance of hybridity theory up until at least the nineteenth century, along with the deep-seated Western antipathy toward the idea of bestiality and the rigid policing of the border between human and animal, meant that a child born resembling in some way an animal and the mother who bore it were objects of suspicion, as were animals born with humanlike characteristics—or characteristics of another species—and their mothers. Malformed children perceived in some way to resemble an animal, and malformed animals in some way perceived to resemble a human being, were often put to death—as, in many cases, were the mothers who birthed them.

In the nineteenth and the first part of the twentieth centuries, individuals presented as human-animal hybrids were stock features of freak shows. Bogdan notes that from approximately 1840 to 1940, "the formally organized exhibition for amusement and profit of people with physical, mental, or behavioral anomalies, both alleged and real, was an accepted part of American life" (Bogdan 2). Such exhibitions would include a variety of nonnormative body types, ranging from the excessively hairy (bearded women and "dog-faced boys") to the extremely tall or short to those with physical deformations. As Fielder discusses, such displays would often routinely include "wild men"—often non–Western people pitched as "savages" and "cannibals"—and "feral children."[6] Stories were woven around these figures by carnival barkers for their audiences,

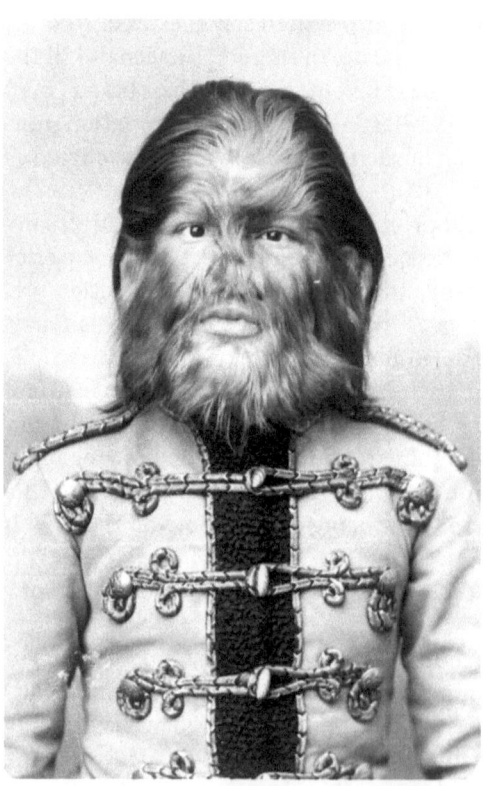

Charles Eisnemann's photograph of Jojo the Dog-Faced Boy (circa 1870).

often explaining the appearance of the performer on display as the consequence of miscegenation, bestiality, or, as will be discussed later, maternal impression. With the waning of the freak show in the mid-twentieth century, fantasies about monstrous hybrid births migrated to science fiction, where hybrids either were the project of "unnatural" human tampering, as in H.G. Wells's *The Island of Dr. Moreau* (1896) or Michael Crichton's *Jurassic Park* (1990), or populated other planets (consider, for example, the famous Cantina scene from George Lucas's first *Star Wars* film, *Episode IV: A New Hope* [1977]).

Maternal Impression

Hybridity theory bears a close connection to another prominent teratological theory—what is sometimes called maternal impression—premised on the idea that what a woman thinks about or sees during conception and the gestation of the embryo can influence its development and appearance. Succinctly presented by Paré as "imagination" in his list of causes of monstrous births, Huet traces this theory back to antiquity, noting the theory, attributed to Empedocles, that "progeny can be modified by the statues and paintings that the mother gazes upon during her pregnancy" (Huet 3-4) and that Pliny wrote that both maternal and paternal thoughts during conception can shape the child (Warkany 30). The belief that the mother's imagination played a crucial role in shaping development of progeny, however, gained traction in the seventeenth and eighteenth centuries. Montaigne, for example, expressed this belief in his essay "On the Power of Imagination" (1850), writing, "We know by experience that women transmit marks of their fancies to the bodies of the children they carry in their wombs."[7] Huet observes that "several stories of monstrosities caused by a mother's troubled contemplation of images became extremely popular in the Renaissance" and were included in the various treatises on monsters of the period, including Paré's (Huet 19).

While, in one sense, maternal impression theory is an extension of hybridity theory, in which one need not physically copulate for hybridization to occur, if followed to its logical conclusion, the consequences of maternal impression theory are significant for patriarchal culture, as paternity is rendered inherently uncertain. Paré mentions, for example, a princess accused of adultery because of having birthed a black child but who was saved by Hippocrates, who pointed out the influence of a portrait of a Moor near her bed (Paré 19). A child could thus differ in appearance from its parents as a consequence of the mother's imagination or images that impressed themselves on her. Huet, however, points out that this logic can work in both directions: an adulterous woman could conceal her crime by thinking about her husband during intercourse with another man. Paternity is thus always speculative.

Maternal impression theory could extend to include the effect not just of imaginative fantasy or the images viewed but also of emotional stimuli experienced by the pregnant woman. The family of Joseph Merrick, the famous "Elephant Man," explained, for example, that his symptoms resulted from his mother being frightened and knocked over by a fairground elephant while she was pregnant. Merrick apparently subscribed to this belief throughout his life (Howell and Ford 128). Stevenson, writing in 1992, notes that maternal impression theory remains widely accepted in parts of the world (Stevenson 353).

Accident

Another common theory for monstrous births from antiquity to today—and one on much safer scientific ground—foregrounds circumstances that affect the development of the fetus, such as intrauterine trauma; ingestion of substances; or conditions, such as illness, that influence the pregnant woman and developing fetus. This theory was at the core of Aristotle's consideration of teratology (although no doubt an understanding that intrauterine trauma, maternal deprivation, or ingestion of particular substances could cause birth defects or induce abortion goes back much further). For Aristotle, gestation is directed by an essence or essential form or character, which ensures that like generates like—a kind of early DNA theory.[8] Aristotle thus proposed that what we call monsters are in fact the consequence of developmental errors introduced during procreation or gestation, resulting in the failure of something to realize its essence fully. Significantly, for Aristotle, monstrous births were not omens or signs. Their monstrosity inhered in their being "contrary to Nature," but this was indicative only of a natural process thwarted, not of the gods' displeasure (Aristotle, 770b: 10). Monstrous births were not augurs of things to come but only indications of a process thwarted or incomplete. Aristotle also dismisses the idea that human copulation with an animal could produce a hybrid, noting, "That ... it is impossible for such a monstrosity to come into existence—I mean one animal in another—is shown by the great difference in the period of gestation between man, sheep, dog, and ox, it being impossible for each to be developed except in its proper time" (Aristotle, 769b: 25).

According to Barrow, the accident theory became more prominent after Paré's inclusion among his causes for monstrous births "a fall or blows struck against the stomach of the mother during pregnancy" and "accidental illness," as well as poor posture or a narrow uterus (Barrow 21). Beginning in the eighteenth century, researchers began to explore the effects of changing environmental conditions on the hatching of eggs. René Antoine Ferchault de Réaumer (1683–1757) investigated artificial incubation of chicken eggs, noting the effect of different temperatures on development. The French naturalist Étienne Geoffroy Saint-Hilaire (1772–1844) explored the effects of manipulating eggs in various ways, including shaking them (Warkany 33). Charles Féré (1852–1907) found that various drugs, including alcohol and nicotine, could induce birth defects in developing eggs, and this then led the way for twentieth-century scientists, including Charles Stockard (1879–1939), who offered increasingly precise explanations for how and why changing environmental conditions could influence the development of embryos in both animals and humans.

The effect that drugs in particular could have on the developing fetus was rendered in stark relief by use of the drug thalidomide in the late 1950s. First marketed in 1957 to alleviate the symptoms of morning sickness, the drug's use resulted in infants being born with malformed limbs and other deformities. Hofland notes that of the more than ten thousand babies born with deformities as a consequence of thalidomide use, over 40 percent died before their first birth- days.[9] In the twenty-first century, various contemporary public health campaigns have sought to highlight the effects of smoking, alcohol, and use of other drugs on developing fetuses. In the literary world, Katherine Dunn's celebrated novel *Geek Love* (1989) concerns a married couple who induce birth defects in their children using various drugs and radioactive material to create a freak show for their traveling carnival.

Genetics

The genetic theory of teratology complements the accident theory by suggesting that malformations may be accounted for by intrinsic genetic causes rather than environmental factors. While the founding of genetics as a science has been credited to Gregor Mendel, who worked in the nineteenth century, the understanding that something like a code directs fetal development and that diseases and anomalies may be inherited goes back much further. As noted, Aristotle believed that species have a kind of essence that directs fetal development such that like generates like. Along these lines, Paré writes that "crookt-back begets crookt-back" and notes among his causes of monstrous births inherited diseases and "corrupt" sperm.[10] The modern understanding of the role of genetics in directing fetal development, however, is primarily a twentieth-century innovation.

Mythology

In medicine and biology, teratology is the scientific study of congenital abnormalities and abnormal formations. Although many reports of monstrous births were apocryphal (like the Papal Ass) or exaggerated, "monstrous births"—deviations from the normal form for a specie—are of course real, and the more striking occurrences, such as conjoined twins or dramatic deformations, have always excited wonder. In contrast to these real-world occurrences are tales of mythical creatures that some claim to have encountered but the existence of which has been discredited or at the very least disputed. We can divide up this discussion into three categories: monstrous races of human beings, monstrous creatures of myth and fantasy, and cryptids—creatures proposed by some to exist but the existence of which is generally disputed by science.

The Monstrous Races

Those who write about monsters are fond of lists—and John Block Friedman's study *The Monstrous Races in Medieval Art and Thought* includes a fascinating one. In his first chapter, Friedman notes that tales of marvelous races of unusual men suffused the ancient world and that such races were speculated about extensively in the works of several authors, including most notably the fifth-century BCE Ctesias, the fourth-century BCE Megasthenes, and the first-century CE Pliny the Elder, as well as in works commissioned by and attributed to Alexander the Great in the fourth century BCE. Far more extensive than Paré's list of causes of monstrous births, Friedman's list consists of forty different races presented as objects of wonder in Ctesias, Megasthenes, Pliny, and the Alexander cycle and is particularly intriguing for the way it includes actual races, such as Pygmies and dark-skinned Ethiopians; individual difference generalized as a characteristic of race, such as the Androgini, who have both male and female sex organs, and Speechless Men, who communicate by gesture; and more fanciful races, such as the Astomi, who lack mouths and live by smell (Friedman 11), the Blemmyae, who lack heads and necks and whose faces are on their chests (Friedman 13), the Cynocephali, who have the heads of dogs (Friedman 15), the Panotii, whose ears reach to their feet and can serve as blankets (Friedman 18), and the Sciapods, who have one leg and a giant foot that they use to shade themselves against the sun (Friedman 18).

Friedman notes that there may be explanations for even the more improbable-sounding races, including perceptual errors—ornamented shields, for example, could have given rise to the belief in men with faces on their chests, and baboons or apes may have been mistaken for dog-headed men—mistranslations, and cultural differences construed as monstrous (Friedman 24). In an observation concerning Greco-Roman accounts of monstrous races, but generalizable far beyond that, Friedman explains that such tales "exhibit a marked ethnocentrism which made the observer's culture, language, and physical appearance the norm by which to evaluate all other people" (Friedman 26). Even a practice such as yoga could have suggested monstrosity to Greek observers: "Probably the Sciapod who shields his head from the sun with his foot while lying on his back derives from observation of people in yoga positions" (Friedman 25). Friedman also notes, however, that while sources for many of the monstrous races can be traced, their elaboration—often "willful, poetic, and imaginative"—filled a psychological need (Friedman 25). Their appeal is rooted in "fantasy, escapism, delight in the exercise of the imagination, and—very important—fear of the unknown." Friedman continues, "If the monstrous races had not existed, it is likely that people would have created them" (Friedman 24). As will be developed more fully later in this chapter, "monsterizing" an existing group, as Asma observes, can also promote imperialist political agendas (Asma 37–38).

As Friedman details, interest in monstrous races persisted through the Middle Ages, with various natural philosophers and theologians grappling with questions of their origins and significance. The questions for St. Augustine in his fifth-century *City of God* were whether monstrous races possessed reason, which would elevate them above animals, and if they are descended from Adam (by way of Noah). Augustine hedges his bets a little, writing, "Wherefore, to conclude this question cautiously and guardedly, either these things which have been told of some races have no existence at all; or if they do exist, they are not human races; or if they are human, they are descended from Adam" (Saint Augustine 16.8, 532). As characterized by Friedman, Augustine "combined missionary zeal with the Roman cosmopolitan tolerance of ethnic diversity" in his consideration of monstrous races as "potential Christians" (Friedman 90). In his seventh-century *Etymologiae*, a wide-ranging encyclopedia, Isidore of Seville draws heavily on Pliny's *Natural History* to discuss monstrous races as those that deviate from a given mean. This allows him to share Augustine's conclusion that monstrous appearance is not necessarily antithetical to Christian salvation.[11] Other works from the Middle Ages were less invested in philosophical theorization than simply in provoking wonder. The eleventh-century Old English *Marvels of the East*, for example, mixes together fantastic tales of dragons and phoenixes with accounts of huge-eared Panotti; half-human, half-donkey Homo-dubii; and cannibalistic Donestre. The fourteenth-century *Travels of Sir John Mandeville* includes among

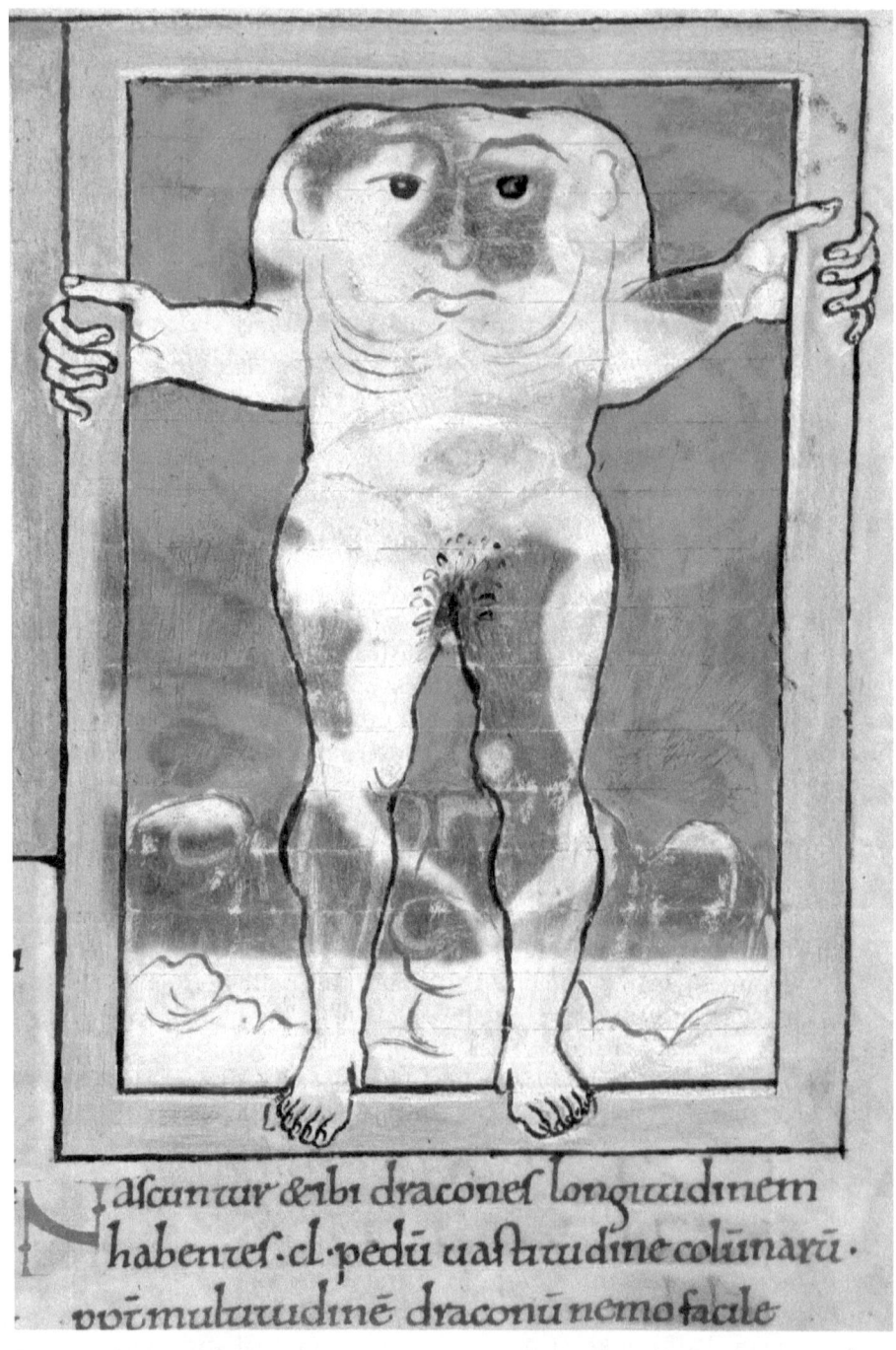

The Blemmyae from The Marvels of the East *(circa fifth century CE).*

Mandeville's famous adventures encounters with one-legged Sciapods and dog-headed Cynocephales—both of which, it is worth noting, come off better than his representation of Jews.

As Davies observes, tales of monstrous peoples continued to circulate in the Renaissance and early modern period: "During the first two centuries of printed books beings such as apple-smellers, troglodytes, anthropophagi, and sciapods, who had sniffed, huddled, chomped, or hopped their way across medieval manuscripts of *The Marvels of the East* and Pliny the Elder's *Historia naturalis*, continued to pass through the hands and minds of European writers, readers, and viewers" (Davies 63). What changed, however, was their proximity. During the Middle Ages, monstrous races were always imagined "at the very edges of the world" (Friedman 46). During the long sixteenth century, in contrast, those edges began to contract as Christopher Columbus and other navigators moved outward—taking their predispositions and expectations with them. Columbus recorded an encounter with cannibals as well as anecdotal accounts of other kinds of monstrous races, including the Cyclops and Cynocephali (Davies 65). Of course, as Davies notes, characterizing indigenous populations as monstrous had significant implications for European colonial enterprises (Davies 69).

Davies argues that beginning in the sixteenth century, the "category of monster expanded enormously, while its subdivisions became less pronounced" (Davies 73). Cabinets of curiosity collected various kinds of unusual artifacts, while exhibitions at fairs and shows mixed deformed human beings and non–European humans (especially Native Americans, notes Davies [73]) with exotic and deformed animals. Davies writes that "from the mid-sixteenth century, such fairs exhibited inhabitants of America, Africa, and even Asia with increasing frequency" (74). Such exhibitions, working in concert with fanciful travel narratives like Mandeville's, arguably influenced and inflected public opinion in ways that facilitated imperialist programs and colonialist endeavors. Indeed, the question of whether the African species of man was fundamentally related to the European variety or of different extraction was central to the debate over African slavery.

Toward the end of the nineteenth century, as it became clear that variation in human morphology was relatively circumscribed—groups of people could have fair skin or dark, be tall or short, but none had dog heads or heads that "do grow beneath their shoulders," as Shakespeare puts it in *Othello* (Shakespeare, *Othello*, 1.3.167–69)—the appeal of the idea of monstrous races discussed by Friedman migrated into literature and, later, film. Science fiction, fantasy, and horror in particular permit authors, artists, and film-makers unchecked expression of the imagination. That depictions of monstrous races in speculative media has often mapped unsubtly onto real-world terrestrial groups suggests the entrenched perniciousness of stereotype.[12]

Mythical Creatures

Despite beginning this survey with a consideration of monstrous births and races, it seems likely that when people think of monsters, what first comes to mind is not conjoined twins or people with exceptionally big ears but the panoply of fantastic creatures that testifies to the fecundity of the human imagination—Godzilla and golems, basilisks and blobs, vampires, ghouls, zombies, werewolves, wendigos, dragons, krakens, and so on: an immense litany of wondrous, fearsome beasties inhabiting the earth, the air, the seas, and worlds beyond. Theorizing the origins of such beasts is a complicated endeavor. In some cases, the possibility of strange or gigantic beasts was certainly suggested by fossils—what is a dragon, after all, if not a kind of dinosaur, the existence of which was made plain by uncovered gigantic bones? In other cases, gigantic specimens of living creatures could suggest even larger ones lurking in inaccessible places—giant squid washed up on the shore could lead one to conjure the kraken, for example. Superstition and incomplete knowledge of the world, of physical processes, and of the self obviously participated in populating the world with monsters—medieval bestiaries mixed together bears, beavers, and bats with unicorns, dragons, phoenixes, and griffins. Tales told by travelers, such as Marco Polo's reports of unicorns and serpents (likely Asian rhinos and crocodiles), must have excited the imagination of audiences, and outright chicanery has played an important role—P.T. Barnum sewed the torso and head of a monkey onto the back half of a fish and marketed it in the nineteenth century as the "Feejee Mermaid," while Bigfoot and Slenderman now have lives of their own despite identifiable origin points. Many monsters, too, have been cut wholesale from the cloth of fancy for various purposes, ranging from prohibition (go here and get eaten, do this and become a monster) to entertainment (often with a profit motive). And then, of course, there are dreams, which have always been a powerful force in suggesting to humans the existence of other worlds and marvelous creatures.

While the origin of each type of monster must be investigated individually (and one must bear in mind that the same monster functions differently in different contexts), theorization of monsters has offered some general insight into the nature and functions of monstrous creatures. As concerns what monsters are, Noël Carroll in "Nightmare and the Horror

Introduction: A Genealogy of Monster Theory

P.T. Barnum and the Feejee Mermaid.

Film: The Symbolic Biology of Fantastic Beings," as well as in his later *The Philosophy of Horror*, offers a straight- forward answer. Restricting his consideration to what he refers to as "art-horror," representations of monsters in art and narrative, Carroll asserts that monsters are entities that represent a threat on some level and evoke disgust as a consequence of "impurity" connected to categorical ambiguity (Carroll 43). In some cases, this impurity is the result of what Carroll calls "fusion," which occurs when something is an "unnatural" or confusing composite, such as the "living dead" or a Minotaur or a Frankenstein's monster literally pieced together from parts of different corpses (Carroll 43). The opposite of fusion, but equally monstrous, is fission, which takes something unified and breaks it into pieces—doppelgangers, alter egos, werewolves, and so on (Carroll 46). Another key strategy for creating a monster is impurity through magnification—take a spider or crab or ape and make it huge, and you have a monster (Carroll 49). Congruent with Cohen's third thesis, Carroll concludes that monsters are essentially defined by what Cohen calls "ontological liminality" (Cohen 6). Neither this nor that—or both this and that—monsters, as Mittman suggests, frustrate our epistemological strategies for making sense of the world.

This raises a question however: if monsters are repulsive and epistemological vertigo is unpleasant, what explains the human fascination with monsters? Carroll's answer in *The Philosophy of Horror* is that we don't so much love monsters as seeing human protagonists contend with them. That is, narrative elicits curiosity—how will the monster be dealt with? Will the heroes win? If our curiosity is stronger than our repulsion, we keep turning the pages, or our eyes stay glued to the screen.

Cohen, however, suggests that there is more to it than this with his sixth thesis, "Fear of the Monster Is Really a Kind of Desire" (Cohen 16). The monster, as Cohen observes, does not just repulse; it simultaneously attracts. The monster is powerful and linked to forbidden desires and practices: "Through the body of the monster fantasies of aggression, domination, and inversion are allowed safe expression in a clearly delimited and permanently liminal space." Monsters are seldom good citizens, decorous and respectful. They instead are bringers of chaos, violators of boundaries: "We distrust and loathe the monster," writes Cohen, "at the same time we envy its freedom, and perhaps its sublime despair" (Cohen 17). Monsters in this sense may be considered a kind of language, a way to give symbolic shape to and communicate affect and experience. The body of the monster is a text expressing human fear and desire—one language we speak through is monsters.

And perhaps we can go even further: we love our monsters because through them we indulge our desire for other worlds (after death, beneath our feet, out in space, all around us). Few thoughts can be more terrifying (if for some liberating) than the consideration that this is all there is: this life, circumscribed by birth and death; this body, subject to disease and decay; this world, the concrete, intersubjective one we perceive through our senses; this universe, and we are the only ones in it. The

Introduction: A Genealogy of Monster Theory

epistemological vertigo evoked by the monster on the local level from a remove becomes euphoria. Ghosts and the undead are impure and threatening, but they also testify to the persistence of spirit after death. Demons, witches, and aliens tell us there are other worlds—eschatological, magical, or extraterrestrial. The one thing that the world's great wealth of monsters shares is that all of them insist that there is more to our world than what we can see and touch. The monster threatens, but also promises liberation—a liberation that itself can seem threatening.

Cryptids

Somewhere between mythical beasts and real animals are cryptids, creatures supposed by some to exist but whose existence has not been confirmed by science. As Bernadette Bosky summarizes, the term *cryptid* is derived from *cryptozoology*, the "study of hidden or mysterious animals," and was invented in 1983 by John E. Wall in the newsletter of the International Society of Cryptozoology (Bosky 105). The category of cryptids, as Bosky explains, can cover creatures amenable to ordinary zoology, including variants that redefine a species and creatures thought to be extinct. "[G]orillas, the Congo peacock, giant pandas, and the okapi, a striped relative of the giraffe, were all cryptids before proof of their existence was established" (Bosky 105). The more famous cryptids, however, are those whose existence is unlikely or impossible—creatures such as the Loch Ness Monster and other surviving dinosaurs, giant hominids such as the Sasquatch or Australian Yowie, the goat-eating Chupacabra alleged to stalk the southwestern deserts of the United States, and the kraken.

In 2005, cryptozoologist George Eberhart proposed (in yet another monster-related list) "10 categories of mystery animal":

1. "distribution anomalies": well-known animal species found in unexpected areas
2. undescribed, unusual, or outsized variations of known species
3. survivals of recently extinct species
4. survivals into the present of species known only from the fossil record
5. survivals of creatures known only from the fossil record into periods much later than previously thought
6. animals not known from the fossil record but related to known species
7. animals not known from the fossil record and not related to any known species

8. mythical animals with a zoological basis
9. seemingly paranormal or supernatural entities with some animal-like characteristics
10. known hoaxes or probably misidentifications.

Eberhart also proposes that cryptozoology should exclude aliens, angels and demons, "bizarre humans," animals relocated by human agency, animals about which there is no controversy, and, curiously, "insignificant" animals whose mysterious features are not "big, weird, dangerous, or significant to humans in some way" (Eberhart 109).

What is perhaps most notable about cryptids is their staying power—once purchase is attained in the imagination, cryptids persist even when their origins can be traced to a hoax, mistake, or misperception. This is because—perhaps to a degree even greater than mythical creatures—cryptids "weird" our world, suggesting that it is stranger than we think: more dangerous, but more interesting. No matter how many investigations into the Loch Ness Monster come up empty or prove that footage of Bigfoot is faked, we still—to borrow from monster theorist Fox Mulder of the program *The X-Files*—want to believe.

Psychology

Our final category of monstrosity shifts our attention from weirdness without to the weird within; to develop this thread, we can focus briefly on another television series—this one about a serial killer. In the television series *Dexter*, which ran for eight seasons from 2006 to 2013 (and returned in 2021), the main character, Dexter Morgan (Michael C. Hall), is a serial killer—but an unusual one. Recognizing homicidal psychopathic tendencies in his adopted son—tendencies we as viewers learn stem from Dexter having observed the brutal murder of his mother as a young child—Dexter's dad, a police officer, taught him to channel his irresistible urges into killing only those guilty of heinous crimes who have somehow escaped justice. Dexter still experiences great pleasure and satisfaction in killing but limits his serial murdering to pedophiles, other serial killers, rapists, and so on. Most considerations of monstrous humans would list serial killers at or near the top. But is Dexter a monster? And if not, is it because we have a sympathetic origin story for his psychosis? Or because we do not feel sympathy for his victims? Or some combination of this and other factors, such as the relationships we see him establish with others on the program?

As the audacious case of Dexter suggests (and I say "audacious" because the premise of asking viewers to sympathize with a serial killer is certainly a bold one), theorizing monstrosity in relation to human psychology is a tricky business and returns us to the vexed issue of definition and the drawing of boundaries. At what point does a human being violate culturally specific expectations to such an extent that he elicits the kind of epistemological vertigo marking monstrosity proposed by Mittman? At what point does deviance make someone a monster? Context is of course key here, because there are few universal human taboos—although prohibitions against cannibalism, murder of group members, and certain sexual practices (necrophilia and incest chief among them) prevail in the majority of societies, nowhere is the idea of monstrosity being in the eye of the beholder more apropos than in considering human monsters.

I would like to suggest that, from a contemporary perspective, human monstrosity is defined most immediately by a lack of sympathy on the part of someone committing or contemplating what are perceived to be physically and/or psychologically harmful acts by an observer who considers those affected as deserving of compassion—particularly if an individual is driven to commit harmful acts by either allegiance to ideology antithetical to that of an observer or sadistic desire. This definition covers the genocidal dictator, on one hand, and the sadistic serial killer who derives enjoyment from his acts, on the other. Also included here are individuals rendered monstrous through their conformity with what Asma calls "monstrous institutional systems" (Asma 244)—that is, those who, acting like machines, participate in what one construes as the immoral abuse of others. The general issue of human psychological deviation from cultural norms of course has received considerable attention for millennia. For the ancient Greeks, such as Socrates and Plato, human monstrosity resulted when human reason failed to govern emotion and appetite (Asma 53). Also originating in antiquity and extending across cultures into the eighteenth century was the idea that temperament was connected to bodily fluids—called *humors*. The four humors proposed by Hippocrates were black bile, yellow bile, phlegm, and blood—and an excess or deficiency of any of them could alter a person's health or psychological condition. Medical practices like bleeding a sick person were intended to restore the balance. An updated version of humorism was eighteenth-century mesmerism. Developed by German doctor Franz Mesmer, mesmerism was premised on the belief in a kind of magnetic fluid that flowed through the body. Physiological and psychological ailments were proposed to be due to the blockage of this fluid, the flow of which could be restored by a trained mesmerist.

In the late nineteenth and early twentieth centuries, Sigmund Freud developed an influential theory concerning human psychology, called *psychoanalysis*, that in interesting ways resonated both with classical Greek philosophy and with theories of internal energy. Freud proposed a divided self—an internal contest between desires (the Id) and internalized social expectations (the Superego) mediated by the Ego. Freud asserted that human beings are divided in another way as well: between the conscious mind and the unconscious, the latter a repository for tabooed desires. For Freud, whose practice focused on those deemed psychologically ill, human behavior (both acceptable and deviant) found its roots in psychosexual development during childhood. Neuroses and psychoses could therefore be traced back to repressed childhood experiences and desires. As Asma explains it, "after Freud, monstrous murderers and abusive people could be theoretically dissected and understood through an examination of their own childhood. Metaphorically speaking, one's childhood is the parent of one's adulthood" (Asma 210). In trying to understand the forces that channeled childhood development toward normative adult behavior, Freud also speculated broadly on religion and culture, with a focus on the incest taboo.

Contemporary theories of psychological illness typically break with Freud's emphasis on childhood psychosexual development but generally accept the notions of repression, unconscious desires, and that childhood experiences (whether real or imagined) can have profound effects on later behavior. The roots of psychological dysfunction in adults still are often traced back to childhood. However, modern treatment of psychological illness also to varying degrees considers physiological causes or triggers for behavior considered deviant, as mental illness can be caused by chemical imbalances, diseases, and physical conditions like tumors.

Comprehending psychological illness as the product of childhood trauma and/or physiological factors may help us feel sympathy for those affected and thus undercut their monstrosity in our eyes. We understand in such instances that individuals do not choose to act in ways considered irrational or deviant but rather are compelled by powerful forces outside their control. Tolerance has its limits, of course—it would be much harder to regard Dexter kindly if his victims were children, even recognizing his traumatic backstory and uncontrollable impulses—and the contemporary media still has a tendency to demonize those with mental illness (most dramatically dissociative identity disorder). Nevertheless, twenty-first-century narratives explaining the causes of mental illness undercut the knee-jerk reaction to categorize those affected as monsters.

The situation, however, is vastly different where action perceived as harmful and motivated by political or religious ideology or mercenary self-interest is concerned. As relates to politics and religion, monstrosity inheres in the perception that one's opponents choose to act immorally. No one, of course, consciously chooses to embrace a belief system they feel to be wrong; nevertheless, the rhetoric of monstrosity that circulates in contemporary culture often assumes that if only one's opponents would think rationally—or sometimes in conformity with the perceiver's understanding of religious or political doctrine—they would reach different decisions. These are monsters due to lack of reflection or understanding.

Monster Politics

The foregoing overview of teratology, mythology, and psychology attempts to trace various threads in the theorization of what monsters are, where they come from, and what they mean. Although far from complete, this consideration suggests the deep psychic investment human beings have had in contemplating monsters for millennia. There is another thread to this discussion of monster theory, however, that has to be briefly introduced—and that is what we could refer to as the strategic deployment of monsters for sociopolitical ends. This perspective on monsters thinks in terms not of "what is this thing?" but rather of "how can I use this thing to achieve my goals?"

Cohen foregrounds the political utility of monsters in his fourth and fifth theses: "The Monster Dwells at the Gates of Difference" and "The Monster Polices the Borders of the Possible" (Cohen 7–16). Where difference is concerned, Cohen observes that representing another culture as monstrous "justifies its displacement or extermination by rendering the act heroic" (Cohen 7–8)—and this is something that demagogues have understood all too well across human history. Whether one is discussing Roman attitudes toward "barbarians" in antiquity, French demonization of Muslims in the Middle Ages, the displacement and destruction of indigenous populations in many parts of the world beginning in the sixteenth century, the Nazi "Final Solution," genocidal campaigns in Bosnia or Rwanda or Armenia, the twenty-first-century immigrant crisis, and so many other instances across time, the exaggeration of cultural difference into monstrosity has always served as an essential preliminary step toward domination. From this perspective, a complete genealogy of monster theory would need to be expanded to include a range of works that explore how manipulation of human fear through the exaggeration of physical and/or cultural difference can and has been used to achieve social or political ends. Such a genealogy would be broad indeed (certainly beyond the scope of this introduction), including primary texts ranging from political screeds against particular groups to propaganda posters, programs, and films.

Nazi propaganda monsterizing Jews during World War II.

Contemporary Monster Theory

What differentiates contemporary monster theory from the theorization of monsters in earlier periods is primarily the position that monstrosity is a socially constructed category reflecting culturally specific anxieties and desires, and often deployed—wittingly or not—to achieve particular sociopolitical objectives. Contemporary monster theory thus disavows (or at least sidesteps the question of) the monstrosity of human subjects based on morphology and instead focuses on the means through which such subjects are "monsterized" and the implications of this process. Adopting a skeptical (or at least agnostic) position in relation to the existence of actual monsters, contemporary monster theory also prefers to focus on images of and narratives involving monsters (human and nonhuman) to tease out what such images and narratives say about their creators and their cultures. Monsters from this perspective remain, as they have been for millennia, texts in need of interpretation; however, they are messages originating from human beings rather than the gods. Put concisely, contemporary monster theory tends to explore "monsters" rather than monsters.

Where contemporary monster theory is concerned, a special position in this monster theory genealogy must be afforded to the work of French philosopher Michel Foucault. Throughout his work, Foucault consistently emphasized the social construction of ideas of normalcy and deviancy, exploring how understandings of what is "natural" and "unnatural" shift across time and from place to place, but invariably participate in the constitution of power hierarchies and the regulation of social behaviors. In *Madness and Civilization* (1961), Foucault explored changing understandings of madness from the Middle Ages to the end of the eighteenth century and the ways in which the label of "mad" created a divide between socially acceptable and unacceptable behavior. Foucault's *The History of Sexuality*—most especially the first volume, *The Will to Knowledge* (1976)—focuses on the way ideas of normalcy and deviancy in relation to sexuality are produced and policed. In *Discipline and Punish: The Birth of the Prison* (1975), Foucault considers in more general terms the coercive regimes that seek to regulate human behavior. In these works and others, Foucault emphasized that, rather than being universal and immutable, understandings of normalcy and deviancy are context dependent and mutable; the result is that what one culture construes as monstrous aberration could be considered normal by another.

Foucault turned his attention explicitly to monsters in his lectures at the Collège de France in 1974–75, which clustered around the theme of the "emergence of the abnormal individual in the nineteenth century" (Davidson xvii) and focused in particular on the "human monster," the "individual to be corrected," and the onanist (Foucault, *Abnormal: Lectures at the Collège de France 1974-1975*, 55). In these lectures, Foucault shows how monstrosity is not only a relational term—monstrosity is always defined against that which is not monstrous—but also part of a regulatory regime that disciplines human beings into acting and thinking in particular ways. In relation to the human monster, Foucault in his lecture of January 22, 1975, asserts that the "frame of reference" for the human monster is always the law (Foucault 55). The human monster, according to Foucault, violates both the laws of society and the laws of nature (Foucault 55-56). Beyond this, though, the human monster exceeds the capacity of the law to respond to it: "the monster's power and its capacity to create anxiety are due to the fact that it violates the law while leaving it with nothing to say.... [It] is a breach of the law that automatically stands outside the law" (Foucault 56). As a consequence, the response evoked by the human monster is either violence or pity.

Indeed, Foucault's interests often extended explicitly to subjects conventionally regarded as monstrous. Representative here as well is Foucault's brief introduction to the English-language publication of *Herculine Barbin (Being the Recently Discovered Memoirs of a Nineteenth-Century French Hermaphrodite)* (1980), in which he considers the history of hermaphroditism and shifting attitudes regarding it—a topic he had touched on in his lectures of 1974-75 (Foucault 70-74). Foucault notes that in the Middle Ages, European hermaphrodites were typically assigned a sex at baptism but were later free to decide for themselves whether they preferred to continue with the sex assigned to them (Foucault, Introduction viii). As time passed, however, sexuality was increasingly regarded as singular and less fluid: "Biological theories of sexuality, juridical conceptions of individuals, forms of administrative control in modern nations, led little by little to rejecting the idea of a mixture of the two sexes in a single body, and consequently to limiting the free choice of indeterminate individuals. Henceforth, everyone was to have one and only one sex" (Foucault viii).

Foucault's concise consideration of the history of and attitudes regarding hermaphroditism in his introduction to *Herculine Barbin* constitutes a pithy and accessible encapsulation not only of Foucault's general method but of the approach of much contemporary monster theory. Through his repeated considerations of the social construction of the ideas of normalcy and deviancy, and the ways in which these ideas vary and shift, as well as coerce certain behaviors while retarding others, Foucault—often referred to as the great theoretician of power—can also be considered as the great theoretician of monstrosity. His work makes clear that monsters are always "monsters"—not "naturally," universally, or eternally monsters but rather constructed as monstrous through the influence of social conventions, expectations, and attitudes.

Foucault's work was part of a larger twentieth-century social milieu in which marginalized populations—women, people of color, gays and lesbians, and so on—were agitating actively for social justice and equal rights, and his research was influenced by and in turn exerted influence on those seeking to explore how entrenched power dynamics rendered particular populations vulnerable to exploitation and exclusion. Foucault's method and research arguably have been central to the development of numerous disciplines within the humanities and social sciences that have been invested in exploring, highlighting, and resisting the forces that have historically marginalized—or monsterized—particular groups, including postcolonial studies, Jewish studies, feminist studies, disability studies, and gender and sexuality studies. Although the rhetoric of monstrosity may not always be explicit, texts that would need to be highlighted in a genealogy of Foucaultian-influenced monster theory would need to include Edward Said's *Orientalism* (1978), which considers how the West's representations of the East as backward and degraded facilitated imperialist agendas; Stephen Greenblatt's *Marvelous Possessions: The Wonders of the New World* (1992), which explores how Europeans in the late Middle Ages and early modern period represented non-Europeans in ways also facilitating an imperialist agenda; Sander Gilman's *The Jew's Body* (1991), which focuses on anti-Semitic representations of Jewish morphology; Rosemarie Garland-Thomson's *Extraordinary Bodies: Figuring Physical Disability in American Culture and Literature* (1997), a foundational text within disability studies; and Gayle Rubin's 1984 essay "Thinking Sex," which explores how value systems are overlaid on sexual behavior.

These titles—and many others—would then supplement a listing of earlier studies that similarly explore the mechanisms through which particular populations are constructed as monstrous others. Such a catalog would need to include, for example, Simone de Beauvoir's *The Second Sex* (1949), which frames women's oppression as rooted in being constructed as other to man; Frantz Fanon's *Black Skins, White Masks* (1952), which addresses the association of Blackness with inadequacy; philosopher René Girard's exploration of scapegoating in *The Scapegoat* (1982); Hannah Arendt's *The Origins of Totalitarianism* (1951), which scrutinizes anti-Semitism but extends beyond that focus; Erving Goffman's research on social stigmas in *Stigma: Notes on the Management of Spoiled Identity* (1963); and Eric Hoffer's *True Believer: Thoughts on the Nature of Mass Movements* (1951), which analyzes how and why mass movements start and the ways in which they position themselves in opposition to other groups perceived as monstrous.

Foucault's work in the second half of the twentieth century arguably constitutes a "tipping point" as concerns monster theory, as it insists that we consider the label of monster as a mechanism of social control and form of oppression—and it is this understanding of monsters as disenfranchised victims of an oppressive dominant culture that informs the twentieth century's most significant development in monstrous representation: giving voice to the monster. As I've pointed out in a different context, beginning arguably in 1971 with John Gardner's retelling of Beowulf from the monster Grendel's perspective, a central contemporary trend in monstrous narrative has been to let monsters tell their own stories, rendering them comprehensible and often sympathetic (see my "Invisible Monsters"). Particularly in films ostensibly targeted at children, such as the *Shrek* and *Monsters, Inc.* franchises, the "true monster" is shown not to be the fairy tale creature or exotic beast but rather the human society that demonizes somatic difference. Such narratives—products of twentieth- and twenty-first-century civil rights movements—clearly convey a message of tolerance and the valuing of diversity. Monstrosity inheres not in looking different but rather in acting in harmful ways.

Notes

1. On this point, see Ulházy.
2. See chapter 4 of McCracken. See also Walsham, 202–203.
3. See Schutte.
4. See Aquinas, I, q. 51, art. 3, rep. 6.
5. See chapter 20 of Paré; see also Warkany, "History of Teratology," 27–29.
6. See Fiedler, chapter 6.
7. Montaigne, quoted in Wes Williams, 696.
8. See book 1, part 1 of Aristotle, *On the Parts of Animals*.
9. See Hofland.
10. Paré, quoted in Barrow, 23.
11. See Friedman, 112–16.
12. See, my "Freaks in Space: 'Extraterrestrialism' and 'Deep-Space Multiculturalism.'" See also Young.

Works Cited

Aristotle, *On the Parts of Animals*, translated by William Ogle, http://classics.mit.edu/Aristotle/parts_animals.html.

Asma, Stephen. *On Monsters: An Unnatural History of Our Worst Fears*. Oxford University Press, 2009.

Barrow, Mark V. "A Brief History of Teratology to the Early 20th Century." *Teratology*, vol. 4, no. 2, 1971, pp. 119–29.

Bates, Alan W. *Emblematic Monsters: Unnatural Conceptions and Deformed Births in Early Modern Europe*. Rodopi, 2004.
Beal, Timothy. *Religion and Its Monsters*. Routledge, 2002.
Bogdan, Robert. *Freak Show: Presenting Human Oddities for Amusement and Profit*. University of Chicago Press, 1988.
Bosky, Bernadette. "Cryptids" in *The Ashgate Encyclopedia of Literary and Cinematic Monsters*, edited by Jeffrey Andrew Weinstock. Ashgate, 2013, pp. 105–14.
Carroll, Noël. *The Philosophy of Horror: or, Paradoxes of the Heart*. Routledge, 1990.
Cohen, Jeffrey Jerome. "Monster Culture (Seven Theses)" in *Monster Theory: Reading Culture*, edited by Jeffrey Jerome Cohen. University of Minnesota Press, 1996, pp. 3–25.
Davidson, Arnold I. "Introduction" to *Abnormal: Lectures at the Collège de France 1974–1975*, by Michel Foucault, edited by Valerio Marchetti and Antonella Salomoni, translated by Graham Burchell, Picador, 1999, pp. xvii–xxvi.
Davies, Surekha. "The Unlucky, the Bad, and the Ugly: Categories of Monstrosity from the Renaissance to the Enlightenment" in *The Ashgate Research Companion to Monsters and the Monstrous*, edited by Asa Simon Mittman. Ashgate, 2013, pp. 49–76.
Eberhart, George M. "Mysterious Creatures: Creating a Cryptozoological Encyclopedia." *Journal of Scientific Exploration*, vol. 19, no. 1, 2005, pp. 103–113.
Fiedler, Leslie. *Freaks: Myths and Images of the Secret Self*. Anchor Books, 1978.
Foucault, Michel. *Abnormal: Lectures at the Collège de France 1974–1975*, translated by Graham Burchell, edited by Valerio Marchetti and Antonella Salomoni. Picador, 1999.
———. "Introduction" to *Herculine Barbin (Being the Recently Discovered Memoirs of a Nineteenth-Century French Hermaphrodite*. Pantheon, 1980, pp. vii–xvii.
Friedman, John Block. *The Monstrous Races in Medieval Art and Thought*. Syracuse University Press, 2003.
Hofland, Peter. "Reversal of Fortune: How a Vilified Drug Became a Life-Saving Agent in the 'War' against Cancer." *Onco'Zine: The International Oncology Nework*, November 30, 2013, https://oncozine.com/reversal-of-fortune-how-a-vilified-drug-became-a-life-saving-agent-in-the-war-against-cancer/.
Howell, Michael, and Peter Ford. *The True History of the Elephant Man*. Penguin, 1981.
Huet, Marie-Hélène. *Monstrous Imagination*. Harvard University Press, 1993.
McCracken, Peggy. *The Curse of Eve, the Wound of the Hero: Blood, Gender, and Medieval Literature*. University of Pennsylvania Press, 2003.
Mittman, Asa Simon. "Introduction: The Impact of Monsters and Character Studies" in *The Ashgate Research Companion to Monsters and the Monstrous*, edited by Asa Simon Mittman. Ashgate, 2013, pp. 1–16.
Paré, Ambrose. *On Monsters and Marvels*, translated by Janis L. Pallister. University of Chicago Press, 1995.
Saint Augustine of Hippo. *The City of God*, translated by Marcus Dods. The Modern Library, 1950.
Saint Thomas of Aquinas. *The "Summa Theologica" of St. Thomas Aquinas*. Burns, Oates, and Washington, 1920–1942.
Schutte, Anne Jacobson. "'Such Monstrous Births': A Neglected Aspect of the Antinomian Controversy." *Renaissance Quarterly*, vol. 38, no. 1, 1985, pp. 85–106.
Smith, Norman R. "Portent Lore and Medieval Popular Culture." *Journal of Popular Culture*, vol. 14, no. 1, 1980, pp. 47–59.
Stevenson, Ian. "A New Look at Maternal Impressions: An Analysis of 50 Published Cases and Reports of Two Recent Examples." *Journal of Scientific Exploration*, vol. 6, no. 4, 1992, pp. 353–73.
Ulházy, Eduard, et al. "Teratology—Past, Present and Future." *Interdisciplinary Toxicology*, vol. 5, no. 4, 2012, pp. 163–68.
Walsham, Alexandra. *Providence in Early Modern England*. Oxford University Press, 1999.
Warkany, Josef. "History of Teratology" in *The Handbook of Teratology: General Principles and Etiology*, edited by James G. Wilson and F. Clarke Fraser. Springer, 1977.
Weinstock, Jeffrey Andrew. "Freaks in Space: 'Extraterrestrialism' and 'Deep-Space

Multiculturalism'" in *Freakery: Cultural Spectacles of the Extraordinary Body*, edited by Rosemarie Garland Thomson. New York University Press, 1996, pp. 327–37.

———. "Invisible Monsters: Vision, Horror, and Contemporary Culture" in *The Ashgate Research Companion to Monsters and the Monstrous*, edited by Asa Simon Mittman. Ashgate, 2012, pp. 275–92.

Williams, Wes. "Montaigne on Imagination" in *The Oxford Handbook of Montaigne*, edited by Phillipe Desan. Oxford University Press, 2016, pp. 679–98.

Young, Helen. *Race and Popular Fantasy Literatures: Habits of Whiteness*. Routledge, 2015.

Invisible Monsters: Vision, Horror, and Contemporary Culture

It takes a village to make a monster.

By this, I mean that nothing or no one is intrinsically or "naturally" monstrous. Instead, as Jeffrey Jerome Cohen points out in "Monster Culture (Seven Theses)," his introduction to his collection of academic essays on monstrosity, *Monster Theory: Reading Culture* (1996), the monster's body is always "pure culture," the embodiment of culturally specific fears, desires, anxieties, and fantasies (Cohen 4). What follows from this is that ideas of monstrosity and the forms that monsters take will differ across time and from place to place. This stands to reason—what scared people (and what they hoped for) in, say, twelfth-century Europe will obviously differ from what scares people (and what they hope for) in twenty-first-century America. We inevitably make our own monsters with the ingredients we have on hand, so the recipe keeps changing—even when the monsters themselves have been passed down from generation to generation.

The implications of the shifting social constructions of ideas of monstrosity are particularly significant when one bears in mind that what is monstrous is always defined in relation to what is human. The monster is, as Cohen appreciates, "difference made flesh" (7); it is the other, the "not us," that which a culture rejects, disowns, disavows, or, to borrow from Julia Kristeva, "abjects" (Kristeva 1). What this means is that to redefine monstrosity is simultaneously to rethink humanity. When our monsters change, it reflects the fact that we—our understanding of what it means to be human, our relations with one another and to the world around us, our conception of our place in the greater scheme of things—have changed as well.

This chapter will discuss a sequence of interrelated trends governing contemporary Western ideas and representations of monstrosity. While there is of course some continuity between present-day representations of monstrosity and those of previous generations, the differences are telling and offer provocative insight into culturally specific anxieties and desires. To consider our current monsters is to reflect on how we think about ourselves and our relation to the world. I will begin by observing the contemporary disconnection of monstrosity from physical appearance. Beginning with the nineteenth-century Romantics and acquiring a substantial degree of momentum in the twentieth century—especially from post–Second World War reconsiderations of ethnic and racial difference—one significant trend in representing the monster has been to decouple physical abnormality from assumptions about intelligence, character, or morals. As presented in Mary Shelley's *Frankenstein* (1818) and elaborated on in Tim Burton's updated version of Shelley's seminal Gothic tale, *Edward Scissorhands* (1990), looking different is no longer sufficient to categorize a creature as monstrous. Instead, such narratives shift the emphasis onto oppressive cultural forces that unjustly ostracize or victimize those who are physically divergent. When the "monster" becomes the protagonist and culture becomes the antagonist, ideas of normality and monstrosity must be reconsidered. This trend of "sympathy for the devil" culminates in contemporary narratives such as the *Twilight* series (both book and film) in which one aspires toward monstrosity as an escape from the stultification of hegemonic social forces of normalization.

What follows from this decoupling of monstrosity from appearance is an important cultural shift that aligns monstrosity not with physical difference, but with antithetical moral values. Monstrosity thus is reconfigured as a kind of invisible disease that eats away at the body and the body politic, and manifests visibly through symptomatic behavior. I will suggest here that this reconfiguration of monstrosity surfaces in contemporary cultural narratives in four connected ways: (1) through the psychopath (and his first cousin, the terrorist) who lives among us and could be anyone; (2) through the faceless corporation or government agency that finds its impetus in greed and corruption, and sends forth its tendrils into the cracks and crevices of everyday life; (3) through the virus that silently infiltrates and infects the body; and (4) through the conceit of the revenge of an anthropomorphized nature that responds to human despoilment of the environment in dramatic and deadly ways. What links these four related manifestations of contemporary monstrosity is their invisibility and potential ubiquity, and the response that they elicit is a form of paranoia most evident in contemporary conspiracy theories.

I will then conclude this discussion of present-day monstrosity with some consideration of one form that the response to the fear that monsters are everywhere takes—what I will refer to as "rational irrationalism" or the construction of nonsensical origins. These are horror stories and monster movies that, to a certain extent circling around to my initial discussion of "sympathy for the devil," go back in time in the attempt to explain the origins of the monster. The attempt here is to offer a rational explanation for irrational behavior by inserting that behavior into a familiar narrative framework, be it childhood neglect and abuse, scientific hubris, or magic. These narratives, however, ultimately offer only a semblance of logic while in actuality failing to demystify anything. The monster, as Cohen notes, always escapes, can never finally be known or captured fully—which is part of its monstrosity (4).

Sympathy for the Devil

Representations of monsters in mainstream media arguably vacillate back and forth between general cycles of identification and non-identification that develop out of and respond to specific cultural conditions. For example, many of the classic horror movies of the 1930s, such as *Frankenstein* (1931), *The Mummy* (1932), and *King Kong* (1933), offer the viewer sympathetic monsters victimized by cultural forces that reflect the shared senses of alienation and persecution felt by those traumatized by the Great Depression, while monster movies of the 1950s, giving shape to cultural anxieties about communism and atomic energy, offer creatures such as giant irradiated ants (*Them!* 1954) and the Blob (*The Blob*, 1958), for which it is difficult to feel anything other than loathing.[1] Despite these localized cycles, however, the overall trend in monstrous representation across the twentieth century and into the twenty-first has been toward not just sympathizing but empathizing with—and ultimately aspiring to be—the monster. Touchstone twentieth-century texts demonstrating this shift in response to established categories of monstrosity are John Gardner's novel *Grendel* (1971), a retelling of the Beowulf myth from the monster's perspective, and Anne Rice's *Vampire Chronicles* series, featuring her vampire heroes Louis and Lestat, which present to the reader a very attractive representation of the vampire. Twenty-first-century mainstream representations of monsters, most notably animated films oriented toward children such as *Shrek* (2001) and *Monsters, Inc.* (2001), and vampire narratives such as the Home Box Office (HBO) adaptation of the Charlaine Harris *Sookie Stackhouse* novels, *True Blood*, and the Stephenie Meyer *Twilight* franchise, forcefully develop this trend of asking the audience to identify with and even esteem the traditional monster while resisting or reviling the cultural forces that define monstrosity based on non-normative appearance or behavior. The result is a reversal of polarities in which evil is associated not with physical difference, but with cultural forces that constrain personal growth and expression.

John Gardner's 1971 novel *Grendel*, which arguably initiated the current trend of first-person monster narratives, is a retelling of the Anglo-Saxon epic poem, *Beowulf*, from the perspective of its antagonist, the monster Grendel. It is, however, much more than this, as it constitutes an extended meditation on the power and seduction of narrative, the pain of isolation, and what existentialist Jean-Paul Sartre refers to as our "monstrous freedom"—the fact that we alone are responsible for our choices.[2] In contrast to many of the autobiographical accounts told by monsters that follow in its wake, *Grendel* arguably does not ask the reader to sympathize with its main character. The reader comes to understand Grendel and his evil nature more fully, but his behavior is never justified and he is perhaps to be pitied but not liked. What subsequent monster narratives rendered from the monster's point of view do tend to share with *Grendel*—and which Gardner's novel articulates more clearly than any of them—is a sense of the confusion and meaninglessness of existence. *Grendel* in essence asks the reader to consider not just what makes a monster, but if there is a difference between a man and a monster at all.

The attempts to understand what it means to exist and what the implications of existing are can also be found at the heart of Anne Rice's *Vampire Chronicles*, and these questions are emphasized most fully in the first novel in the series, *Interview with the Vampire* (1976), which introduces the reader to Louis, the angst-ridden vampire protagonist, and Lestat, his charismatic and devil-may-care companion. Rice, despite the commonly held misconception, was not the first author to feature the vampire telling his own story—that achievement arguably lies with Fred Saberhagen's *The Dracula Tape*, a novel published one year prior to *Interview* that features Dracula, depicted as the historical figure Vlad Tepes, telling his own story and coming off decidedly better than Van Helsing and the bungling vampire hunters whom he thwarts. Rice's achievement, however, is to create a rich, sensual world in which the traditional monster, the vampire, emerges as the complex and conflicted hero. Gifted with immortality, physical beauty, extraordinary speed and strength, and even the ability to fly, Rice's vampires are essentially transformed into superheroes. At the end of *Interview with the Vampire*, the young interviewer, Daniel, seduced by the power which the vampire possesses, encapsulates the thrust of much post–1970s monster fiction by desiring to *become* a vampire. He aspires to escape the world of the mundane by becoming monster.

Jumping ahead to the twenty-first century, this reversal of polarities, in which the traditional monster becomes the hero, is explicitly combined with an interrogation of the social construction of ideas of normality in works such as *Shrek*, *Monsters, Inc.*, *Twilight*, and *True Blood*. *Shrek* and *Monsters, Inc.*, animated films ostensibly for children but appealing to adults, vigorously decouple monstrosity from physical appearance. The hero of *Shrek* is a traditional fairytale villain, an ogre. His eventual love-interest, Princess Fiona, is a sort of were-ogre—human during the day, ogre at night—and, running contrary to conventional narrative expectations, when presented with the option, she ultimately chooses to remain in her ogre form and to surrender her human one. The villain in the first *Shrek* film is the existing power structure as represented by Lord Farquaad, the diminutive ruler of the kingdom of Duloc. Conventional expectations are reversed even more fully in *Shrek 2* (2004) in which the villains are the physically attractive but morally bankrupt Fairy Godmother and Charming, her vain, spoiled, and egotistical son (who is also the villain in the third *Shrek* incarnation, *Shrek the Third* [2007]). *Monsters, Inc.* presents an even more straightforward disconnection of appearance from monstrosity and interrogation of normality as it presents a world of monsters—most notably kindly monsters Sully (voiced by John Goodman) and Mike (voiced by Billy Crystal)—who are scared of humans. *Monsters, Inc.* is thus entirely the product of contemporary cultural relativism—the awareness that what one culture considers normal may be considered exotic by another.

The *Shrek* films and *Monsters, Inc.* teach the lesson that it is moral values and behavior, not physical appearance, that define monstrosity. The hip HBO series *True Blood*, targeted at a more mature audience, adds to this contemporary awareness of cultural relativism attentiveness to the ways in which monstrosity is a socially constructed category used to police behavior and empower the arbiters of right and wrong. The premise of the series is that, co-opting a metaphor from the gay rights movement, vampires—who have always lived among humans—have decided to "come out of the coffin" and reveal their existence to the world. The push for "vampire rights" prompts a conservative backlash, as expressed in the opening credits of each episode by a billboard reading "God hates fangs," a tongue-in-cheek parody of evangelical homophobia. By paralleling vampires with homosexuals, each group unjustly demonized by a society with narrow ideas of socially correct behavior, the series prompts the awareness not just of the ways in which the term "monster" has functioned as a convenient catch-all rubric for any individual, group, race, or culture whose appearance, behavior, or values run contrary to prevailing social norms in a given time and place, but also of how the deployment of the term "monster" is a powerful political tool for the furthering of particular political designs. Expressed in *True Blood*, as in other contemporary revisions of traditional monster narratives, is the suspicion that it is those who refer to others as monsters who themselves are most deserving of the label.

The contemporary reversal of values, in which traditional monsters and individuals with non-normative appearances are recast as heroes, is at the center of any number of modern literary and cinematic narratives—most notably comic books and their cinematic adaptations, such as the *Hellboy* films (*Hellboy* [2004], *Hellboy II: The Golden Army* [2008]) featuring a demon fighting on the side of good, the X-Men stories in which "mutants" advocate for their freedom from conservative forces of bigotry, *The League of Extraordinary Gentleman* (film, 2003) which features Mr. Hyde cast in an heroic role and Mina Harker from Bram Stoker's *Dracula* (1897) as both a vampire and a hero, the Incredible Hulk stories, and so on—but nowhere is the attractiveness of monstrosity more vividly illustrated than in the novels and film adaptations of Stephenie Meyer's *Twilight* series, in which vampires and werewolves are presented as powerful and beautiful. As anyone with even a passing familiarity with these narratives is aware, at the center of the series is protagonist Bella, who falls in love with, essentially, the perfect man, Edward (played by Robert Pattinson in the films), who turns out to be a vampire—albeit a "vegetarian" one who resists drinking human blood. Although a monster as conceived of in traditional thinking, Edward in the *Twilight* narratives is represented as more angelic than demonic. Indeed, he is the apotheosis of the modern sensitive man rather than a repellent monster, and he offers to Bella love, excitement, protection, and escape from the mundane.

The Monster Among Us: The Psychokiller

What first-person narrative accounts told from the monster's perspective and monster tales highlighting cultural relativism effectively assert is that, while we still recognize and refer to traditional monsters as such, the idea of monstrosity has been decoupled from physical appearance and today refers first and foremost to the intention and desire to do harm to the innocent. This redefinition of monstrosity, however, creates a conundrum for contemporary citizens: how does one remain safe in a world in which anyone could be a monster? This is the powerful epistemological anxiety underpinning the popularity of contemporary crime programs like the *CSI: Crime Scene Investigation* franchise, narratives of psychopaths and serial killers, and in a twist with very practical "real world" implications, paranoia concerning terrorists. What Shrek and Sully and Lestat and Edward Cullen present to us are traditional monsters that act humanely—that demonstrate the care and concern for others and the range of emotional responses which we currently define as characteristic of humanity; what *Psycho*'s Norman Bates (1960), and his figurative offspring, *American Psycho*'s Patrick Bateman (book, 1991; film, 2000), *The Silence of the Lambs*'

Hannibal Lecter (book, 1988; film, 1991), to a certain extent the Showtime series *Dexter*'s eponymous antihero, and popular conceptualizations of terrorists such as the September 11 hijackers all have in common is that they look human while in reality being, from the contemporary perspective, monsters. Through his antisocial actions, the psychopath and the murderous terrorist make visible the internal lack of humanity obscured by their human facades—they are monsters on the inside.

Norman Bates, the antagonist of Alfred Hitchcock's film *Psycho*, famously played by Anthony Perkins, is arguably the poster boy for contemporary monstrosity. What is so disconcerting about Norman is just how *normal* and average he appears. Clean-cut, polite, and diffident, Norman disarms those whom he encounters with the appearance of wholesomeness. What the viewer dramatically discovers at the end of the film, however, is that Norman is not one person, but two—he suffers from multiple personality disorder and has internalized his "mother," who refuses to allow him to express adult male sexuality and instead orders him to kill any woman who arouses his lust. Norman thereby defies the conventional expectation that an individual personality be singular and coherent. He is in a sense possessed, compelled by a demonic force within to commit monstrous acts. The result is a disconnection between his external wholesomeness and his internal diseased state. He is a monster whose monstrousness only becomes visible through his actions.

The shock of *Psycho* is the revelation of Norman's mental disorder. Bret Easton Ellis tips his hat to *Psycho* both through the title of his novel, *American Psycho*, and through the name of his antihero protagonist, Patrick Bateman. Ellis, however, in curious ways inverts *Psycho*. To begin with, the narrative is a first-person account told from Bateman's perspective, in which he first reveals his obsessive materialist "yuppie" concerns with wealth and status, and then increasingly details his sadistic murders involving rape, torture, cannibalism, and necrophilia. Who the murderer is in *American Psycho* is not concealed and, as a result, the narrative suspense is shifted to when and whether he will be caught. In the end, though, Ellis undercuts the reader's expectations by raising questions as to whether Bateman has actually committed the horrendous acts that he narrates or if they were instead all in his mind—sick fantasies. Like Norman Bates, however, Patrick Bateman presents a facade of normality that obscures his monstrous, sadistic desires and, again like Norman, Patrick is clearly mentally deranged. Whether a murderer in fact or in fantasy, Patrick nevertheless is a Harvard-educated Wall Street monster whose monstrosity defies easy visual detection.

In contrast to Norman Bates and Patrick Bateman, who are made easy to revile in the end, Thomas Harris's creation, Hannibal Lecter, and

Dexter of the Showtime series of the same name, based on the novels by Jeff Lindsay, are especially interesting—and troubling—manifestations of the psychopathic serial killer, as each is presented to varying degrees as simultaneously monstrous and heroic. Hannibal Lecter is a brilliant, soft-spoken, and cultured psychologist—which jars greatly with his murderous and cannibalistic impulses. As with Norman Bates and Patrick Bateman, one wouldn't know Lecter for the monster he is were his psychotic tendencies not explained to the viewer and then revealed through his actions. Nevertheless, despite knowing Lecter for a monster—indeed, in *Silence of the Lambs*' most brutal sequence the viewer observes Lecter reveal himself from beneath the flayed face of one of his guards that he has used to disguise himself—the narrative still manages to present Lecter as an attractive and compelling force. Because he is cultured; because his foil in villainy, Buffalo Bill, is so repulsive; because of the bond he forms with Detective Starling (Jodie Foster) whom he assists; and because he is so vastly more interesting than the repressive system of law and order that underestimates him, our sympathies are strangely enlisted on behalf of Lecter.

Showtime's Dexter, who is essentially Hannibal Lecter with a stricter moral system, engages those same sympathies. Dexter is the monster aware of his own monstrosity—he takes pains to hide it, but cannot suppress it entirely. As revealed in the series, Dexter is a sociopath who was taught by his adoptive police officer father to direct his murderous tendencies only toward other killers. Dexter must have proof that an individual is guilty of murdering an innocent person, lacks remorse, and intends to kill again before he murders the murderer. Dexter (who in interesting ways seems indebted to Kevin Spacey's character, John Doe, in *Se7en* [1995] who is a sociopath that kills those he considers reprehensible) is the dark side to the superhero narrative—he is essentially Batman if Batman did not only brutally apprehend villains but also intentionally killed them. And the trick of the series is to seduce the viewer into not just excusing but indeed sanctioning Dexter's "eye-for-an-eye" system of justice that allows him to be both hero and murderer. What Dexter, however, has in common with almost all accounts of serial killers and psychopaths is that, on the surface, he looks like a normal, average person. His monstrosity is an internal, irresistible force that compels him to harm others.

Monsters, as I have suggested above, give shape to culturally specific anxieties and desires. It is no surprise then that, in the wake of the contemporary decoupling of appearance from monstrosity, concerns that anyone could be a monster and monsters could be anywhere should find, in our post–9/11 world, especially compelling embodiment in the figure of the terrorist. The terrorist—more a convention of the action genre in film and literature than horror—is essentially the sociopath with a focused and often more political impetus for his monstrous desire to do harm and, as such, terrorist narratives are often more explicitly ideological than conventional monster narratives. When Jack Bauer (Kiefer Sutherland) saves the President and the United States from violent extremists on *24*, he is supporting a particular set of beliefs and way of life. The problem for Jack Bauer and Homeland Security, and citizens riding the New York subway, however, is that—racial profiling notwithstanding—the terrorist, like the serial killer, presents no obvious external markers of his monstrosity. This is why old women and young children must go through metal detectors at airports. All of us are potentially psychopathic terrorists. We are subjected to these visual prostheses because vision is not enough to separate out the monsters from the rank and file of humanity. We no longer recognize a monster when we see one.

The Monster is Everywhere: Corporations, Governments, and Conspiracy Theories

It is really only a small step from the concern that anyone could be a monster and the monster could be anywhere to the paranoiac fantasy that *everyone* is a monster and the monster is *everywhere*. The invisibility of the monster allows it to infiltrate the city, the countryside, even the intimate domestic space of the home. In her excellent study of monsters, *Pretend We're Dead: Capitalist Monsters in American Pop Culture*, Annalee Newitz surveys contemporary manifestations of a particular monster narrative, stories in which capitalism transforms human beings into monsters that cannot distinguish between commodities and people (Newitz 2). In the course of her analysis, she considers serial killers, mad doctors, the undead, robots, and—curiously—people involved in the media industry. What she omits from her discussion are corporate and government officers dedicated to furthering the greed-driven, insidious ambitions of power-hungry, capitalist organizations.

In the 1950s—as expressed in "Red Scare" monster movies such as *The Thing from Another World* (1951) and *Invasion of the Body Snatchers* (1956)—the anxiety that "communism" was infecting American democracy was rife. The problem with a communist—like a sociopath or terrorist—is that he is not immediately visually distinguishable. You could have Bolsheviks in your company washroom, as the famous propaganda poster states, and not even know it! Following the Vietnam War and the Watergate scandal—as well as the dissolution of the USSR and the fall of the Berlin Wall—social anxieties shifted from concerns about communist infiltration to concerns about corporate and government encroachment into everyday life, and these concerns have found expression in science fiction, fantasy, and horror narratives from *Alien* (1979) to *Avatar* (2009), and most notably in *The X-Files* television series which ran from 1993 until 2002, which are all linked by an emphasis on the monstrousness of capitalist corporations and corrupt government organizations.

The ostensible monster in *Alien* and its various sequels is obviously the nightmarish double-mouthed extraterrestrial designed by H.R. Giger. Just as monstrous and more insidious, however, is the corporation (unnamed in the first film, but subsequently identified in later films as the "Weyland-Yutani Corporation") that desires a specimen of the alien life form and considers the crew expendable in achieving this objective. In *Alien*, the agent of the corporation is the android, Ash (Ian Holm). In the 1986 sequel, *Aliens*, the corporate agent is Carter Burke (Paul Reiser at his most smarmy), a human. Both, however, have been "programmed" by the corporation to disregard human life and safety if it promotes the corporation's capitalist agenda. The *Alien* films thus essentially have two monsters—the alien itself and the bigger monster, the monstrous corporation, that just as clearly feeds off the lives of the human characters.

This monsterization of the corporation (with an eco-friendly twist) becomes the motor force propelling the blockbuster *Avatar* (2009)—which, in keeping with the decoupling of appearance from monstrosity addressed above, casts the "traditional" monsters in the roles of sympathetic victims and heroes. *Avatar* is about a rapacious corporation conducting mining operations on the distant planet Pandora inhabited by the Na'vi, ten-foot tall, blue-skinned sapient humanoids who live in harmony with nature. When the RDA Corporation discovers a huge mineral deposit under the massive tree which constitutes the Na'vi home, the Na'vi are attacked and forced to leave, the tree is destroyed, and the area despoiled. Eventually, the Na'vi—led by human Jake Sully, a paraplegic former marine whose consciousness animates an "avatar" Na'vi body—band together and, assisted by other Pandoran creatures, fight back and successfully repel the human invaders. The heroes in this film, upending the conventions of science fiction, are giant blue extraterrestrials. The monster is the human-run RDA Corporation—especially as represented by the head of RDA's private security force, Colonel Miles Quaritch (Stephen Lang)—which has no compunction about displacing and killing the Na'vi and destroying both their way of life and their planet.

Post-Watergate suspicion of the government as a monster furthering its own clandestine and menacing agenda without regard for the health or welfare of the general populace is the recurring theme of any number of films, including *Three Days of the Condor* (1976), *JFK* (1991), and *Enemy of the State* (1998), but finds its fullest expression through the hit 1990s television series, *The X-Files*. One of the primary slogans of the program (flashed during the opening credits of each episode), "Trust No One," clearly indicates the disposition of the program's primary detective, Fox Mulder (David Duchovny), who believes that a vast government conspiracy to hide evidence of extraterrestrial contact has occurred and that the U.S. government is conspiring with aliens and other governments on a range of sinister projects. While approximately two out of every three X-Files episodes were stand-alone, in which Mulder, together with his partner, the skeptic Dana Scully (Gillian Anderson), investigated bizarre cases involving paranormal phenomena, the main story arc involving government conspiracy and a shadowy division of the government called "The Syndicate"—represented by the Smoking Man (William B. Davis), a merciless killer and masterful political strategist—effectively characterized the government itself as the series' most ruthless and craftiest monster.

As is the case in narratives about serial killers and terrorists, what is most unsettling in stories of corporate greed and government conspiracy is that the monster defies visual identification. And it is not just that hidden behind the facades of business executives and government officers lurk consuming lusts for power and wealth; beyond this, what is most disturbing about such narratives is the diffuse nature of the Kafka-esque monster that cannot be located, much less killed. Like a classical monster, the hydra, corporations and governments have many heads and if *The X-Files* teaches us anything, it is that for every "Smoking Man" apprehended, two more spring up in his place.

The Monster Is Inside Us: The Virus

If the monster can be everywhere by virtue of its invisibility, if the snaky tendrils of corporate greed or government manipulation can bypass one's defenses and penetrate the intimate spaces of one's life, the logical final extension of this infiltration is the possibility that the invisible monster (invisible, at least, to the naked eye) is already within us. This fear is at the heart of the subgenre of film (also generalizable to literature) that Murray Pomerance has referred to as the "infection film"—films governed by the "omnipresent suggestion that the body (a body politic, a body of cultural wisdom, and most essentially, of course, a protagonist's [usually beautiful] personal body) has been surreptitiously invaded, and that defenses treated in some central way as 'natural' and hegemonic have been outwitted, outmanned, outperformed, overrun, or bypassed" (Pomerance 205). The monster in such narratives is microscopic and the threat it presents is generally either death—often on a massive scale—or monstrous transformation. The virus as bringer of death is the underlying premise of films such as *The Andromeda Strain* (book, 1969; film, 1971) and *Outbreak* (1995). The virus as agent of monstrous transformation is the recurring premise of many zombie and vampire films such as *28 Days Later* (2002) and *I Am Legend* (1997).

The Andromeda Strain interestingly shares a basic conceit with the seminal zombie horror movie, *Night of the Living Dead*, released only one year prior to Michael Crichton's novel—that of extraterrestrial infection. In George A. Romero's *Night of the Living Dead*, the reanimation of the recently deceased and their cannibalistic appetite is credited to radiation released by the explosion of a returning space probe in the Earth's atmosphere. In *The Andromeda Strain*, the concern is over an extraterrestrial microorganism returned to Earth on a military satellite. The microorganism, dubbed the "Andromeda Strain," fatally clots human blood in most people, while causing suicidal or psychotic behavior in others, and the basic plot of both book and film is to isolate the organism, keep it from spreading, and develop a cure. In Wolfgang Petersen's *Outbreak*—which derives its impetus from the late twentieth-century AIDS pandemic—the culprit is a lethal virus originating in Africa. Combining the infection theme with the government conspiracy theme, the revelation in *Outbreak* is that the military discovered the virus 30 years prior to the California-based epidemic and has been experimenting with it as a form of germ warfare. *Outbreak*, like *Alien*, thus has two monsters: the virus itself and the military, especially as represented by Major General Donald McClintock (Donald Sutherland), who is willing to bomb the infected town of Cedar Creek to cover up his culpability in the viral epidemic and to continue his weapons development unimpeded.

In *28 Days Later* and *I Am Legend*, scientific experimentation goes horribly awry. In *28 Days Later*, animal rights activists break into a scientific research facility to free chimpanzees being used for medical research. In the process, they become infected with a disease referred to only as "Rage," which turns individuals psychotic. (While not technically a zombie film, the movie is often classified as such, given the resemblance of the infected to the living dead.) The virus spreads quickly throughout England and the plot centers on the struggle of the main characters to survive in a post-apocalyptic landscape. The plot of Will Smith's *I Am Legend*—the most recent adaptation of Richard Matheson's 1954 novel of the same name—is similar. A re-engineered strain of measles virus, developed as a treatment for cancer, mutates and becomes lethal, killing 90 percent of the world's population. Of those remaining, most are transformed into animalistic, aggressive creatures intolerant of sunlight. (Matheson's novel actually has vampires in it; the 2007 film adaptation does not.) The plot of the film concerns U.S. Army virologist Lieutenant Colonel Robert Neville's (Will Smith) dual quests to stay alive and to develop a cure for the virus.

All four films are representative of contemporary infection paranoia in which the virus takes center stage as a modern variant of the monster. Such films clearly reflect contemporary anxieties concerning both germ warfare and pandemics such as AIDS, the Ebola virus, Bird Flu, and Swine Flu. By virtue of its invisibility to the naked eye, not only does the virus have the potential to be everywhere and to bypass all boundaries, but the real concern is that we may already be infected without knowing it. The monster may not only be lurking without, but within, defying visibility until its horrific effects occur.

Reaping What We Have Sown: Nature as the Monster

Closely related to the viral pandemic is the recurring contemporary nightmare of nature's revenge. Indeed, in monster virus narratives such as *I Am Legend*, the holocaust is often shown to be the product of man's tampering with nature—human hubris, sometimes with benevolent intentions, sometimes not, results in tragedy. In these instances, we literally make our own monsters. This is essentially the same story that gets played out in eco-disaster films in which human beings must contend for survival against an anthropomorphized mother nature. In films such as *The Day After Tomorrow* (2004) and most interestingly in M. Night Shyamalan's *The Happening* (2008), nature becomes monster as it actively—and with seeming intentionality—threatens human survival.

The Day After Tomorrow offers the most vivid representation of nature's revenge through its depiction of the catastrophic effects of global warming. What takes place in *The Day After Tomorrow* is a sequence of extreme weather events—including snowstorms in India, devastating hail in Japan, monster tornadoes in Los Angeles, and a massive super-hurricane that swamps New York with a 40-foot storm surge—all of which culminate in the ushering in of a new ice age. In this film, nature is the enemy—a monster of irresistible force seemingly punishing the human race for its failure to care for the environment. The thrust of the film, therefore, is that—just like any mad scientist in the typical "overreacher" horror film—humanity's overstepping of natural boundaries gives rise to the monster that wreaks its bloody revenge upon its arrogant creator. The nature-as-monster plot takes the idea of the monster being everywhere to its fullest possible expression: the world as monster bent on human destruction.

In *The Happening*, writer and director M. Night Shyamalan combines the themes of nature as monster and virus as monster to give us one of the most unsettling portrayals of the potential consequences of human alteration of the environment. The plot of the film is, in keeping with disaster films in general, the struggle for survival of a small group of people in a decimated landscape. In this instance, the struggle is against a mysterious neurotoxin that is carried by the wind and causes those infected to commit suicide. While there is no definitive explanation for the existence of the neurotoxin, the primary hypothesis presented in the film is that it is being released by trees and other plants that have developed a capacity to defend themselves against human encroachment. At the end of the film, the pandemic gripping the east coast of the United States abruptly abates, but an expert on television, comparing the outbreak to a red tide (aquatic algal blooms of harmful phytoplankton), warns that the epidemic may have just been a first sally, as plants respond to the human threat to the planet by releasing toxins. The film then concludes with a recurrence of the pandemic beginning in Paris.

What stands out about *The Happening* is the literal form of intentionality attributed to nature. The proposition presented in the film is that nature is aggressively responding to human desecration of the environment by fighting back in a particularly dramatic and perversely poetic way—we are literally killing ourselves, stresses the film, as a result of destroying nature. Of particular note within the film are shots that normally would be considered pastoral and soothing—of the wind blowing across fields of grass, for example, and of trees swaying in the breeze—that are infused by the plot with a sense of dread and fear. As Eliot (Mark Wahlberg), Alma (Zooey Deschanel), and Jess (Ashlyn Sanchez) attempt to flee nature's wrath, nature itself seems consciously to be pursuing them with the intention of killing them. But how does one run from the wind and where can one hide when the monster is the earth itself?

Rational Irrationalism or the Search for False Origins

The progression that this chapter has charted in terms of conceiving present-day monstrosity is one that has moved from the idea that, in the wake of decoupling monstrosity from appearance, anyone could be a monster (the psychopath), to the concern that everyone is a monster (the corporate or governmental conspiracy), to the concern that the monster is everywhere, including potentially within us (the virus and nature as antagonists). What links these four manifestations of contemporary monstrosity (psychopath, corporation, virus, nature) is epistemological anxiety related to visibility. We used to be able to recognize a monster when we saw one and therefore to act accordingly in the name of self-preservation. But how do you avoid a monster that you cannot see? How do you identify the monster when it could be anyone or anywhere? The recurring concern underlying contemporary monster narratives is that, through a sort of retroactive causality, we can now only determine the monster's presence through its effects. We know a serial killer is on the loose, that a corporation has prioritized wealth over health, that a deadly virus is spreading, or that nature is "angry," only after people start dying and the bodies begin to pile up—and the casualties then continue to mount as the protagonist is forced to determine who the monster is and how to combat it (assuming resistance is even possible).

I would like to suggest as a conclusion to this chapter that one cultural response to the epistemological barrier erected by invisibility and the anxiety attending it is the attempt to extend vision temporally and to augment it prosthetically so as to define, situate, and comprehend monstrosity and thus to be able to predict it. The attempt is to create narratives that allow us to see the invisible—to determine the origins of the monster and thus to understand—to see—what we are dealing with. More often than not, however, rather than producing actual understanding, the monster is inserted into a familiar, but nonsensical, narrative—an origin story that presents the semblance of logic, but under closer scrutiny is revealed to explain very little at all. Norman Bates's murderous inclinations in *Psycho* are revealed to be the product of a controlling mother, and the psychologist at the end of *Psycho* presents a compelling narrativization of Norman's psychoses, but what, in fact, is actually explained? Similarly, the hypothesis in *The Happening* is that nature is responding to human encroachment by producing deadly neurotoxins—an explanation that makes a kind of narrative sense, but very little from a scientific perspective. This is what I call "rational irrationalism"—a logical narration of nonsensical origins that has three significant effects: it responds to the reader or viewer's desire to make sense of what is taking place; however, it does not fully satisfy this desire, and it therefore leaves a residue of mystery and a sense of unease that allows for further elaboration in a sequel.

Vampire narratives in particular tend to be obsessed with making visible the invisible and providing origin stories that make no actual sense. One sees this in Rice's *Vampire Chronicles* when the origins of the vampire are traced back to ancient Egypt and demonic possession. One sees it repeatedly in vampire films such as *Blade* (1998) that attempt to offer a veneer of scientific plausibility, as well as in infection films, through the now-iconic shot of the scientist looking through the microscope and observing infected blood cells, indicating the presence of different or diseased blood. And one sees it in romantic horror films, such as Francis Ford Coppola's *Bram Stoker's Dracula* (1992), which trace the origins of the vampire back to heresy, magic, and the "true love conquers all" narrative; since this movie offers the most explicit example of what I am calling rational irrationalism, I would like to close by focusing on it in a bit more detail.

Bram Stoker's novel, *Dracula*, provides no explanation for the vampire's existence. In the 1992 film adaptation, however, Coppola felt the need to supply one and thus invented a beginning that, while explaining the vampire's existence, in actuality explains nothing. What the viewer learns is that, in 1462, Vlad Dracula, aka Vlad Țepeș, returned from battling the Turks to discover that his wife and the love of his live, Elisabeta, had committed suicide after receiving false reports of his death. Enraged by this ironic twist of fate, Dracula desecrates a chapel and renounces God, as blood dramatically wells up from candles, the communion font, and the heart of a large cross that he stabs with his sword. Developing this thwarted love plot further, the film then has the infamous Count stalking Mina Harker because he believes her to be the reincarnation of his lost love, Elisabeta.

Despite being titled *Bram Stoker's Dracula*, this origin story for Dracula and the explanation of his pursuit of Mina finds no basis in Stoker's narrative. Rather, it is Coppola's invention and satisfies the modern desire for explanations. It tells the viewer how and why Dracula transformed into a monster, what animates him, and why he pursues Mina Harker in the way that he does. It makes the monster comprehensible by inserting him into the familiar narrative paradigm "love never dies." This is, of course, the same underlying explanatory framework that structures a large number of ostensible "monster" movies; from tales of the mummy, in which the animated mummy pursues the reincarnation of his ancient bride, to ghost stories such as the paradigmatic *Ghost* (1990), starring Patrick Swayze and Demi Moore, in which the murdered Sam Wheat (Swayze) hovers around his wife, Molly (Moore), until she is out of danger and his murderers are brought to justice, the desire to believe that departed loved ones are still "out there," looking out for us, is powerful indeed. The narrative is comforting because it is familiar, but in actuality it makes sense of nothing. The "logical" origin story that it conveys remains irrational, but it does powerful ideological work in supporting the cultural investment in the ideas of marriage, monogamous love, and divine justice, so it is received as making sense.

In *Bram Stoker's Dracula*, Mina recalls her previous life as Elisabeta; in *Ghost*, Molly "sees" Sam through the mediation of the psychic Oda Mae Brown (Whoopi Goldberg); in *Blade*, we see the vampire blood cells; in *Dexter*, we learn how Dexter became what he is. In other contemporary horror films centered on invisibility and vision—such as *Predator* (1987), in which the alien monster has a cloaking device, and *Pitch Black* (2000), in which the monsters only come out at night and when an eclipse is looming—the drive is toward visualization, both figurative and literal. Recalling the repeated mantra of *Avatar*, the "I see you" expression of love, the attempt is again and again to *see* our monsters for what they are, to bring them into view, to understand them, and thus to gain some control over them. Underlying this obsessive emphasis on the visual, including the rational irrationalism of familiar but illogical origin stories, is the deeply seated contemporary anxiety that our monsters are no longer visible until they kill. In the wake of the modern decoupling of monstrosity from appearance, the monster can be anyone and anywhere, and we only know it when it springs upon us or emerges from within us.

Notes

1. Inasmuch as these monsters from the 1950s are thinly veiled metaphors for communism, they are on some level "human." Nevertheless, while we may recognize them as such, the films prevent us from overcoming our fundamental aversion to them.
2. On the idea of monstrous freedom, see Sartre, 22.

Works Cited

Cohen, Jeffrey Jerome. "Monster Culture (Seven Theses)" in *Monster Theory: Reading Culture*, edited by Jeffrey Jerome Cohen. University of Minnesota Press, 1996, pp. 3–25.
Kristeva, Julia. *The Powers of Horror: An Essay on Abjection*, translated by Leon S. Roudiez. Columbia University Press, 1982.
Newitz, Annalee. *Pretend We're Dead: Capitalist Monsters in American Pop Culture*. Duke University Press, 2006.
Pomerance, Murray. "What is *Happening* to M. Night Shyamalan: Meditation on an 'Infection' Film" in *Critical Approaches to the Films of M. Night Shyamalan: Spoiler Warnings*, edited by Jeffrey Andrew Weinstock. Palgrave Macmillan, 2010, pp. 203–18.
Sartre, Jean-Paul. *The Family Idiot: Gustave Flaubert 1821–1857*, translated by Carol Cosman. University of Chicago Press, 1989.

What Is IT? Ambient Dread and Modern Paranoia in *It* (2017), *It Follows* (2014), and *It Comes at Night* (2017)

This essay finds its impetus in the curious convergence of three twenty-first-century horror films around the ambiguous "It" foregrounded by their titles: Andrés Muschietti's 2017 adaptation of the first half of Stephen King's 1986 novel *IT*, David Robert Mitchell's 2014 *It Follows*, and Trey Edward Shults's 2017 *It Comes at Night*. In each of these films, the titular "it" is difficult or impossible to pin down; it can assume the form of anyone (or, in the case of Shults's film, infect anyone) and appear anywhere; it cannot be reasoned with, explained, or swayed from its course; and conventional sources of protection—the law, and particularly the family—all come up short when confronting it. In this way, the ambiguous "its" of these three films can be seen as crystallizations of a twenty-first-century zeitgeist in which monstrosity seems particularly difficult to locate and defuse. While it is certainly true that horror has a long history of invisible, mysterious forces that are difficult to pin down or name, my argument here is that, in the age of terrorism, mass shootings and what is called in the U.S. "stranger danger," climate change, global pandemics and the related "social distancing," the omnipresence and ambiguity of modern threat has become a central theme. These three films, clustering as they do around questions of how to identify and grapple with an "IT," a menace that can appear anywhere and assume different forms, thus exemplify the ways in which horror films serve as a barometer of pervasive cultural anxieties. How does one respond to a threat that could come from anywhere or anyone—particularly when others can't believe or won't admit that the threat is even real?

By raising monstrous ambiguity to the level of central theme, these three films offer particular insight into how monsters and horror films featuring them function in general. As Jeffrey Jerome Cohen discusses in his seminal "Monster Culture (Seven Theses)," monsters are by nature ambiguous as they violate the categorical distinctions human beings prefer to keep their world tidy and intelligible: living/dead, animal/human, machine/human, sentient/insentient, and so on. A good bit of what is threatening about monsters, according to Asa Mittman, inheres in the ways their categorical ambiguity throws our interpretive schemas out the window, inducing what Mittman describes as a kind of epistemological "vertigo": "the monstrous is that which creates this sense of vertigo, that which calls into question our (their, anyone's) epistemological worldview, highlights its fragmentary and inadequate nature, and thereby asks us ... to acknowledge the failures of our systems of categorization" (8). "Monster" thus serves as a kind of catch-all category, the miscellaneous folder for things that don't otherwise fit. Ambiguity is in this way a defining feature of monstrosity—all monsters are in this sense "its" in the sense of "my God, what is it?!"

Monsters are by nature ambiguous in another way as well: they represent more than one thing at the same time. Jack Halberstam (writing as Judith Halberstam) makes this case asserting that "monsters are meaning machines. They can represent gender, race, nationality, class, and sexuality in one body" (21–22). Chief among Halberstam's examples of this is Bram Stoker's vampire Dracula from his 1897 novel, which can be interpreted as condensing Victorian anxieties about masculinity in crisis, uppity women, homosexuality, foreigners, Jews, the waning of conventional religious observance, and so on. Monsters in this sense are like overdetermined elements in a dream—they are an effect traceable back to multiple causes.

That said, what is so compelling about the ambiguous its of *IT*, *It Follows*, and *It Comes at Night* is the way they take the inherent ambiguity of the monster as their primary theme. In this way, they not only function as kinds of "meta-monsters," laying bare the structure of monstrosity in general through a type of hyperbolic ambiguity, but also act as canny commentary on contemporary anxieties clustering around visibility and the ability to identify threat. If monsters are "pure culture" condensing, as Cohen suggests, "a time, a feeling, and a place" (4), the protean and/or invisible Its of these three films render in stark relief a pervasive contemporary anxiety related to the ambiguity of modern threat and the insufficiency of conventional safeguards to contain or combat it. Not adhering strictly to convention of addressing films in chronological order, this essay will begin with a consideration of Muschietti's 2017 *It*, which achieved unprecedented levels of cultural saturation, breaking box office records and, at least as of late 2018, becoming the highest-grossing horror film of all time (D'Alessandro); it will then jump back in time three years to Mitchell's *It Follows*, which, although preceding Muschietti's *It* chronologically, in some respects seems to naturally follow it as the ambiguity of threat is amplified; I then close the essay by returning to 2017 with a discussion of Shults's *It Comes at Night*—a film in which invisible threat becomes all pervasive. My argument is that the modern, monstrous Its of these films emerge from the fog of a kind of contemporary ambient dread, embodying the paranoia we feel when danger seems everywhere but nowhere we can put our finger on.

The Losers' Club: Muschietti's It

Muschietti's *IT*, one should note at the start, is not complete in itself; rather, in keeping with the two-part structure of King's sprawling novel that divides between the initial battle with the shapeshifting Pennywise the Clown (ITs preferred form) and the final confrontation 27 years later, the 2017 film gives us the first half of the story. This essay focuses on the first film not just because the essay was drafted before the release of *It: Chapter Two* in 2019, but because the first film offers such a clear demonstration of the thesis being advanced here concerning the inscrutability and ubiquity of twenty-first-century threat.[1] One must also acknowledge that Muschietti's film is an adaption of a novel from 1986; however, the focus of this present essay is less on where King got his idea, or how it was received and interpreted over three decades ago when it was first released, than on why the ambiguous nature of the narrative's monstrous threat might resonate especially well with viewers in the second decade of the twenty-first century.

As in many of King's stories, it also must be pointed out that *IT* has two monsters, with the latter being essentially a distillation of the former. In keeping with Tony Magistrale's observation that "real horrors in King's novels ... are neither new nor supernatural" ("Defining," 2), the first monster in a Stephen King story is often a small town that looks quaint on the surface and turns out to be rotten underneath. These towns—including Derry, Maine, where *IT* is set; Chamberlain, Maine, in *Carrie* (1974); Jerusalem's Lot in *'Salem's Lot* (1975); and Castle Rock, Maine, in a number of stories including *Needful Things* (1991)—are places where a charming small-town façade obscures a range of vices and crimes ranging from petty jealousy and vindictiveness, bullying, and bigotry to child abuse, incest, and murder. The wholesome façade of these towns is frequently ripped in particular by plots involving children who are victims of neglect and abuse from both parents and peers.

Although less developed than in King's novel, Muschietti's adaptation of *IT* certainly conforms to this framework. At the center of both book and cinematic adaptation is the "Losers' Club," a cobbled together family of misfits and outcasts. Bill Denbrough (Jaeden Lieberher) stutters and has lost his brother Georgie (Jackson Robert Scott) to the monstrous IT (Bill Skarsgård); Ben Hanscom (Jeremy Ray Taylor) is bullied at school for being both the new kid and overweight; Beverly Marsh (Sophia Lillis) is bullied as well for not fitting in and for false rumors of her promiscuity; Stan Uris (Wyatt Oleff) is Jewish and suffers from a form of OCD; Eddie Kaspbrak (Jack Dylan Grazer) is a hypochondriac; Mike Hanlon (Chosen Jacobs) is black and home schooled; and Richie Tozier (Finn Wolfhard) is a loudmouth who wears glasses. Neglected or abused by parents and bullied by their peers, the members of the Losers' Club band together to confront the doubled monstrosity of both the world in general and IT in particular.[2]

Concerning the former, a remarkable aspect of Muschietti's adaptation is the complete absence of nurturing adults or sympathetic peers. As in King's novel, "grownups don't really 'see' their own children, or if they do, it is only long enough to abuse them" (Magistrale, *Landscapes* 113).[3] Bill's dad (Geoffrey Pounsett), grieving over the loss of Georgie, is distant and dismissive—and Bill's mother is barely present in the film; Stan's dad (a rabbi, played by Ari Cohen) is disappointed in him for a lack of interest in Judaism; Eddie's mother (Molly Jane Atkinson) is the source of his hypochondria, having convinced him that he is ill and must stay close to her for his own protection; Beverly's father (Stephen Bogaert), the worst of the lot, is both physically and sexually abusive—Beverly has no mother. Ben and Richie's parents are never shown; Mike literally has no parents as they died in a fire set by racists. The handful of other adults present in the film is equally useless or damaged. Officer Bowers (Stuart Hughes) is just as much of a bully as his son Henry Bowers (Nicholas Hamilton); the pharmacist at the convenience store, Mr. Keene (Joe Bostick), seems more than ready to flirt with the 12-year-old Beverly. And, apart from the members of the Losers' Club, all the other kids represented mimic the cold and sadistic tendencies of the adults that surround them—aside from IT, the film's primary antagonists are bully Henry Bowers and his cronies Patrick Hockstetter (Owen Teague), Vic Criss (Logan Thompson), and Reginald Huggins (Jake Sim), who together terrorize the members of the Losers' Club. Even apparently nice gestures, such as when a girl at the drug store offers to sign Eddie's cast after he breaks his arm in a confrontation with Pennywise, turn out to be cruel jokes—she simply writes "Loser" on it. The result of this is that these outsiders are entirely on their own—no one will come to their aid or assist them; they must hang together or, as the saying goes, they will hang separately. It is tempting to say that what IT robs the children of is their safety; but that's not right because they were never safe to begin with.

Where IT is concerned, it is often difficult to know in a Stephen King narrative whether the monster is conjured up by the preexisting evil of the town or if the town's evil is the product of some monstrous spirit of place. King often seems to try to split the difference, asserting at the same time—to borrow a metaphor from King's *Pet Sematary*—that the people are sour because the ground is, and that the ground is sour because the people are. What is clear, however, is that, regardless of which came first, it is a reinforcing cycle, and the supernatural menace that emerges is a concentrated reflection of the town's more diffuse evil—Carrie White has natural psionic abilities but goes ballistic in *Carrie* due to her mother's abusive religious mania combined with vicious bullying; the Overlook Hotel in *The Shining* (1977) may have been built on a Native American burial ground (where else?) but also harbors within its walls the depraved evil of those who stayed within its walls; Jerusalem's Lot in *'Salem's Lot* is a nasty town even before the vampire Barlow arrives, and this may be the reason he chooses the town; the same can be said for Castle Rock before the demonic Leland Gaunt sets up shop in *Needful Things*, and so on. And in *IT*, as Magistrale asserts, "Derry's accumulated moral wastes coalesce into Pennywise" (*Landscapes* 110) who inhabits the sewers beneath their feet. Ben's research into the history of Derry discovers that the town, going back to its origins in the eighteenth century, has indeed always been plagued by cycles of kidnappings and child murder. Kids disappear and then seem quickly forgotten. Apart from this, what we learn about IT is what can be extrapolated from the children's encounters with Pennywise: IT attacks children, it feeds on fear, it can change shape, it can appear anywhere, and it seems invisible to those whom it is not targeting.

In its Pennywise form, IT of course inverts what at least used to be a privileged figure of childhood enjoyment: the clown. It lures Georgie at the start, enticing him from beneath a storm grate with promises of cotton candy and popcorn, before severing his arm and dragging him into the sewer. And IT's calling card, the now-iconic red balloon, similarly functions as the ironic inversion of conventional associations as it renders dreadful a potent symbol of childhood innocence.[4] But IT appears in other forms as well, playing on the fears and guilt of its victims. It lures Ben into the basement of the library and attacks him in the form of a headless child; it seeks to lure Bill into his house's basement in the guise of his dead brother, Georgie (a form it will reinhabit at the end of the film); it explodes as a fountain of blood from Bev's sink after we've seen her awkwardly shopping for Tampax; it attacks the hypochondriac Eddie in the form of a filthy, leprous hobo; and it attacks Stan in the guise of a creepy woman from a Modigliani-inspired portrait that hangs in his father's office.[5]

IT in its various forms, especially Pennywise with his red balloon,

IT in its Pennywise form with red balloon.

certainly embodies the corruption of innocence and the various ways adults actively and passively fail children. In 1986, this could have been correlated with the phenomenon of "latchkey kids"—children who return from school to an empty house—which itself was connected to anxieties connected with changing social roles for women, shifting family dynamics, and rising divorce rates resulting in more one-parent households. IT, in keeping with monsters in general, is also a protean metaphor condensing anxieties related to fear of loss, of being an outsider, of growing up, and of betrayal by supposed protectors. I would like to suggest however that the same monster resonates differently today. While it remains all the things it was, we are different. Post 9/11, when babies in strollers and grandparents in wheelchairs have to go through airport security and everyone gets patted down entering sports events, the protean monster we can't see despite being right before our eyes is the terrorist. Relatedly, we live in the era of mass shootings—toddlers in preschool, introduced from the moment they can walk in the U.S. to "stranger danger," practice emergency drills in the event there should be an active shooter—who again could be anyone—even as a significant percentage of the American population rejects the notion that firearms are part of the problem. We live in the era of climate change—something we can't actually see or touch but the consequences of which are before our eyes daily even as its reality is denied by the Trump administration.[6] We live in the era of #metoo and #timesup, with women speaking up about sexual harassment and abuse, making clear the pervasiveness of the problem, how many "respectable" men in prominent positions are culpable, and how many people saw something but said nothing.

In King's novel, published in 1986, IT goes dormant after three years of terror, returning 27 years later to mirror the anxieties and feed on the fears of a new generation of children. Thirty-one years after the novel was published—and 27 years after the 1990 TV mini-series starring Tim Curry!—IT is back, giving shape to the anxieties of a new generation of media consumers concerned in particular about the ambiguity of threat—its protean nature, omnipresence, and invisibility. It is no wonder the film, as of late 2018, was the highest-grossing horror film of all time (D'Alessandro).

It should be pointed out that the *It* films, in keeping with the novel on which they are based, end on a hopeful note. The members of the Losers Club, by trusting in one another and, ultimately, themselves, are able to defeat the supernatural menace. This victory is not without its casualties however. Adult Stan (Andy Bean in *It: Chapter Two*) slashes his wrists at the start rather than return to Derry to confront the returned Pennywise, and Eddie (James Ransone) dies in the final confrontation. Nevertheless, as a kind of wish fulfillment, order is restored at the end as the chaotic shapeshifting threat is expunged. The happy ending, of course, may in part explain the immense success of the two films: confronted by the ambiguity of daily threat in their own lives, viewers find satisfaction in a conclusion reflecting their own desires. If we just trust in each other, the film seems to say, clarity will be restored, threat contained, and things will get better. But this hopeful note is tempered by the profound amnesia that sets in as soon as Pennywise disappears. We cannot learn from our mistakes, the narrative seems to say. And thus we will not recognize the next threat for what it is until it strikes.

That's Just What It Does: It Follows

The next step forward in this consideration of ambiguous threat and omnipresent dread in modern horror cinema takes us back three years to a film certainly well-known to horror aficionados but that did not achieve the same level of cultural saturation as Muschietti's *It*: David Robert Mitchell's *It Follows* (2014). A "high concept"[7] film if there ever was one, the film's plot can be reduced succinctly to Randy Meeks' (Jamie Kennedy) first rule to survive a horror film from Wes Craven's *Scream* (1996), itself a metatextual meditation on 70s and 80s horror: "You can never have sex. The minute you get a little nookie—you're as good as gone. Sex always equals death." In brief, the film focuses on Oakland University student Jaimie "Jay" Height (Maika Monroe) who, after having sex with her new boyfriend Hugh (Jake Weary), is pursued by a murderous supernatural entity that can assume any form and that others that have not previously experienced it cannot see. Tracking Hugh down (whose real name turns out to be Jeff Redmond) after he has abandoned her to her fate, he explains to her that the creature began pursuing him after a one-night stand and that it will kill Jay unless she passes it off to someone else through having sex—and when one person is killed, the entity then pursues the preceding person in the train of sexual transmission. Jay has various near misses with the creature—at school, in her home, at a friend's lake house—before she and her friends shoot it in a swimming pool. This seems to solve the problem but, in keeping with horror film logic, the possibility of the entity's return is left open and suggested by an ominous walking figure in the film's final shot.

The "It" of *It Follows* shares a number of features with the IT of Muschietti's *IT*—most notably its abilities to shift its appearance and appear anywhere, its invisibility to those haven't had sex with an "infected" person, its inscrutability, and its implacability. Like Pennywise, the It of *It Follows* assumes various forms, with little in most cases to distinguish it from a normal human being. In some cases, it appears as a stranger—Jay first sees it as a young, naked woman; she then sees it school as an old woman in a hospital gown; at home, she sees it as disheveled, middle-aged woman who urinates on herself; later, she sees it as a naked man standing on the roof of her house. It can, however, also appear as someone familiar—at the lake house, it appears in the form of her friend Yara (Olivia Luccardi); having had sex with a boy named Greg (Daniel Zovatto) who has agreed to assume the risk, Jay then sees it first in the form of Greg entering his house across the street, then in the form of Greg's mother as it attacks Greg. Perhaps most disturbingly, in her final confrontation with it at a swimming pool, Jay sees it in the form of her own father.

That the film's It can assume any form, including that of friends and family, highlights the absence of conventional safeguards in *It Follows*. As in Muschietti's *IT*, parents and authority figures are absent or powerless to stop the creature. After Jay's initial sexual encounter with Hugh results in her being kidnapped and taken to a secluded location where Hugh explains the curse, the police are indeed called, but can find no evidence of the creature or information about Hugh and then cease to play a role in the film. Parents are almost entirely absent and play no part in addressing the teenagers' concerns—indeed, Jay's father only appears in the film near the very end when the entity assumes his form. Tellingly, when Greg offers his lake house as a refuge to try to get away from It, Jay asks him what his mother will think of his disappearing for a few days—his response is simply "she won't even know." This seems to be the case for Jay, her sister Kelly (Lili Sepe), and her other friends as well.[8] While not as abusive as *IT*'s Mr.

Marsh and Mrs. Kaspbrack, parents in *It Follows* are every bit as absent and impotent to address their kids' concerns.

Instead of relying on conventional authority figures as sources of protection, it is up to the teens in *It Follows*, in keeping with many horror films, to band together to confront the supernatural threat. Although they cannot see the entity, Jay's sister and friends Paul (Keir Gilchrist), Yara, and Greg believe her enough to come to her aid and comfort her, and then to drop everything to go to the lake house with her; at the lake house, Jay's story is confirmed as, although they cannot see the entity, they witness its effects as first Jay and then Paul are attacked. To be fair, the boys in *It Follows* are not entirely selfless in their concern. As in Muschietti's *IT*, *It Follows* also has its own love triangle (which the ages of the characters allows to be developed more fully). In *IT*, the overweight Ben has a crush on Beverly, but Beverly has a crush on Bill; in *It Follows*, Paul is in love with Jay, but Jay is attracted to Greg—the latter of which is more than willing to take advantage of the opportunity to sleep with Jay, particularly because he is not entirely convinced of the reality of the supernatural entity. (When interrogated about her choice of partner by the jealous Paul, Jay responds simply that she thought the more manly Greg would be better able to grapple with the threat.) Near the end of *It Follows*, after Greg has died and the rest of the group believes the entity has been killed, Paul and Jay finally have sex, and then Paul is shown driving past prostitutes through a run-down part of Detroit, implying that he has his doubts about the demise of the creature and is contemplating passing along the curse by paying for sex (that he doesn't follow through with this plan is then suggested by the ending of the film—see below).

The most straight-forward way to interpret *It Follows* is as an allegory of sexually transmitted disease—an interpretation that is congruent with the "throw-back" aesthetic of the film, with its washed-out color palette and periodic soundtrack emphasis on analog synthesizer. Indeed, *It Follows*, in both its aesthetics and themes, is very much indebted to and patterned after 1970s and 1980s slasher films like those of the *Halloween*, *Friday the 13th*, and *Nightmare on Elm Street* franchises in which an implacable supernatural assailant terrorizes a group of teens.[9] Nods to such films seem liberally sprinkled across *It Follows*, such as the zombie-like movement of the entity, its transformational abilities (as in John Carpenter's *The Thing*), Jay being menaced at school (*Nightmare on Elm Street*), the teens seeking refuge in a lake house (suggesting the *Friday the 13th* films), and Rich Vreeland's synthesizer-heavy score (*Halloween*); given the basic premise of the film that, to avoid death, the curse must be passed along to another, its closest parallel may be to *Ringu / The Ring*, substituting sex for watching a videotape. More centrally, the linking of sexual activity to threat echoes the familiar pattern of slasher films discussed famously by Carol Clover in *Men, Women and Chainsaws*—and summarized by Randy Meeks in *Scream*—in which those teens who engage in premarital intercourse die. Were *It Follows* a film from the 1980s or '90s, one might even be inclined to interpret it as an AIDS film, expressing panic over the pandemic in the form of a monster transmitted through sexual intimacy that can appear as anyone.

The film, one hastens to add, can still reasonably be interpreted in this way; indeed, it would be difficult to discuss the film without acknowledging the straight-forward interpretation introduced in most reviews of it: the film expresses anxieties about sexually transmitted diseases that can infect anyone and cannot be visually distinguished in a partner.[10] But, in keeping with the overdetermined nature of monsters in general, making a one-to-one correspondence between the film's monster and sexually transmitted disease is too limited. Instead, debuting in 2014, the film expresses the ambient dread that suffuses our current moment—and it does this in large measure through 360-degree pans and shots of people walking that conspire to create an overwhelming sense of paranoia. Our expectancy of something bad happening—an attack out of the blue—colors our appreciation of every shot in the film as the monster, which is spread sexually but attacks viciously, could be anywhere and anyone.

The film's impressive 360-pans are central to the creation of ambient dread as they suggest an invisible all-seeing force watching the characters. Indeed, the film begins with a 360-degree shot with several zooms that focuses on a character named Annie (Bailey Spry) who emerges distraught from her house, runs into the middle of her suburban street, and then circles back around to her house. The camera's panoptic view tracks her the entire time. An even more dizzying pan—closer to 540 degrees than 360—takes place when the group, pursuing a clue to Hugh's real identity, visits a local high school to look through yearbooks. The camera, located in an interior hallway, starts by showing us the outside through a window, and then slowly and methodically circles, taking in Jay and Greg as they walk past the camera and enter the open door to a classroom and the continuing around in a circle, showing us the windows again and a sparsely populated hallway before finally coming to rest and zooming in on the open classroom door. In each of these pans, the steady, methodical movement of the camera parallels it with the entity itself, an unseen, implacable assailant, creating the impression of a malevolent observer.

Implicated even more extensively in the film's evocation of ambient dread and paranoia is the way the film's shots of people walking render ominous the most mundane of human activities. What indeed stands out about the monster's pursuit of its victims in *It Follows* is its methodical slowness. The entity in the film does not run after its victims; rather, it plods relentlessly. Given that the creature can assume any shape and appear anywhere, the consequence is that anyone walking slowly is an object of concern. The film occasionally plays this for laughs; having tracked Hugh (AKA Jeff) down to his suburban home, the group sits outside as he attempts to explain himself. At one point, he becomes panicked when a young woman wearing headphones approaches. Pointing at her, he asks the group in an excited tone, "Do you guys see that girl right there?"—to which they all calmly reply "yeah." But this is the point: having seen It, it is impossible to regard the world in the same way ever again. Everyone is potentially a monster.

The laugh evoked from the viewer by Hugh/Jeff's panic is thus not one of ridicule, but of relief—because what the film conditions us to do is to respond exactly as Jeff does to every person who walks toward the camera, or who Jay sees walking slowly. It does this by first establishing the connection between slow walking and monstrosity. Jay's first encounters with the creature in the forms of naked younger woman, old woman in hospital gown, and middle-aged woman in her home establish that it can change its form, that it can appear anywhere, and that it walks deliberately and doggedly toward its victim. This premise is fundamental to the film's aura of ambient dread as it leads to paranoia—both in Jay's case and the viewer's. In some cases, the viewer is sutured to Jay's perspective, sharing her concern; this is the case, for example, when, having pursued the clues regarding Hugh to the dilapidated home in which he was living, Jay peeks out the window, sees a black man walking by slowly, and quickly backs away from the window. It's the classic shot/reverse shot/shot triad that obscures the camera's mediating role by allowing us to share Jay's view and affect: we see her look, we see what she sees through her eyes, we see her again. She doesn't know if the man walking by is human or a monster and, having seen the world through her eyes, neither do we—and thus we share her anxiety.

In other cases, having conditioned the viewer through Jay to regard all deliberately walking figures as suspect, the camera then flirts directly with the viewer, showing us walking figures not observed by the characters and asking us to consider whether or not they are human. For example, as the group prepares to leave the High School after investigating Hugh/Jeff, a shot from the backseat of their car shows us a lone girl in jeans and a white jacket walking slowly toward the car. She is unremarked by characters, but the camera brings her into focus for a few moments. Is she the creature?[11] Even more unsettlingly, at the very end of the film, we are shown Jay and Paul walking down the sidewalk, holding hands. First, we are shown them from the front, with no one behind them; then we get a shot of them from behind, and a close-up of their hands; the camera then shoots them from the front again, but this time, there is a lone figure on the sidewalk behind them in the distance also walking slowly. The film's final shot is again the walking couple from behind, the camera slowly getting closer. These shots are for the viewer, who is invited to consider whether or not the solitary walking figure briefly shown behind them is simply another pedestrian, or a supernatural killer hunting the two kids. As A.A. Dowd notes for his review in *AV/Film*, "Gradually, the background space of every shot becomes a source of menace, and every extra on screen becomes a potential threat. The film turns its viewers into paranoid spectators, scanning the frame for signs of trouble" (Dowd).

In Muschietti's *IT*, the kids in the Losers' Club are stalked by a shape-changing supernatural menace that plays on their worst fears and that they are on their own to confront. Tapping into cultural anxieties is of course the modus operandi of horror, and the protean, invisible nature of threat in the 2017 *IT* seems congruent with contemporary dread over unseen, omnipresent, seemingly unreasonable threats that can strike at any time. Cut from the same cloth, *It Follows* amplifies the threatening ambiguity of *IT*. As summarized by Jordan Crucchiola in a 2015 review for *Wired*, "The 'It' can be anyone you know. Or anyone you don't. It can fill a different vessel whenever It wants. It doesn't speak. It doesn't run. It just walks. It walks right towards you on a deliberate, direct path until It finally has you. And then you die. It is not personal or passionate about killing you. That's just what It does" (Crucchiola). We know why Pennywise terrorizes kids (it feeds on fear) and, at least in King's novel, we get ITs backstory. We therefore may recognize IT as evil and horrifying, but we can comprehend ITs motivations—it is a sort of rational horror. The It of *It Follows*, however, is something different. We understand the mode of transmission, but not its motivation. We don't know where it came from and have no sense of whether or not it can be killed. Unlike Pennywise, it does not speak, nor does it show any affect at all. What differentiates the It of *It Follows* most immediately from the monstrous IT of King's *IT* is its affectless implacability—it moves with slow, relentless determination. In a psychoanalytic register, it is pure drive, pursuing its goal relentlessly and without deviating from its course.[12] And most crucially, there is no process of discrimination involved in the selection of Its victims— It does not *choose* its victims; rather, It is simply passed on from sexual partner to partner, each jeopardizing the safety of the next. The appearance of It within *It Follows* is the only symptom of a potentially fatal sexually transmitted disease. In Leslie A. Hahner and Scott J. Varda's analysis of the film, they assert that the "use of ambient horror [in *It Follows*] epitomizes the continuous perils of rape culture" (253). In Casey Ryan Kelly's examination of the film, he argues that the film's "ambient horror" (236) expresses the "precarity" of those "antagonized by systemic, structured vulnerability: unemployment, environmental degradation, and divestment in the public good" (235). My take on the film is more general than that of Hahner and Varda and more specific than that of Kelly: The manifestation of It within *It Follows* is a symptom of larger cultural anxieties over the irrationality and ambiguity of modern threat.[13] We can't see it until we do. The ultimate unknowable Other, we can't reason with it or understand It. It can appear anywhere, in the shape of anyone, and traditional sources of authority are simply impotent to protect us from it. It could be watching us right now, in the room with us, and we would never know until it struck. It therefore is the crystallization of contemporary paranoia, the shape of modern ambient dread. It follows in our wake, an irrational consequence of our actions that we must attempt to survive without truly knowing how to combat or address its threat. Our modern ailment is ambient dread and we are all infected.

The Open Door: It Comes At Night

In some ways, there is an obvious progression from *It Follows* to *It Comes at Night*, which shifts our attention from a sexually transmitted disease to a large-scale pandemic, and from an apocalypse predicted to one accomplished. Like both *It* and *It Follows*, *It Comes at Night* is about a lack of safety in the modern world and the inability to trust to anyone. Rather than being set in a past or present world that resembles our own however, *It Comes at Night*, in keeping with contemporary trends in fiction and film, presents us with a country—possibly a world—ravaged by a highly contagious viral pandemic. Despite this speculative premise (although, in the wake of Covid-19, far less speculative than it once appeared), *It Comes at Night* is arguably the most gut wrenching of the three films here because of its otherwise realistic representation of a family trying desperately but, in the end, futilely, to protect itself from a non-rational and pervasive deadly threat.

It Comes at Night pulls no punches; indeed, its very first scene features a painful interaction between an obvious sick older man (David Pendleton), covered with boils and sores, and two figures in gas masks. A distraught woman (Sarah, played by Carmen Ejogo) tells the older man that she loves him, before embracing the other gasmasked figure, her husband, Paul (Joel Edgerton). The sick man is then removed from the house to a spot in the woods by Paul and another figure in a gasmask, Sarah and Paul's teenage son, Travis (Kelvin Harrison, Jr.). Travis says "goodbye,

Grandpa. I love you." Paul then apologizes, covers the sick man's face with a pillow, and shoots him in the head. The old man, wrapped in a tarp, is rolled into a shallow grave, and set ablaze with gasoline.

What we soon come to understand is that Paul, Sarah, and Travis are survivors of some kind of deadly pandemic that appears to have devastated the country. This interracial family—Paul is white, Sarah is black, and their son Travis is also dark skinned—lives in a secluded forest cabin with their dog, Stanley, with no knowledge of the outside world. Their routine is interrupted one night when someone tries to break into the house, and Paul captures Will (Christopher Abbott) who claims he was looking for supplies for his family and thought the house was abandoned. After a prolonged interrogation, Paul goes with Will to retrieve his wife, Kim (Riley Keough) and their young son Andrew (Griffin Robert Faulkner), and the two families, reasoning that they will be safer together, set up an uneasy coexistence together in the same house. Precipitating later plot events, one evening, the dog, Stanley, runs off after having been barking at something in the woods.

The tension in the film ratchets up after Travis (Paul and Sarah's son) finds Andrew (Will and Kim's young son) sleeping one night in the living room—presumably having sleepwalked there. Travis takes Andrew by the hand and leads him back to his parents' room, but commotion is then heard in the house and Travis discovers the front door slightly ajar. The two families then discover the dog, Stanley, lying on the kitchen floor, bleeding and ill. It is unclear who opened the door—Sarah suggests that Andrew might have done it while sleepwalking, while Will and Kim maintain that it was Travis—but concerns have now been introduced about possible infection, and Paul decides that the two families should isolate themselves for a few days in different parts of the house.

The next morning, Travis overhears Andrew coughing and Kim telling Will that they need to leave. Distrust now boils over and Paul and Sarah, wearing gasmasks and protective gloves, move to confront the other couple. A standoff ensues with Will initially holding Paul at gunpoint, insisting his family is healthy, and asking for a share of food and water so they can leave. Paul and Sarah turn the tables forcing the other family outside, where a brutal fight between Paul and Will ensues. Sarah then shoots Will, while Kim and Andrew flee. Paul fires after them, killing Andrew. Kim, hysterical, begs Paul to shoot her too, which he does. Sarah at this point notices that Travis, who has been watching, looks unwell. The wrenching conclusion then reveals a dying Travis being comforted by his heartbroken mother while his father weeps in another room. The final devastating shot is of Paul and Sarah, both visibly sick, sitting across from each other at an empty table, hopeless.

Paul and Sarah at the end as darkness descends.

    This final shot is emblematic of the horror of *It Comes at Night*. In the same way that *It Follows* most obviously condenses anxieties about sexually transmitted diseases, *It Comes at Night* is, in the era of Ebola, SARS, H1N1, Avian Flu, antibiotic resistant strains of more familiar viruses, and, most recently the Coronavirus, a clear expression of contemporary anxieties regarding global pandemics—as such, it is part of a growing body of narratives that focus specifically on the aftermath of plague (some involving zombies, some not), meditating as it does on what would happen should an unstoppable fatal virus spread rapidly. And this specific variant of the post-apocalyptic narrative shares with other versions, such as *The Day After* (Nicholas Meyer, 1983) nuclear war scenario and the *Day After Tomorrow* (Roland Emmerich, 2004) climate change approach, the simultaneous sense of culpability and helplessness: human beings are responsible for unleashing forces of destruction they cannot control. The apocalypse, it seems, is always just around the corner—when the sun sets, tomorrow, the day after tomorrow.

    But like *IT* and *It Follows*, the horror of *It Comes at Night* is more diffuse and ambiguous than simply anxiety about viral pandemics. Although there is no supernatural component to *It Comes at Night*, it is nevertheless tempting to classify it as a film about the living dead. This is not just because those afflicted by the mysterious disease resemble zombies; it is also because the virus robs the world of safety and the ability to trust others. As in both *It* and *It Follows*, one cannot trust appearances in *It Comes at Night* as anyone may be infected with the disease and be initially asymptomatic. For this reason, Paul and Sarah can never be entirely comfortable with Will and Kim. In Peter Bradshaw's review of the film for *The Guardian*, he writes that the film "mirrors what life would be like for survivors and their attitude to strangers or even friends whose motivations can't truly be known. These are people who might have to lie, to cheat, to betray even those they like, who under other circumstances they would feel a debt of gratitude towards—but this is what is needed to live and the old rules have been superseded" (Bradshaw). Everyone in Paul and Sarah and Travis's world is a potential bomb waiting to go off, including family members—and those infected or who come in contact with someone infected are already dead; they just don't know it yet.

Beyond even this, the true horror of *It Comes at Night* is what one could call Lovecraftian cosmic horror—existential dread over human helplessness in the face of overwhelming non-rational forces and the contingency of events. Despite the unfair odds, one can fight a Pennywise or invisible killer entity, but there is no fighting a virus that could be anywhere and for which there is no cure. As Brian Tallerico observes in his review of the film, there are no zombies to fight here; rather, "the villains are loss, grief, pain, fear, and distrust—very human emotions" (Tallerico). And then there is the crushing unfairness of it all—Paul and Sarah clearly love each other and their son, Travis. Paul, we learn, was a history teacher before the pandemic, an educator. They are trying to survive together in the complete absence of any assistance from anyone. They make a decision, cautious and calculated as it is, to try to help another family but, in the end, "no good deed goes unpunished." Whether they would have survived had they acted differently, or for how long, is impossible to know, but we do know that they are caught up in a horror story not of their own making.

Paul and Sarah are, in sum, what we could consider normal people confronting tragedy on both a personal and epic scale—which returns us to the film's devastating final shot of them, defeated, grief-stricken, and dying, looking at each other across an empty table. *IT* and *It Follows* both involve plucky bands of kids who successfully (or at least with partial success) confront a supernatural menace, leaving us with hope at the end (despite our awareness that the conventions of the horror film dictate that the monster always returns). Paul and Sarah are left with—and leave us with—only a sense of loss and despondency. There will be no second act—at least not for them—and no return from the grave.[14] *IT* and *It Follows* leave us with a clear sense that there is more to the universe than we imagine—malevolent forces, certainly, but this suggests at least the possibility of benevolent ones as well. The closest thing *It Comes at Night* gives us is a dream-like shot of Travis, as he is dying, walking down a hallway toward the outside door to the house—perhaps to join a larger universe one might suggest, but perhaps also to wink out of existence. The final shot of his sick, exhausted, and despondent parents certainly gives us little cause to hope for a heavenly reunion.

It Comes at Night is thus a horror film most obviously giving shape to contemporary anxieties about global pandemics and, more broadly, channeling contemporary concerns about the ways human beings are creating the conditions of our own destruction. In the end though, it is also a tragedy about the lack of trust and safety in the modern world. Tallerico even goes so far as to call it a "reverse horror film," writing that the message of the film is, "Sure, the outside world is scary, but it's distrust and paranoia that will truly be your undoing. The real enemy is already inside. Now try and get some sleep" (Tallerico). When anyone can be infected, be a monster on the inside, trust becomes impossible. And when there is no safe place to hide, and structures of containment such as the government, law enforcement, and, finally, the family, are absent or fail, it is impossible to feel secure. In this way, the horror of *It Comes at Night* is an allegory of our modern moment—the monster could be anyone and anywhere, even within us without our even knowing.

Looking at *IT*, *It Follows*, and *It Comes at Night* suggests that our present moment is one of perpetual twilight, with ambiguous Its watching and waiting to emerge. While one must be careful about generalizing on the basis of one—or even three—films, nevertheless I'd like to propose that the ambiguous Its of these three horror movies function as objective correlatives for a contemporary structure of feeling defined by a sense of ambient dread related to invisible and ambiguous threats. The monster can take many shapes and wears many faces—terrorist, serial killer, virus, climate change. It can strike anywhere—is even possibly already within us—and conventional structures of containment fail. The consequence then is pervasive paranoia: stranger danger, if you see something say something, active shooter drills for preschoolers, full body screenings looking for incipient cancers, and so on. The twenty-first-century monster is an "It"; we just don't know what it is, where it came from, how to spot it, or what exactly to do about it.

Notes

1. Indeed, *It: Chapter Two* can arguably be interpreted as a kind of wish fulfillment in several respects as the now-grown members of the Losers' Club track the source of horror to its source, uncover its origins, and defeat it. As a result, it is less about what we fear than what we hope for.

2. On the outsider status of the Losers' Club members and the "mythical power of childhood friendship" (151), see Hansen.

3. Taking a cue from Magistrale, Strengell also addresses the ways in which grownups are the real enemies in many of King's narratives. See Strengell, especially 209–11.

4. Indeed, IT's red balloon, supernaturally unaffected by wind, is the evil inversion of the apparently sentient red balloon in Albert Lamorisse's 1956 fantasy, *The Red Balloon* (*Le balloon rouge*).

5. Sears notes in his analysis of the novel that "*It*, seeking a rhetoric to describe its own excessive monstrosity, initially offers that monstrosity as polymorphous and many-faced" (183). Sears goes on to the notes that the novel ultimately compresses the otherness of IT into "a single, disturbingly obvious image of feminine monstrosity" (184). On King and gender, see also Hansen and Pharr.

6. Particularly where climate change is concerned, Timothy Morton's discussion of "hyperobjects"—things "massively distributed in time and space relative to humans" is apropos. We can't touch hyperobject directly, although we experience their effects in profound ways. See *Hyperobjects*.

7. "High concept" in relation to a film or television show refers to a premise that can be succinctly stated.

8. Paying careful attention to the absence of Jay's father and her mother's behavior, M.J. Pack ingeniously theorizes that the father has committed suicide and the mother has developed a drinking problem. See Pack.

9. Much of the critical commentary on *It Follows* has focused on the film's indebtedness to slasher films of the 1970s and '80s. Joshua Grimm draws out these connections in his short monograph on the film for example, as does Casey Ryan Kelly. The big difference between *It Follows* and the cinematic predecessors to which it tips its hat, as I will develop below, is the ambiguity of the threat at the heart of the film. My argument is that it is precisely this that marks it as a reflection of twenty-first-century anxieties.

10. See, for example, *The Guardian* review by Peter Bradshaw titled "Sexual dread fuels a modern horror classic" in which Bradshaw writes that the film, "with its viral spread of horror and shame, could be read as an abstinence parable or a herpes nightmare or a metaphorical account of Aids [sic]." Peter Travers likens the entity to a "pernicious lethal STD" is his review for *Rolling Stone* (Travers). In his interesting scholarly analysis of *It Follows*, David Church offers a queer inflection of this standard approach to the film, arguing that the film's "true source of horror is living under a regime of sexual shame wherein our heteronormative culture compels sexual subjects toward monogamy." The curse, he notes, "would become moot in a society embracing the value of a multiplicity of sexual partners" (4).

11. Abrams adds in relation to shots from the backseats of cars in general, "We're also given the impression of infinite space whenever Mitchell's camera stands in for, or is positioned inside Paul or Jay's cars. In these scenes, the road that stretches out in front of them/us is long, and there is never a set destination in sight" (Abrams).

12. I have in mind here particularly Žižek's discussion of zombies in *Looking Awry*. See 22–23.

13. Although tangential to the focus of this essay, M.J. Pack offers an insightful analysis of other irrational elements to the film, focusing on the facts that film's time period and season are inconsistent, and speculating on the absence of Jay's mother and father. See Pack. Joshua Grimm also focuses on temporal ambiguity in the film; see Grimm, especially chapter 1.

14. Adding to the poignancy of the somber denouement is the unremarked centrality of race to the film. The fact that Paul, Sarah, and Travis are an interracial family is never mentioned. It is obvious to the viewer from the opening scene, but plays no role. If we take their demise to signal the victory of plague over humanity, the Red Death's dominion established, then humanity has moved through a brief idyllic window of being post-racial to being simply post-humous.

Works Cited

Abrams, Simon. Rev. of *It Follows*, *RogerEbert.com*, 13 March 2015. https://www.rogerebert.com/reviews/it-follows-2015.

Bradshaw, Peter. "It Follows review—sexual dread fuels a modern horror classic." *The Guardian*, 26 Feb. 2015. https://www.theguardian.com/film/2015/feb/26/it-follows-review-horror-sex-death.

Chuch, David. "Queer Ethics, Urban Spaces, and the Horror of Monogamy in *It Follows*." *Cinema Journal*, vol. 57, no. 3, Spring 2018, pp. 3–28.

Clover, Carol. *Men, Women and Chainsaws*. Princeton University Press, 1992.

Cohen, Jeffrey Jerome. "Monster Culture (Seven Theses)" in *Monster Theory: Reading Culture*, edited by Jeffrey Jerome Cohen. University of Minnesota Press, 1996, pp. 3–25.

Crucchiola, Jordan. "What Makes the New Horror Film *It Follows* So Damn Good." *Wired*, 17 March 2015. https://www.wired.com/2015/03/it-follows-unholy-trinity/.

D'Alessandro, Anthony. "No. 5 'It' Box Office Profits—2017 Most Valuable Blockbuster Tournament." *Deadline Hollywood*, 23 March 2018. https://deadline.com/2018/03/it-stephen-king-box-office-movie-profits-1202351455/.

Dowd, A.A. "*It Follows* is a new classic of both horror and coming-of-age cinema." *AV/Film*, 12 March 2015. https://film.avclub.com/it-follows-is-a-new-classic-of-both-horror-and-coming-o-1798183055.

Grimm, Joshua. *It Follows*. Auteur, 2018.

Hahner, Leslie A., and Scott. J. Varda. "*It Follows* and Rape Culture: Critical Response as Disavowal." *Women's Studies in Communication*, vol. 40, no. 3, 2017, pp. 251–69.

Halberstam, Judith. *Skin Shows: Gothic Horror and the Technology of Monsters*. Duke University Press, 1995.

Hansen, Regina. "Stephen King's *It* and *Dreamcatcher* on Screen: Hegemonic White Masculinity and Nostalgia for Underdog Boyhood." *Science Fiction Film and Television*, vol. 10, no. 2, Summer 2017, pp. 161–76.

Kelly, Casey Ryan. "*It Follows*: Precarity, Thanatopolitics, and the Ambient Horror Film." *Critical Studies in Media Communication*, vol. 34, no. 3, 2017, pp. 234–49.

Magistrale, Tony. "Defining Stephen King's Horrorscape: An Introduction" in *The Dark Descent: Essays Defining Stephen King's Horrorscape*, edited by Tony Magistrale. Greenwood Press, 1992, pp. 1–4.

———. *Landscape of Fear: Stephen King's American Gothic*. Bowling Green State University Popular Press, 1988.

Mittman, Asa Simon. "Introduction: the Impact of Monsters and Monster Studies" in *The Ashgate Research Companion to Monsters and the Monstrous*, edited by Asa Simon Mittman. Ashgate, 2013, pp. 1–14.

Morton, Timothy. *Hyperobjects: Philosophy and Ecology After the End of the World*. University of Minnesota Press, 2013.

Pack, M.J. "Here's Why You Missed the Scariest Part of 'It Follows.'" *Thought Catalog*, 20 August 2015. https://thoughtcatalog.com/m-j-pack/2015/08/heres-why-you-missed-the-scariest-part-of-it-follows/.

Pharr, Mary. "Partners in the *Danse*: Women in Stephen King's Fiction" in *The Dark Descent: Essays Defining Stephen King's Horrorscapes*, edited by Tony Magistrale. Greenwood Press, 1992, pp. 19–32.

Sears, John. *Stephen King's Gothic*. University of Wales Press, 2011.

Strengell, Heidi. *Dissecting Stephen King: From the Gothic to Literary Naturalism*. University of Wisconsin Press, 2005.

Tallerico, Brian. Rev. of *It Comes at Night*. *RogerEbert.com*, 9 June 2017, https://www.rogerebert.com/reviews/it-comes-at-night-2017.

Travers, Peter. rev. of *It Follows*. *Rolling Stone*, 11 March 2015. https://www.rollingstone.com/movies/movie-reviews/it-follows-252145/.

Žižek, Slavoj. *Looking Awry: An Introduction to Jacques Lacan through Popular Culture*. The MIT Press, 1991.

Index

Numbers in **_bold italics_** indicate pages with illustrations

Abbott, Christopher 219
Abbott, Stacey 92, 93
Abbott and Costello Meet Frankenstein 93
Abnormal: Lectures at the Collège de France 1974-1975 184
Abraham Lincoln: Vampire Hunter 87, 91, 101-102, 106
Abrams, Robert E. 35, 36
Abrams, Simon 223n11
"Afterward" (short story) 15
AIDS 100, 104, 147, 155, 200, 201, 215, 223n10
Al Saud, Faisal bin Abdulaziz 111
Alas Poor Ghost! Traditions of Belief in Story and Discourse 24
Alexander the Great 170
Alfred Hitchcock's Haunted Houseful 2
Alfredson, Tomas 87, 97, 123
Alien *see* extraterrestrial
Alien (franchise) 153, 198, 200
Allen, Irwin 155
Ally McBeal 23
Always (film) 28n1
American Nightmares: The Haunted House Formula in American Popular Fiction 24
American Psycho (film) 194
American Psycho (novel) 194, 195
Americans, Indigenous 9-10, 11-13, 21, 28n4, 74-75, 101, 142-144, 146, 149, 173
The Amityville Horror 9, 12-13
Amplas, John 84
Anaconda 155
Anderson, Gillian 199
Androgini (monstrous race) 170
android 198; *see also* cyborg; robot
Andromeda Strain (film) 155, 200
The Andromeda Strain (novel) 155, 200
angel 178
Angel (TV series) 120, 135, 136
Angel Heart 147
Angels in America, Part One: Millennium Approaches 23
animal, monstrous 152, 154-155, 176
Anson, Jay 9

The Antichrist 114
anti-Semitism *see* monsters and anti-Semitism; vampires and Anti-semitism
Aquinas, Thomas 164, 186n4
Arachnophobia 155
Arata, Stephen 101
Ardat lili 164
Arendt, Hannah 185
Aristotle 165, 168, 169, 186n8
Arterton, Geema 102
Ashgate Encyclopedia of Literary and Cinematic Monsters 3-4
Ashgate Research Companion to Monsters and the Monstrous 139
Asimov, Isaac 151
Asma, Stephen 142, 158, 171, 179, 180
Astomi 170
Atkinson, Mollie Jane 209
atomic energy 191; *see also* monster and radiation
Attack of the Crab Monsters 150
Attack of the Giant Leeches 151
Attebery, Brian 4, 5
Auerbach, Nina 96
Augustine of Hippo (St. Augustine) 162, 164, 171
Avalos, Stefan 154
Avatar 153, 198, 205
Aykroyd, Dan 23

Bacon, Kevin 28n1
Badham, John 96
Bailey, Dale 24
Balderston, John L. 93
Bandaras, Antonio 97
Bara, Theda 78
Barber, Patricia 42-43
Barker, Roy Ward 95
Barnett, Louise K. 47n2
Barnum, P.T. 144, 174, **_175_**
Barrow, Mark V. 161, 165, 168
Bartleby (character) 2, 3, 7
"Bartleby, the Scrivener" 30-49

225

Index

Barton, Charles 93
basilisk 174
Bates, Alan W. 160
Báthory, Elizabeth 95–96
Batman 196
Bava, Mario 1
Beal, Timothy K. 146, 158
Bean, Andy 212
Beckinsale, Kate 83, 132
Beetlejuice 28n1
Bekmambetov, Timur 87, 91, 98, 101
Bell, Book and Candle 147
Beloved (novel) 2, 3, 7, 16–17, 23, 50–69, 149
Ben (1972 film) 155
Benchley, Peter 155
Benito Cereno 75, 144
Benjamin, Walter 57
Bennett, Gillian 24
Ben-Sasson, Haim Hillel 111
Benshoff, Harry 79–80, 84–84
Bentley, Christopher 112
Benz, Julie 136
Beowulf 191, 192
"Berenice" 148
Bergland, Renée 24, 26, 28n4
Berlin Wall 197
bestiality 164–65
bestiary 174
Bewitched (TV series) 147
Beyond the Gates 20
Bickley, Bruce R. 47n3
Bierce, Ambrose 17, 76, 78, 148–49
Bigelow, Gordon E. 39–40
Bigelow, Kathryn 99
Bigfoot 154, 174, 177, 178
Bird, Robert Montgomery 75, 143
The Birds 155
"The Birth-Mark" 77, 150
"The Black Cat" 148
Black Skins, White Masks 185
Black Sabbath (film) 1
Blacula 120
Blade (1998 film) 98, 204–205
Blade (character) 98
Blade II 98
Blade (franchise) 83, 87, 88, 98, 101, 134–135
Blade Runner 151
Blade: Trinity 98
The Blair Witch Project 28n1
Blanchot, Maurice 32–33
Blemmyae 170, **172**
The Blob 191
Bloch, Robert 80
blood libel 109–112, 116
Bloom, Harold 85
Bogaert, Stephen 209
Bogdan, Robert 166
"Booth's Jews: The Presentation of Jews and Judaism in Life and Labour of the People of London" 115
Bordwell, David 93
Boreanaz, David 136
Bosky, Bernadette 177
Bostick, Joe 209
Boucicault, Dion 77
Bouson, J. Brooks 67n9
Bowie, David 96
Bradbury, Ray 147
Bradford, William 143
Bradshaw, Peter 221, 223n10
Bradstreet, Anne 146
Bram Stoker's Dracula (1992 film) 80, 84–85, 96, 204
Braud, Ann 20
Breaking Dawn 136
Brewster, Scott 4
Briggs, Julia 28n2
Brodwin, Stanley 47n3
Brogan, Kathleen 16, 24, 26, 28n3, 149
Brown, Charles Brockden 143
Browning, Tod 79, 84, 93, 144
bubonic plague 112–113
Buffy the Vampire Slayer 9, 23, 84, 120, 135, 147
Bugs Bunny 4
Bunston, Herbert 93
burial grounds, Native American 9–10, 12–13, 15, 16, 210
Burton, Tim 28n1, 86, 96–97, 101, 147, 190
Buse, Peter 24
Butler, Octavia 83, 87
Byzantium 91, 97, 102–104, 105, 106

cabinets of curiosity 173
Cameron, James 153
cannibalism 75, 173, 179, 195, 196, 200
Canterbury Tales 110
Capital (book by Karl Marx) 115
capitalism 100–101, 105–106, 115–116
captivity narrative 73
Card, Orson Scott 153
Cardos, John 155
Carlberg, Peter 123
Carmilla (novella) 78, 93, 95, 103
Carpenter, John 214
Carpenter, Lynette 24, 26, 28n3
Carradine, John 94
Carrie (novel) 208, 210
Carroll, Noël 158, 174–176
Caruth, Cathy 63, 65, 66n2
Cat's Eye (film) 1
Cell (2006 novel) 151
Celluloid Vampires: Life and Death in the Modern World 92
Chandler, Helen 93
Chaney, Lon, Jr. 94
Chan-wook, Park 120, 125
Charnas, Suzy McKee 117n3
Chase, Cynthia 50
Chaucer, Geoffrey 110

Index

Child of Glass 2
Chopin, Kate 14
Christol, Helene 67n8
Christophersen, Bill 143
Chupacabra 154, 177
Chupacabra: The Island of Terror 154
Church, David 223n10
Churchill, Marguerite 79
cinema *see* film
Cisneros, Sandra 16
City of God 162, 164, 171
Civil War (American) 20, 21, 87, 143
Cixous, Hélène 36
climate change 206, 211, 220, 222
Clover, Carol 215
Cohen, Ari 209
Cohen, Jeffrey Jerome 2–3, 4, 5, 7, 73, 82, 106, 120–121, 141, 142–134, 157, 165–166, 176, 183, 189, 191, 207
Coleridge, Samuel Taylor 76, 117n4
Collin, Barnabas 97
colonialism, British 114
colonization, North American 9
Columbus, Christopher 143, 173
communism 131, 197–198, 205n1
A Companion to the Ghost Story 7
Constantine (2005 film) 147
The Constitution (American) 12
consumerism 195
Cooper, Alice 87
Cooper, Dominic 101
Cooper, James Fenimore 74–75, 143
Cooper, Merian C. 154
Coppola, Francis Ford 80, 84–85, 96, 204
Cornell, Drucilla 47n1, 60–61
corporation, as monster 153, 190, 197–199, 202–203
cosmic horror 154, 221
Costner, Kevin 28n1
Count Chocula 108, 117n2
Count Count (character) 108, 117n2
Covid 100, 147, 155, 218, 220
Cowan, Douglas E. 141, 143
Crain, William 120
Crane, Stephen 141, 149
Craven, Wes 212
Craver, Donald H. 39
Crawford, F. Marion 78
Creepshow (film) 1
Crichton, Michael 151, 155, 167
Crossing Over with John Edwards 23
The Crow 28n1, 105
Crow, Charles L. 24, 139
Crowley, John W. 24
Crucchiola, Jordan 217
The Crucible 147
Cruise, Tom 97
cryptid 152, 154, 177–178
Crystal, Billy 193
CSI: Crime Scene Investigation 194

Csokas, Marton 87, 101
Ctesias 170
Cthulhu 154
Cujo (film) 155
Cujo (novel) 155
Cultural Haunting: Ghosts and Ethnicity in Recent American Literature 24
Cundieff, Rusty 1
Curry, Tim 212
The Curse of Eve 164
Cusack, John 20
Cushing, Peter 94
cyborg 151
Cyclops 173
Cynocephali 170, 173

Dafoe, Willem 85, 99
D'Alessandro, Anthony 207, 212
Dance of the Damned 3
Danielewski, Mark Z. 17
Dark Shadows (2012 film) 86–87, 96–97, 101
Darling, Marsha 67n3
Daughters of Darkness 95–96, 102, 103, 105
Davidson, Arnold I 184
Davies, Surekha 162, 173
Davis, Christina 57
Davis, William B. 199
The Day After 220
The Day After Tomorrow 152, 201, 220
Day Watch (film) 98
Daybreakers 91, 99–101, 104, 105, 106, 123
dead letter 3, 30, 31, 33, 44–47
Dead Like Me 23
Dead Men Walk 3
Dead of Night 1
Deane, Hamilton 78, 93
Dear, William 154
"The Death of Halpin Frayser" 77, 79, 148
de Beauvoir, Simone 185
del Toro, Guillermo 88, 98, 155
de Man, Paul 67n5
demon 147, 150, 164, 177, 178, 194
de Montaigne, Michel 167, 186n7
Denbrough, Geoffrey 209
Deneuve, Catherine 96
Depp, Johnny 86–87, 97
de Réaumer, René Antoine Ferchault 196
Derleth, August 80
Derounian-Stodola, Kathryn 73–74
Derrida, Jacques 4, 24, 30, 46, 47n1, 51–52, 59–61, 64, 66, 67n5, 67n10
Deschanel, Zooey 202
The Devil 12, 92, 114, 118n6, 143, 147, 150, 164
The Devil's Advocate 147
Dexter (TV series) 145, 178–179, 180, 195, 196, 205
dhampir 98, 135, 164
Dick, Philip K. 151
dinosaur 151, 155

Index

Discipline and Punish: The Birth of the Prison 183
disease 81, 88, 95, 99, 112–114, 126, 147, 151, 152, 155, 190, 199–201, 202–203, 214–215, 218–222, 223n10
Do Androids Dream of Electric Sheep? 151
Dr. Terror's House of Horrors 1
Donestre 171
doppelganger 176
Dorff, Stephen 98
Douglas, Mary 36
Dowd, A. A. 217
Dracula (character) 71, 78, 79, 84–85, 98, 100, 118n6, 118n8, 207
Dracula (1931 film) 79, 84, 93, 117n4
Dracula (1979 film) 114n4
Dracula (novel) 71, 73, 74, 75, 78–79, 80, 85, 88, 92, 96, 100, 101, 107, 112, 114–115, 117n4, 118n6, 118n8, 118n9, 120, 194, 204, 207
Dracula (stage production) 78–79
Dracula: Prince of Darkness 103
The Dracula Tape 82, 192
Dracula's Daughter 79–80, 82, 93–94, 95
dragon 174
dread 206, 215–218, 221, 222, 223n9
Dreyer, Carl-Theodor 92, 93
Duchovny, David 199
Dumas, Alexander 77
du Maurier, Daphne 155
du Maurier, George 118n8
Dunn, Katherine 169
Dyer, Mary 164

Eberhart, George 177–178
eco-disaster film 151–152
Edgar Huntly 143
Edgerton, Joel 218
Edward Scissorhands 190
Edwards, Jonathan 146–147, 154
Eisnemann, Charles **166**
Eisner, Lotte H. 92
Ejogo, Carmen 218
The Elephant Man *see* Merrick, Joseph
Elis, Brett Easton 195
Ellis, David R. 155
Emmerich, Roland 152, 220
Empedocles 167
Ender's Game 153
Enemy Mine (film) 153
"Enemy Mine" (short story) 153
Enemy of the State (1998 film) 198–199
Englander, David 115
epitaph 7, 47, 50–55, 58, 66
Erdrich, Louise 16, 23, 149
Erman, John 2
ethics 7–8
Etymologiae 171
eugenics 145
Eusebius 162
The Exorcist 28n1

Extraordinary Bodies: Figuring Disability in American Culture and Literature 185
extraterrestrial 152–154, 177, 178, 198, 199, 200, 205

Faces of Degeneration: A European Disorder, c. 1848–c. 1918 115
The Fall (novel) 88
"The Fall of the House of Usher" 17, 76, 77, 79, 148
Fanon, Frantz 185
Fantasm and Fiction 25
the fantastic (genre) 18
Faulkner, Griffin Robert 219
The Fearless Vampire Killers 117n1
Feejee Mermaid 174, **175**
Felman, Shoshana 63, 64
female Gothic 13–17
feminism 3, 13–17
Féré, Charles 169
Fiedler, Leslie 166, 186n6
Field of Dreams 28n1
Finucane, F.C. 24
Fisher, Terence 94, 103
Fledgling 83, 87
Fleischer, Ruben 155
"The Fly" 151
A Fool There Was 78
"For the Blood is the Life" 78
"Force of Law: The 'Mystical Foundation of Authority'" 46, 47n1, 67n10
Ford, Harrison 23, 151
Ford, Peter 168
forgery 34
Foster, Jodie 196
Foucault, Michel 183–185, 186
1408 (film) 20
"1408" (short story) 20
Fowkes, Katherine A. 24, 26
Francis, Freddie 1
Franco, Jesús 95
Frankenstein (1931 film) 79, 191
Frankenstein (novel) 150, 190
Frankenstein's monster (character) 94, 176
freak show 143, 144, 153, 166–167, 169
Freaks (1932 film) 144–145
"Freaks in Space: 'Extraterrestrialism' and 'Deep-Space Multiculturalism'" 186n12
Freneau, Philip 12
Freud, Sigmund 35–36, 38, 179–180
Friday the 13th (franchise) 214
Friedman, John Block 170–171, 173, 186n11
Friedman, Maurice 47n3
Furman, Jan 56

García, Christina 16
Gardner, Helen 78
Gardner, John 186, 191, 192
Garland-Thomson, Rosemarie 185
The Gates Ajar 20

Index 229

The Gates Between 20
Gavriel, Uri 103
Geek Love 169
Gelder, Ken 100, 108, 113, 114–116, 118n7, 118n9
Geller, Sarah Michelle 84
Geoffrey of Monmouth 164
George, Melissa 135
ghost 2, 3, 7–69, 148–149, 177; and burial 10, 37–38; as consolation 10, 19–21, 26, 177; as critique 10, 13–17, 28n3, 149; and ethnicity 16–17, 25, 28n3, 50–69; and history 25–26, 57–67; and justice 10, 13, 26, 57–67, 204; and literary theory 24–25; and national myth 10–13, 20; and reality 17–19; stories by women 149
Ghost (1990 film) 20, 23, 204
Ghostbusters 2, 23
Ghostly Matters: Haunting and the Sociological Imagination 24, 55–56
Ghosts: Appearances of the Dead and Cultural Transformation 24
Ghosts: Deconstruction, Psychoanalysis, History
Ghosts in the Middle Ages: The Living and the Dead in Medieval Society 24
The Ghosts of Modernity 24
ghoul 174
"The Giant Wisteria" 14
Gibson, Alex 94
Giger, H.R. 153, 198
Gil, José Ramón Larraz 95
Gilchrist, Keir 214
The Gilda Stories 82–83, 87
Gilman, Charlotte Perkins 14–15
Gilman, Sanders 185
Girard, René 185
Given Time: I. Counterfeit Money 51–52
Giving Up the Ghost: Spirits, Ghosts, and Angels in Mainstream American Comedy Films 24
Glasgow, Ellen 14
Glaum, Louise 78
global warming 202
Godzilla 150, 174
Goffman, Erving 185
Goldberg, Whoopi 204
golem 174
Gomez, Jewelle 82–83, 87
Goodman, John 193
Gordon, Avery 24, 25, 26, 28n3, 55–58
Gorn, Elliott J. 67n8
Gornick, Michael 84
Gossett, Louis, Jr. 153
Gothic (genre) 2, 28n2, 76, 92, 121, 142, 148, 149, 150, 152, 154–155
Gough, Michael 94
Goyer, David S. 98
Grady, Frank 117n2, 118n7
Grahame-Smith, Seth 101

"The Gray Champion" 11, 12, 14
Grazer, Jack Dylan 209
The Great Depression 79, 191
Greenblatt, Stephen 185
Greenquist, Brad 10
Grendel (novel) 191, 192
griffin 174
Griffiths, Lucy 131
Grimm, Joshua 223n9, 223n13
Grosz, Elizabeth 159

Hackford, Taylor 147
Håfström, Mikael 20
Haggard, Piers 155
Hahner, Leslie A. 217, 218
Ha-kyn, Shin 126
Halberstam, Jack 91, 100, 142, 207
Hale, Gregg 1
Hall, Michael C. 145, 178
Halloween (film franchise) 214
Hamilton, Nicholas 209
Hamlet 38
Hammer Film Productions 93, 94–95, 103, 117n4
Hammond, Jeffrey 20
Haney-Jardine, Lux 101
Hansen, Regina 222n2, 222n5
The Happening 152, 202, 203
Harlib, Amy 83
Harris, Charlaine 86, 120, 191
Harris, Curtis 101
Harris, Thomas 195–196
Harrison, Kelvin, Jr. 218
Harry and the Hendersons 154
Hartnett, Josh 135
Haskin, Byron 155
The Haunted Dusk: American Supernatural Fiction, 1820–1920 24
The Haunted Mansion (attraction) 2
The Haunted Screen: Ghosts in Literature and Film 24
haunting 7, 10, 12–13, 16, 19, 20, 24–28, 30, 55–56; see also ghost
The Haunting (1999) 28n1
The Haunting of Hill House 17–19, 149
Haunting the House of Fiction: Feminist Perspectives on Ghost Stories by American Women 24
Hawke, Ethan 100
Hawthorne, Nathaniel 11, 12, 14–15, 17, 76–77, 147, 150
Hay, Malcolm 111
Hays Code 80
HBO (Home Box Office) 86
Headless Horseman 10–11
Hedebrant, Kare 97
Hegel, Georg Wilhelm Friedrich 51
Hellboy 194
Hellboy II: The Golden Army 194
Henderson, May G. 53, 67n3

Index

Herculine Barbin (Being the Recently Discovered Memoirs of a Nineteenth-Century French Hermaphrodite) 184
hermaphrodism 184
Herzog, Werner 96
Hessian 10–11, 148
Heston, Charlton 98
Hiddleston, Tom 104, 132
Hill, Leslie 32–33
Hillyer, Lambert 79, 93–94
Hilton, Daisy 145
Hilton, Violet 145
Hindle, Maurice 118*n*7
Hippocrites 167, 179
Hiroshima, Mon Amour 63
History of Sexuality (Foucault) 183
Hitchcock, Alfred 145, 155, 195
Hitler, Adolf 145
Hoag, Ronald Wesley 47*n*3
Hoffer, Eric 185
Hofland, Peter 169, 186*n*9
Hogan, Chuck 88, 155
Holden, Gloria 79, 93–94
Holm, Ian 198
Homo-dubii 171
Hooper, Tobe 2, 9, 23
horror 1, 9
horror films, anthology 1
The Horror of Dracula 94
Horror Stories 80
Horror Studies (journal) 4, 139
Horvitz, Deborah 52
Hough, John 95
house, haunted 17
House of Dracula 93
House of Frankenstein 93
The House of Leaves 17
The House of the Seven Gables 17, 76
House on Haunted Hill (1999) 28*n*1
Howard, Robert E. 80
Howell, Michael 168
Hudson, Henry 11, 12
Huet, Marie-Hélène 167, 168
Hugh of Lincoln 110
Hughes, Stuart 209
humors, bodily 179
The Hunger 96, 103, 117*n*3
Hunt, Marvin 41
Hurt, William 105
Huston, Danny 136
Hutchinson, Anne 164
Hyde, Allan 130
hyperobject 223*n*6

I Am Legend (film) 98, 105, 151, 200–201
I Am Legend (novel) 81–82, 85, 97–98, 99, 151, 200–201
I, Robot 151
"I, the Vampire" 80–81
"Imp of the Perverse" 148

incest 179
Incredible Hulk 194
incubus 164
Independence Day 152
Indian *see* Americans, Indigenous
"The Indian Burying Ground" 12
Interview with the Vampire (film) 97, 102
Interview with the Vampire (novel) 82, 124, 128, 129, 192
Invasion of the Body Snatchers 197
Irdu lili 164
Irving, Washington 10–11, 12, 28*n*2, 147, 148
Isidore of Seville 171
The Island of Dr. Moreau 167
IT (novel) 208, 209, 212
IT (2017 film) 2, 4, 206, 207, 208–212, 213–214, 217, 220, 221, 222, 222*n*1, 222*n*2, 222*n*3, 222*n*4, 222*n*5
IT: Chapter Two 208, 212, 222*n*1
It Comes at Night 2, 4, 206, 207, 208, 218–222, **220**
It Follows 2, 4, 206, 207, 208, 212–218, 220, 221, 222, 223*n*8, 223*n*9, 223*n*10, 223*n*11

Jackson, Peter 154–155
Jackson, Shirley 17–19, 149
Jacobs, Chosen 209
Jacobs, Lewis 92
James, Henry 17–19, 26, 108, 148, 149
Janicker, Rebecca 17
Jarmusch, Jim 89, 91, 104, 120, 132
Jaws (franchise) 155
Jenks, Carol 95
The Jersey Devil 154
Jessee, Sharon 67*n*7, 67*n*8
Jewett, Sarah Orne 14
The Jew's Body 185
JFK (1991 film) 198
Johnson, Barbara 47*n*1
Johnson, E.C. 118*n*9
Johnston, Joe 151
Jojo the Dog-Faced Boy **166**
Jones, Brennon 154
Jones, Caleb Landry 102
Jordan, Neil 91, 97, 102
The Journal of the Fantastic in the Arts 2, 4, 71–72
Judaism *see* Vampire and anti-Semitism
Julius Obsequens 161
Jurassic Park (franchise) 151, 167
justice 7, 10, 13, 15, 17, 26, 30, 44–47, 51, 58–66, 67*n*10, 106, 178, 185, 196, 204; *see also* ghost and justice

Kang-ho, Song 126
Karlen, John 95
Karlson, Phil 155
Kazui, Fran Rubel 84
Keaton, Michael 28*n*1
Keenan, Sally 55, 56, 65, 67*n*3

Keenan, Tom 47*n*1
Keller, Nora Okja 16
Kelly, Casey Ryan 217–218, 223*n*9
Kennedy, Jamie 212
Kenton, Erle C. 94
Keough, Riley 219
"Kerfol" 15, 17, 149
Kerr, Howard 24, 27
Kidman, Nicole 23
King, Stephen 9, 10, 13, 20, 23, 82, 84, 85, 88, 116, 117*n*4, 118*n*6, 148, 149, 151, 155, 206, 208, 209, 210, 212, 217, 222*n*3, 222*n*5
King Kong 79, 154–155
King Kong (1933 film) 79, 154, 191
King Kong (2005 film) 154–155
Kingdom of the Spiders 155
Kingston, Maxine Hong 16, 23
Kinski, Klaus 96
Kipling, Rudyard 78
Kolmar, Wendy K. 24, 26, 28*n*3
Kovacs, Lee 24, 26
kraken 174, 177
Kristeva, Julia 189
Kruger, Otto 79, 94
Krumholz, Linda 61
Kubrick, Stanley 149
Kümel, Harry 95, 102, 103, 105
Kushner, Tony 23
Kuttner, Henry 80–81

Lambert, Mary 10
Lamorisse, Albert 222*n*4
Lang, Stephen 198
Langelaan, George 151
Langella, Frank 96, 117*n*4
Langmuir, G.I. 110
Lanzmann, Claude 63
The Last Broadcast 154
The Last Man on Earth 98
Last of the Mohicans 74, 143
latchkey kids 211
Laub, Dori 65
Lawrence, D.H. 108
Lawrence, Francis 98, 105, 147, 151
The League of Extraordinary Gentlemen 194
Leandersson, Lina 97, 123
Lee, Brandon 28*n*1
Lee, Christopher 94–95
Le Fanu, Sheridan 78, 93, 95, 103
"The Legend of Sleepy Hollow" 10–11, 12, 147, 148
Leone, Massimo 158
Let Me In 87
Let the Right One In 87, 97, 122
Levernier, James Arthur 73–74
Lieberher, Jaeden 209
"Ligeia" 76, 148
Lillis, Sophia 209
Lindqvist, John Ajvide 97
Lindsay, Jeff 145, 196

Livy 161
Llosa, Luis 155
Loch Ness Monster 154, 177, 178
Long, Frank Belknap 80
Longyear, Barry B. 153
Looking Awry: An Introduction to Jacques Lacan Through Popular Culture 223*n*12
Lormer, Jon 1
"The Lost Ghost" 149
love 42–47, 52
Lovecraft, H.P. 3, 28*n*2, 80–81, 154, 221
Lucas, George 167
Lucas, Isabel 123
Luccardi, Olivia 213
"Luella Miller" 77, 79
Lugosi, Bela 78, 79, 93, 116, 117*n*4
Lukyanenko, Sergey 98
Lundie, Catherine 26, 28*n*3
Lust for a Vampire 95
Luther, Martin 162
lycanthrope *see* werewolf
Lycosthenes, Conradus 162

Maazel, Lincoln 84
mad scientist 150–152, 197
Madness and Civilization 183
Magistrale, Tony 208, 209, 210, 222*n*3
Malkovich, John 86
"The Man of the Crowd" 37, 47*n*3, 148
Mandeville, John 173
Le Manoir du Diable 92
Mann, Daniel 155
Marco Polo 174
Marlowe, Christopher 134
Marsh, Carol 94
Marshall, Frank 155
Marshall, Paule 16
Martin 84, 99
Marvelous Possessions: The Wonders of the New World 185
Marvels of the East 171, **172**, 173
Marx, Karl 100, 115–116
mass shootings 206, 211
Mather, Cotton 143, 147
Matheson, Richard 81–82, 85, 88, 97–98, 99, 151, 200
The Matrix (franchise) 151
Mays, Daniel 102
McCall, Dan 44
McCracken, Peggy 164, 186*n*2
Megasthenes 170
Méliès, Georges 92
Melville, Herman 3, 7, 30–49, 75, 144
Memnoch the Devil 125
Memoires for Paul de Man 67*n*5
Men in Black (franchise) 153
Men, Women and Chainsaws: Gender in the Modern Horror Film 215
Mendel, Gregor 169
Meredith, Burgess 1

232 Index

Merhige, E. Elias 81, 85–86, 99
Merlin 164
Merrick (novel) 124, 125
Merrick, Joseph 168
Mesmer, Franz 179
#metoo 211
Meyer, Nicholas 220
Meyer, Stephenie 86, 97, 128, 136, 191, 194
The Middle Passage 52, 54–56, 60, 62–63, 64, 67n7, 149
"The Middle Toe of the Right Foot" 17, 148–149
Midkiff, Dale 10
millennial anxiety 25–26
Miller, Arthur 147
Miller, George 164
Miller, J. Hillis 33, 36–37, 38, 40–41, 44–46, 47n3
Miller, Jonny Lee 102
mimesis 32–33
Minotaur 162–164, 176
"The Minster's Black Veil" 150
Mitchell, David Robert 206, 208, 212
Mittman, Asa 158–159, 166, 176, 179, 207
Mobley, Marilyn Sanders 63
Monroe, Maika 212
monster 2, 4–5, 73, 79, 81–82, 106, 120–121, 139–223; ambiguity 206–222, 222n5; and anti-Semitism 173, **182**; and category crisis 7, 165–166, 175–176, 207; and desire 176–177; etymology 141, 158; origins 161–170; overdetermination 142, 207; and politics 171, 180–182; and psychology 178–181; and radiation 150–151; and religion 146–147; and visibility 139–140, 145, 189–205, 206–223
The Monster (novella) 141, 149
"Monster Culture (Seven Theses)" 7, 73, 157, 176, 180, 189, 191, 207
monster theory 2, 157–186
The Monster Theory Reader 2, 4, 157
Monster Theory: Reading Culture 3, 157, 189
Monsters in the Closet: Homosexuality and the Horror Film 79–80
Monsters, Inc. 81, 145, 186, 191, 192–193
monstrosity 81–82, 84–86, 91, 118n8
monstrous races 170–174
The Monstrous Races in Medieval Art and Thought 170
Montaigne, Michel *see* de Montaigne, Michel
Monty Python 2
Moore, Demi 23, 204
"Morella" 76, 79, 148
Moretti, Franco 115, 118n7
Moretz, Chloe Grace 87
Morgenstern, Naomi 63, 67n6
Morrison, Toni 3, 7, 16–17, 23, 50–69, 149
Morton, Timothy 223n6
The Mortuary Collection (film) 1

mourning 19–20, 26, 46–47, 51, 53, 55, 57, 58–59, 60–62, 64, 66, 67n2
mummy 148, 204
The Mummy (1932 film) 79, 191
Murnau, F.W. 71, 79, 85–86, 92–93, 96, 99, 112–113, 117n3
Murray, Bill 23
Muschietti, Andrés 206, 207, 208, 209, 212, 213, 214, 217
The Mysterious Stranger 147

The Naked Jungle 155
The Narrative of Arthur Gordon Pym of Nantucket 144
A Narrative of the Captivity and Restoration of Mrs. Mary Rowlandson 143
Nat Turner Revolt 144
The National Uncanny: Indian Ghosts and American Subjects 24
Native Americans *see* Americans Indigenous
Natural History (Pliny) 171
nature, as monster 190, 201–202
Naylor, Gloria 16, 23
Nazi Party 111, **182**
Near Dark 99
Neary, Gwen Margaret 26, 28n3
necrophilia 179, 195
Needful Things 208, 210
Neill, Sam 100
New Woman (social movement) 78
Newfield, Sam 3
Newitz, Annalee 197
Newman, Kim 120
Nick of the Woods 75, 143
The Night Eternal 88
Night of the Living Dead 151, 200
Night Visitors: The Rise and Fall of the English Ghost Story 28n2
Night Watch 98
"Nightmare and the Horror Film: The Symbolic Biology of Fantastic Beings" 174–176
Nightmare on Elm Street (franchise) 214
Niles, Steve 88
Nodier, Charles 77
Nord, Ika 123
Norrington, Stephen 98
Nosferatu: A Symphony of Horror 71, 79, 85–86, 92–93, 96, 99, 112–113, 117n3
Nosferatu the Vampyre 96
NoSleep Podcast 7
Nosowitz, Dan 9
nuclear war 220
NYPD Blue 23

Ok-bin, Kim 126
Oldman, Gary 84, 96
Oleff, Wyatt 209
Olivier, Laurence 117n4

Index

The Omega Man 98
Omen (film franchise) 164
On Monsters and Marvels 160
"On the Jewish Question" 116
On the Track of the Crescent 118n9
Only Lovers Left Alive 89, 91, 104–106, 120, 132–134
Orientalism (Edward Said) 185
The Origins of Totalitarianism 185
Ostow, Mortimer 110
Othello 173
The Others (film) 23
Ouimet, Danielle 95
Our Vampires, Ourselves 96
Outbreak (1995 film) 155, 200
"The Oval Portrait" 76–77

Pack, M.J. 223n8, 223n13
Pal, George 152
Palimpsest (podcast) 7
Panotii 170, 171
The Papal Ass 162, **163**, 170
paranoia 206, 215–218, 222
Paré, Ambroise 160–161, 164, 165, 167, 168–169, 186n5, 186n10
Paris, Matthew 110
Parker, Alan 147
Parkes, James 111, 112
Parks and Recreation (TV show) 9
Patrick, Barbara Constance 26, 28n3
Pattinson, Robert 86, 97, 194
Pendleton, David 218
penny dreadful 75
Pennywise 208–212, **211**, 213, 217, 221
Perkins, Anthony 195
Pet Sematary 9, 10, 210
Petersen, Wolfgang 153, 155, 200
Pfeiffer, Michelle 23
Pharr, Mary 222n5
Phelps, Elizabeth Stuart 20
The Philosophy of Horror 175, 176
phoenix 174
The Piano Lesson 23
Pichel, Irving 79
Pick, Daniel 115
The Picture of Dorian Gray 76
Pitch Black (2000 film) 205
Pitt, Brad 97
Pitt, Ingrid 95
Plante, Patricia R. 39
Plato 179
Pliny the Elder (Gaius Plinius Secundus) 167, 170, 171, 173
Poe, Edgar Allan 17, 26, 28n2, 37, 47n3, 76–77, 78, 79, 144, 148
Polanski, Roman 117n1, 147, 164
Poliakov, Leon 109–110
Polidori, John 77, 103
Poltergeist 2, 9, 23
"Pomegranate Seed" 15, 149

Pomerance, Murray 199
Poole, W. Scott 144
postmodernism 25–26, 82
post-structuralism see postmodernism
Powell, Frank 78
Prager, Dennis 110, 111, 112, 114
plague see disease
Predator (1987 film) 205
Pretend We're Dead: Capitalist Monsters in American Pop Culture 197
Price, Vincent 98
Pride and Prejudice and Zombies 101
Prodigiorum ac Ostentorum Chronicon 162
Proyas, Alex 151
Psycho (film) 145, 194, 195, 203
Psycho (novel) 80
psychoanalysis 179–180, 203
psychopath 145, 178–179, 190, 194–197, 202–203, 222
Pulitzer prize 23
pulp magazines 80
Puritans (American) 19–20, 142–143, 146–147, 164
Purity and Danger: An Analysis of the Concepts of Pollution and Taboo 36
pygmies 170

Quaid, Dennis 153
Queen of the Damned 82
Quine, Richard 147
Quinn, Seabury 80

Rabaté, Jean-Michel 24
radiation 150–151, 169, 200
Randian, Prince 145
Ransone, James 212
Rappaccini's Daughter" 150
rational irrationalism 190–191, 202–205
Rau, Andrea 95
"Reading Epitaphs" 50
Reading the Vampire 108, 118n7
The Red Balloon (Le balloon rouge) 222n4
Red Scare 197
Regona, Ubaldo 98
reincarnation 80, 84–85, 96
Reiser, Paul 198
Reitman, Ivan 2
Religion and Its Monsters 158
repetition 35, 37–38, 47n2, 51, 60, 92
Requiem for a Vampire 95
Resident Evil (film franchise) 155
Revolutionary War (American) 10–11, 148
Rice, Anne 82, 88, 97, 105, 117n4, 120, 123–126, 128, 129, 130, 132, 145, 191, 192
Riley, Sam 102
Rime of the Ancient Mariner 76
The Ring (film) 28n1, 214
Ringu 214
"Rip Van Winkle" 10–11, 12

ritual murder *see* blood libel; vampires and anti–Semitism
Roberts, Bette B. 122, 123
robot 151, 197
The Rocky Horror Picture Show 3
Rody, Caroline 52, 54, 56, 57, 61
Rollin, Jean 95
Romero, George A. 1, 84, 99, 151, 2000
Ronan, Saoirse 102
Rose Red 149
Rosemary's Baby 147, 164
Roth, Cecil 110
Routledge Handbook to the American Ghost Story 4
Rowe, John Carlos 34, 35, 37, 42
Rowlandson, Mary 74, 143, 153
Rubin, Gayle 185
Ryder, Winona 84, 96
Rymer, James Malcolm 75, 117n4, 120, 122

Saberhagen, Fred 82, 192
Sabrina the Teenage Witch 147
Sagal, Boris 98
Said, Edward 185
Saint-Hilaire, Étienne Geoffroy 169
Sale, Maggie 67n8
Salem Witch Trials 147
'Salem's Lot 82, 84, 85, 116, 117n4, 118n6, 208, 210
Salkow, Sidney 98
Salmonson, Jessica Amanda 28n3
Sanchez, Ashlyn 202
Sangster, Jimmy 95
Sartre, Jean-Paul 133, 192, 205n2
Sasquatch *see* Bigfoot
Satan *see* the Devil
The Satanic Rites of Dracula 94–95
The Scapegoat 185
Scarborough, Dorothy 28n2
Scare Tactics: Supernatural Fiction by American Women 3, 13
The Scarlet Letter 14–15, 76, 150
Schmitt, Jean-Claude 24
Schreck, Max 92
Schröder, Greta 71, 92
Schutte, Anne Jacobson 186n3
Schwenger, Peter 24–25
Sci Fi Channel 23
Sciapods 170, 173
Scott, Ridley 151
Scott, Jackson Robert 209
Scott, Tony 96, 103, 117n3
Scream (1996 film) 212, 215
Scruggs, Charles 66n1
Sears, John 222n5
The Second Sex 185
Sepe, Lili 213
serial killer *see* psychopath
Sesame Street 108
Se7en (1995 film) 196

Sewell, Rufus 101
sexual harassment 211
Seyrig, Delphine 95
Shadow of the Vampire 81, 85–86, 99
Shakespeare, William 173
Shaviro, Steven 104, 105
Shea, Katt 3
Shelley, Mary 150, 190
The Shining (1980 film) 149
The Shining (novel) 9, 13, 149, 210
Shrek 81, 145, 186, 191, 192–193
Shults, Trey Edward 206, 208
"The Shunned House" 80–81
Shyamalan, M. Night 152, 202
Signs (2002 film) 152–153
Signs Taken for Wonders: On the Sociology of Literary Forms 118n7
Silence of the Lambs (film) 194–195, 196
Silence of the Lambs (novel) 194–195
Silko, Leslie Marmon 16
Sim, Jake 209
Simpson, Philip L. 145
The Simpsons 1, 9
"Sinners in the Hands of an Angry God" 146–147
Siodmak, Robert 94
"The Site of Memory" 58, 67n4
The Sixth Sense 23
Skal, David J. 92
Skarsgård, Alexander 130
Skarsgård, Bill 209
Sketch Boo of Geoffrey Crayon, Gent. 10–11
Skin Shows: Gothic Horror and the Technologies of Monsters 100
Skull in the Stars (website) 122
Slade, David 88, 98, 135
slavery 16–17, 21, 50–69, 83, 87, 101–102, 143, 144, 149, 173
Sleepy Hollow (1999 film) 28n1, 147
Slenderman 174
Smit-McPhee, Kodi 87
Smith, Andrew 13
Smith, Clark Ashton 80
Smith, John 143
Smith, Norman R. 161, 162
Smith, Valerie 53, 63
Smith, Will 98, 153, 200–201
Smock, Ann 38
Snakes on a Plane 155
Snipes, Wesley 83, 98, 135
Socrates 179
Something Wicked This Way Comes 147
Sommers, Stephen 98
Son of Dracula 94
South Park 2
Sovereignty and Goodness of God: Being a Narrative of the Captivity and Restoration of Mrs. Mary Rowlandson 74
Spacey, Kevin 196

Index

Specters of Marx, 4, 24, 59–60, 64
Spectral America: Phantoms and the National Imagination 3, 7
spectral turn 23–28
spectrality see ghosts
spectrality studies 27
Speechless Men 170
Speedman, Scott 83
Spielberg, Steven 23, 28n1, 151, 152
Spierig, Michael 91, 99, 123
Spierig, Peter 91, 99, 123
Spillers, Hortense 25, 57
Spindell, Ryan 1
spiritualism 20
Spofford, Harriet Prescott 14
Spry, Bailey 215
Star Trek (franchise) 152
Star Wars (franchise) 153, 167
Star Wars: Episode IV: A New Hope 167
Steel, Pippa 95
Stensgaard, Yutte 95
Stern, Milton R. 38–39
Stevenson, Ian 168
Stewart, Kristen 86, 97
Stigma: Notes on the Management of Spoiled Identity 185
Stir of Echoes 28n1
Stockard, Charles 169
Stoker, Bram 71, 73, 74, 75, 78, 80, 84–85, 88, 92, 96, 100, 101, 107, 114, 115, 117n4, 118n8, 118n9, 120, 194, 204, 207
Stotts, Andrew 24
Stowe, Harriet Beecher 13
The Strain 88, 155
The Strain Trilogy 88
Strange, Glenn 94
Strange Tales of Mystery and Terror 80
Strengell, Heidi 222n3
Stribling, Melissa 94
Stuart, Roxana 76
succubus 164
suicide 72, 84, 120–137, 202, 223n8
Supernatural Horror in Literature 28n2
The Supernatural in Modern English Fiction 28n2
Surandon, Susan 96
Suratt, Valeska 78
Sutherland, Donald 200
Sutherland, Kiefer 197
Svengali 118n8
The Swarm 155
Swayze, Patrick 23, 204
Swinton, Tilda 104, 132
"A Sympathetic Vibration: Dracula and the Jews" 115

Tacitus 161
Tales from the Crypt 1
Tales from the Hood 1
Tallerico, Brian 221, 222

Tan, Amy 16
Tarantula (1955 film) 151
Tate, Allen 76
Tatopoulos, Patrick 98
Taylor, Edward 146
Taylor, Jeremy Ray 209
Teague, Lewis 1, 155
Teague, Owen 209
Telushkin, Joseph 110, 111, 112, 114
teratology see monster theory
Terminator (franchise) 151
Terror Tales 80
terrorism 145, 190, 195, 196–197, 206, 211, 222
Tertullian 162
Testimony: Crises of Witnessing in Literature, Psychoanalysis and History 64
thalidomide 169
theater 73, 77, 78, 88, 93
Them! 150, 191
The Thing (1982 film) 214
The Thing from Another World 197
"Thinking Sex" (Gayle Rubin) 185
Thirst (2009 film) 120, 125–129
30 Days of Night (film) 88, 98, 135–136
30 Days of Night (graphic novel) 88, 98
Thomas of Monmouth 110
Thompson, Logan 209
Three Days of the Condor 198
Through the Custom-House: Nineteenth-Century American Fiction and Modern Theory 35
#timesup 211
Todorov, Tzetvan 18
Torture Garden 1
Totem and Taboo 35
Trachtenberg, Joshua 111, 112, 114
Tracks 149
transubstantiation 113–114
Traoré, Ousseynou B. 67n8
trauma 10, 16–17, 25, 56, 60, 62–65, 66n2, 67n4, 67n9, 147, 180, 191
Travels of Sir John Mandeville 171–173
Travers, Peter 223n10
Trilby 188n8
Tru Calling 23
True Believer: Thoughts on the Nature of Mass Movements 185
True Blood (franchise) 86, 120, 130–132, 134, 145, 191, 193
The Turn of the Screw 17–19, 149
Twain, Mark 147
24 (TV series) 145, 197
28 Days Later 200
Twilight (franchise) 86, 97, 128, 136, 145, 190, 191, 194
The Twilight Zone 1
Twins of Evil 95
Twitchell, James 108
Typee: A Peep at Polynesian Life 75

Ulházy, Eduard 186n1
uncanniness 34–42, 93
"The Uncanny" 35–36, 38
Underworld (franchise) 83, 87, 101, 135
Underworld (2003 film) 98
Underworld: Evolution 98
Underworld: Rise of the Lycans 98
unicorn 174
Universal Studios 93, 94
USSR, dissolution of 197

vampire 2, 3, 71–137, 148, 155, 174, 192, 203–204, 207; and action films 98; American 73–90; and anti-Semitism 72, 107–118; and class 84, 99, 100; and disease 100, 112–113; and environmentalism 100, 105–106; female 76–77, 78; and gender 84, 102–104; and intertextuality 103; and race 74–75, 83, 87, 88, 98, 101–102; relationship to film 92–93; and religion 85; and sexuality 79–80, 82–83, 86, 88, 94, 95–97, 193; and sunlight 71, 83, 100, 123, 127, 131, 136
Vampire, A Phantasm in Three Dramas 77
Vampire Chronicles 82, 124–125, 126, 128, 130, 145, 191, 192, 203
"Vampire Culture" 117n2, 118n7
The Vampire Diaries 89
The Vampire Film: Undead Cinema 3, 91, 95, 97, 98, 103
The Vampire Lestat 82, 130
The Vampire Lovers 95
The Vampire Tapestry 117n3
Vampirella 117n4
vamps 78; *see also* vampire, female
Vampyr (1932 film) 92, 93
"The Vampyre" 77, 103
Vampyres (1974 film) 95
Vampyros Lesbos 95
Van Helsing 98
Van Helsing, Abraham (character) 79, 93, 94, 108, 113, 117n3, 117n4, 118n5, 118n6, 192
Van Sloan, Edward 79, 93
Varda, Scott J. 217, 218
Varney the Vampire; or, The Feast of Blood 75, 85, 117n4, 120, 122–123, 127, 129, 132
Venom (1981 film) 155
Versions of Pygmalion 36–37, 47n3
V/H/S/2 1
Victorian Gothic (website) 122
Vietnam War 197
virus *see* disease
Vreeland, Rich 214

Wahlberg, Mark 202
Wald, Priscilla 155
Walker, Benjamin 87, 101
The Walking Dead 142
Wall, John E. 177
Wallace, Diana 13

Walsham, Alexandra 186n2
Walt Disney 2
Walt Disney World 2
War of the Worlds (1953 film) 152
War of the Worlds (novel) 152
War of the Worlds (radio play) 152
War of the Worlds (2005 film) 152
Warkany, Josef 161, 165, 169, 186n5
Wasikowski, Mia 104
Watergate scandal 197, 198
Weary, Jake 212
Weird Tales 80
Welcome to Night Vale 2
Weller, Lance 154
Welles, Orson 152
Wells, H.G. 152, 167
wendigo 174
werewolf 83, 86, 98, 135, 148, 174, 176
Werewolf of London 79
West, Julian 93
The West Wing 23
Wharton, Edith 2, 14–15, 17, 149
What Lies Beneath 23
What Remains of Edith Finch (videogame) 7
Whedon, Joss 84, 136, 147
White, Jack 134
"Why Every Horror Film of the 1980s Was Built on 'Indian Burial Grounds'" 9
Wilde, Oscar 76, 108
Wilkins-Freeman, Mary E. 14, 76, 77, 78, 79, 149
The Will to Knowledge 183
Willard 155
"William Wilson" 148
Williams, Wes 186n7
Willis, Bruce 23
Wilson, August 16, 23
Wilson, Edmund 18
"The Wind in the Rose-bush" 149
Winthrop, John 143
Wired (magazine) 217
Wise, Robert 155
Wiseman, Len 98
witch 3, 147, 164, 177
The Witches of Eastwick (film) 164
the Wolf Man 94
Wolfhard, Finn 209
The Wonders of the Invisible World 143
A World of Difference 47n1
Worthington, Sam 153
Wright, Jeffrey 104
Wyatt, Jean 67n3

The X-Files 23, 145, 154, 178, 198, 199
xenophobia 114, 153

Yelchin, Anton 104, 132
"The Yellow Wall-paper" 14
Young, Helen 186n12

"Young Goodman Brown" 12, 147, 150
yowie 177

Zanger, Jules 115, 118*n*8
Žižek, Slavoj 37–38, 223*n*12

zombie 3, 142, 151, 174, 220
Zombieland 155
Zovatto, Daniel 213
Zucker, Jerry 20